John Todd and the
Underground Railroad

John Todd and the Underground Railroad

Biography of an Iowa Abolitionist

JAMES PATRICK MORGANS

McFarland & Company, Inc., Publishers
Jefferson, North Carolina, and London

LIBRARY OF CONGRESS ONLINE CATALOG

Morgans, James Patrick.
    John Todd and the Underground Railroad : biography of an Iowa
abolitionist / James Patrick Morgans.
        p.   cm.
    Includes bibliographical references and index.

    ISBN-13: 978-0-7864-2783-3
    softcover : 50# alkaline paper ∞

    1. Todd, John, 1818–1894.   2. Abolitionists—Iowa—Tabor—
Biography.   3. Clergy—Iowa—Tabor—Biography.   4. Under-
ground railroad—Iowa—Tabor.   5. Antislavery movements—
Iowa—Tabor—History.   6. Tabor (Iowa)—Biography.   7. Tabor
(Iowa)—Race relations—History—20th century.   I. Title.
F629.T334 M67 2006
326'.8092B—dc22

                                                2006026546

British Library cataloguing data are available

On the cover: John Todd (*Library of Congress*);
the Nishnabota River (*Todd House Museum Archives*)

Manufactured in the United States of America

McFarland & Company, Inc., Publishers
  Box 611, Jefferson, North Carolina 28640
  www.mcfarlandpub.com

I lovingly dedicate this book to the memory of
my mother, Bernice Morgans,
and my grandparents, Selma and Joe Johnson.

ACKNOWLEDGMENTS

The first person I would like to thank is Wanda Ewalt, president of the Tabor Historical Society. Without her encouragement and help this book probably would not have been written. The Tabor Historical Society has been an inspiration to me for their hard work in keeping the Underground Railroad alive. I feel fortunate that the society and Ms. Ewalt gave me full access to the material in the Todd House Museum. I would also like to thank the Iowa Humanities for giving me a grant to begin work on the Todd papers.

I would like to acknowledge the help that Jan Frank-de Ois and her staff, especially Carrie Falk, at the Shenandoah, Iowa, Public Library provided in finding the sometimes out-of-print and century old publications I needed for research. William Overbey's map and other work was also much appreciated.

I would also like to thank Robert Gaston of Longview, Washington, and Dale Matthews of Shenandoah for their historical family papers. I would like to thank Dr. Lowell Soike of the Iowa State Historical Society for his help in pointing out research materials. I much appreciated the material that Sandy Fairbairn of the Hitchcock House, in Lewis, Iowa, provided. Also, the assistance that John Zeller of the Iowa State Historical Society and Dennis Bateman of the *Sidney Argus-Herald* provided was very much valued. Lynn Handy of Percival, Iowa, contributed materials to the Todd House Museum, and this was appreciated, as was the early pioneers list made by Carlos Harrison. I also valued the comments made by James Hill of the National Parks Service's "Network to Freedom Program."

I would like to thank the organization at the Kansas State Historical Society for their assistance. The staff at the Iowa State Historical Society is always so obliging and helpful. Also, the Oberlin College Archives provided useful materials, and the staff was always accommodating. The Kenneth Spencer Research Library at the University of Kansas also has a nice collection of Todd materials. A special thanks as well to historian Louis Waddell at the Pennsylvania State Archives in Harrisburg, Pennsylvania. Also, the libraries in Tabor, Iowa, and Nebraska City, Nebraska, were helpful.

I would like to acknowledge the help my two children, Patrick James Morgans and Meredith Joy Morgans, provided. I also appreciate the encouragement of my family and friends during this project. Finally, without the help of my wife, Judith A. Morgans, I don't think I could have completed this book. Her handwriting interpretation skills are phenomenal and as we went through more than two thousand handwritten documents, I was always amazed at her ability. Also, her support for this project and inspiration were always much prized.

Table of Contents

Preface

This book, while ostensibly a biography of John Todd, is in fact the story of an Underground Railroad (UGRR) station. How this station town was begun and the noble purposes of its birth, its work on the UGRR and other abolitionist labor—such as the Kansas Free State Movement—are discussed. John Todd is the glue that holds this account together.

Perhaps no other historical subject is as well known as the Underground Railroad with so little material available. Because the activities were illegal the conductors were reluctant to write about their actions in journals or letters. Local newspapers didn't publish names, methods, times or dates. Thousands of escapees on the Underground Railroad made their way to freedom without their names or stories being known. One thing that is certain is the undeniable courage and thirst for freedom that characterized "passengers" on this railroad. This is an important part of America's history that needs to be examined.

This account focuses on one Underground Railroad station in Tabor, Iowa, and what may be considered a subsidiary station in Civil Bend, Iowa. This station was unique in that it was the first station on the Western frontier of the United States. Iowa was the westernmost of the contiguous states at that time. To its west were the territories of Nebraska and Kansas. Sometimes in these territories the rule of law was at the end of a gun or a mob's rope. Once in Tabor, the escaping slaves and their hunters knew that the rule of law of the United States would apply for better or worse. Also, Tabor's closeness to slave state Missouri made it inevitable that chases of all kinds by bounty hunters and slave posses would occur for the recapture of the runaway slaves.

I tried to show not only the importance of the Underground Railroad

1

but also the harshness of life on the frontier, as illustrated in the letters in
the Appendix. In the 1850's when the UGRR activities were at their height
in Tabor, it was a new frontier town. The residents of this village sometimes
struggled just to earn their daily bread. Land speculation was rampant and
the gold rush in 1859 put the future of the town in doubt. Many of the
accounts of the Underground Railroad seem to indicate that the conductors had nothing else to do but wait for the next escapees to come through.
This was not the case in Tabor. The realities of their pioneer life made their
days long and hard.

Most of the original pioneers of Tabor had graduated from or attended
Oberlin College in Oberlin, Ohio. Oberlin was one of the most important
colleges in that century. At a time in America's history when colleges were
segregated or restrictive to women and minorities, Oberlin allowed men,
women and blacks to attend the same classes. The people of Tabor wanted
to establish a college like Oberlin in the Missouri Valley. Their struggle with
this task and the eventual establishment of a college are told.

John Brown, the man who some say started the Civil War, found Tabor
to be a most hospitable place. Brown had lived in Ohio, and he found these
fellow Buckeyes to be as staunch abolitionists as he had ever seen. When
warrants were issued in Kansas by pro-slavery governments for the arrests
of Brown, James Lane or others, they found Tabor to be the perfect spot to
go. The residents were most accommodating in hiding them out and they
were close enough to the action in "Bleeding Kansas" to be able to jump
into the fray when the time was right in that territory.

The book is journalistic in nature. I have organized it this way. In Chapter 1 several of the escapes on the Underground Railroad are discussed. The
chases by slave posses trying to recapture runaways in Tabor are detailed.
John Brown is introduced, along with the fact that John Todd was hiding
the weapons Brown would use on his raid of Harper's Ferry. Chapter 2 talks
about John Todd's family history, the importance of Oberlin College in his
life and the significant history of this institution, which Todd's brother and
his future wife also attended. In Chapter 3 John accepts his first pastorate
in Ohio, which turns out to be a disappointment. The red hot atmosphere
of Oberlin is replaced by the dull realities of a town not all that interested
in the betterment of mankind. Mrs. Martha Todd's fascinating family background and family members are discussed. The chapter ends with the Todds
looking for more of a challenge in life.

Chapter 4 introduces George and Maria Gaston. Although he never
attends Oberlin, George is considered an "Oberlin" person. The Gastons
decide to become missionaries and government farmers to the Pawnee
Indians in Nebraska. On the way out to Nebraska they pass through Southwest Iowa. They have many trials and tribulations, mostly with the other

missionaries. Finally, sickness and attacks by the Pawnees' long time foe, the Sioux, force them back to Ohio. Chapter 5 finds George Gaston unable to get the area of Southwest Iowa out of his mind. He organizes a group of people to move to Iowa to start an Oberlin style college. He finds a restless minister, John Todd, to fill the important role of spiritual advisor for the group. The group heads out to Iowa but finds their first attempt to settle at Civil Bend to be unsuccessful. They finally settle in Tabor. They begin abolitionist activities almost immediately.

Chapter 6 discusses the politics of Iowa at this time and the racist tendencies of the state. Iowa certainly puts out an unwelcome mat for blacks free or slave who wanted to settle there. The national politics seemed to mirror this attitude. Chapter 7 discusses some of the tactics used by the Underground Railroad in and around Tabor. It also talks about other Underground Railroad stations in the area, and how the people of Tabor would transport escapees to these locations. Chapter 8 examines some more of the escapes on the Underground Railroad. There were many brutalities involved in these escapes. Some of the atrocious violence visited upon the free blacks in Southwest Iowa are also discussed. Chapter 9 involves Tabor and its participation in the Jim Lane Trail and its commitment to the Kansas Free State Movement. Lane's charismatic personality is discussed, as is his participation with the Underground Railroad.

Chapter 10 brings John Brown on stage again. Brown first began to plot the over throw of slavery in the United States while in Tabor. Brown's actions on the Underground Railroad are examined, including his use of Tabor as a hideout and the utilization of the town by his men. Then finally, Brown's rejection by the town that had been so often his oasis is detailed. The Civil War breaks out in Chapter 11, which chronicles Tabor's reaction to it, John Todd's participation in the Union Army, and finally the war's result that Tabor has longed for—the end of slavery. In Chapter 12, Tabor turns its attention to building a college like Oberlin and struggles with financing it. The death of John Todd and the other lions of Tabor are conversed. The letters and documents in the Appendix add life to the story.

IOWA

Grinnell o →

Iowa City o →

o Winterset

o Council Bluffs

Bellevue o

West Nishnabotna River

East Nishnabotna River

o Lewis

NEBR. TERR.

Tabor
o

o Quincy

Wyoming o

o Civil Bend

Nebraska City o

Amity
o

o Linden

o Rock Port

MISSOURI

Brownville o

KANSAS TERR.

o St. Joseph

o Holton

o Lecompton

Lawrence
o

o Independence

Topeka o

o
Kansas City

A map of the general four-state area discussed in this book.
(William Overbey.)

1

All Aboard for the Queen's Dominions

Three heavily armed slave hunters from Missouri were banging loudly on the door of George Gaston's house on a cold December day in 1856. Yelling piercing curses and oaths, the men demanded the return of two runaway slaves. The men suspected these slaves had been aided by Gaston, the Reverend John Todd and the rest of Tabor, Iowa's Underground Railroad apparatus.

The men-folk in town heard the ruckus and went to the aid of Gaston. The town's men, while every inch pious Christians, were not pacifists and felt they had the right to defend themselves, their friends and their cause. They calmly told the slavers they were also heavily armed, and if the Missourians did not leave, there would be trouble. The slave hunters, seeing that they were badly outnumbered, left. However, they threatened to return with search warrants.[1]

The slave hunters knew that the fugitive slave laws were on their side. These laws stated that even if a runaway slave escaped to a northern state such as Iowa where slavery was illegal, the slaves were still not safe. If a runaway slave was caught in Iowa, where slavery was illegal, the runaway by law must be returned to bondage in the slave state where the runaway and his master resided. The slave hunters thought they would eventually prevail, and the human contraband would be returned to Missouri.

The runaway slaves had escaped from the Kansas City area in Missouri and had gone through Kansas up to Nebraska, where the slave hunters recaptured them. Crossing the Missouri River at Nebraska City, the slavers and their captives sliced across Fremont County in Iowa. The slaves, tied and bound, found themselves back into slave state Missouri at the little hamlet know as Linden just across the border.[2]

Captured just a stone's throw away from freedom in Iowa, the two runaways were incarcerated in the Missouri jail with only a pan full of coals to keep them warm on a winter's night. The slavers had asked their captives where they were headed, and they told them Tabor. The bounty hunters told the runaways that they had better not go to Tabor, as the people there got rich by selling fleeing slaves down the river to New Orleans. Slaves in Missouri were often told that if they didn't work harder or change their attitudes, they would be sold down the Mississippi River to slave auctions in New Orleans.

During the night, the fugitives took the smoldering coals and burned a hole in the floor of the prison. The jail was set upon posts three feet off the ground and after they burned a hole they made their second getaway. They got an early Christmas present in 1856—their freedom—and made their escape to the Missouri River bottoms in Iowa. Despite the dubious advice of the slavers, the escapees were savvy enough to realize that if the slave hunters told them not to go to Tabor then this was exactly where they should go. Without compass or map under cloudless night skies, they made their way north to the Iowa town. On their trek to freedom, a blinding winter storm blew up, causing whiteout conditions, and the two runaways were separated. One of them made his way to Tabor, and contrary to the slavers' false propaganda about the town, it proved extremely hospitable to the lone runaway. The people of Tabor made preparations to forward the former slave in his passage on the Underground Railroad.

However, the escapee in Tabor wouldn't leave until his fellow runaway showed up in the Iowa town. Days passed with no sign of the other runaway. The former slave, who was not used to idleness, asked if he could perform chores while he waited for his partner. Every day he went out into the timbers surrounding Tabor and cut wood. After more days had passed and much timber harvested, his fellow runaway finally showed up. At last, this happy pair, again reunited, made their way on the Underground Railroad to what John Todd called the "Queen's Dominions" and freedom in Canada.[3] The Underground Railroad these men had used for travel was neither a railroad nor underground; railroad terms were used to describe the secret places, methods of travel and people who assisted in this cause.

By the time the slave hunters were loudly banging on George Gaston's door, the two united former slaves were long gone from Tabor. However, when the slave hunters threatened to come back with search warrants, this worried John Todd's wife, Martha. She was the daughter of a prominent attorney from Ohio, and she knew the power of a search warrant. She would write to her father, also a conductor on the Underground Railroad,[4] that she knew the former slaves were safe out of the reach of the bounty hunters, but the Todds had other secrets they were hiding.[5]

Concealed in the basement of the Reverend Todd's house were 200 Sharps rifles. These rifles were sometimes called "Beecher's Bibles" by abolitionists. To avoid detection by unfriendly persons, the outside shipping crates of these rifles would sometimes be stamped "Beecher's Bibles" in honor of the Reverend Henry Ward Beecher. Beecher felt the abolitionists in Kansas had the right to protect themselves with guns if necessary. Beecher was a well-known abolitionist and brother of Harriet Beecher Stowe, author of *Uncle Tom's Cabin.*

The rifles had been delivered by wagon to Tabor. In the Todds' barn and around their property were hidden two cannons and an arsenal of shells and ammunition. This munitions store was meant for the Free State immigrants headed into Kansas. It was felt these immigrants would need protection from the sometimes-murderous actions of pro-slavery men in Kansas. Mrs. Todd feared questions would be raised by authorities about this arsenal, if search warrants were produced.

While the citizens of Tabor were overwhelmingly anti-slavery, outside the town in the countryside some of the residents of Fremont County, Iowa, were diametrically opposed to Tabor's wish for freedom for all human beings. Many residents of Fremont County, which borders on Missouri's northern boundary, were from Missouri and other Southern slave states.[6] Sheriffs and other public officials in Northern states were obligated to carry out fugitive slave and other obnoxious laws protecting slavery and their human "property" in free states such as Iowa. It was also easy to find people outside of Tabor who would join posses hunting for runaway slaves in rural Fremont County. Escaping slaves would be captured in Fremont County by slave hunters or slave posses from Missouri hoping to collect reward money. Much to the distress of the abolitionists in Tabor, this had been done on a number of occasions. A preacher in the vicinity of Tabor was most adamantly against the work on the Underground Railroad and felt he was doing the work of the Lord by denouncing Tabor's Underground Railroad activity.[7]

Those slave hunters who pounded on George Gaston's door never returned to Tabor with warrants, but the armory hidden by the Congregational minister had a very dubious history. John Brown, after some infighting amongst various abolitionist groups over the ownership of these weapons, took possession of the arms, and with his small army, went to Harper's Ferry, Virginia. Brown had hoped to attack the federal arsenal at Harper's Ferry, take the rifles and other arms stored there and distribute them to slaves throughout the South in hopes of overthrowing the institution of slavery. The weapons used by Brown and his men on his ill-fated uprising against the United States arsenal were the same weapons stored in John

Todd's cellar during 1856–57. Thus the parson from Tabor could have been, but was not, officially implicated in Brown's plot to start a slave revolt.[8]

If one looked at John Todd's and George Gaston's past, there would be little doubt they would become involved in this nation's struggle over slavery. Todd graduated from Oberlin College with an undergraduate degree and then later received his theological degree from Oberlin Seminary. While at Oberlin College, Todd soaked up that institution's philosophy of equality. In the 19th century Oberlin College became the leading integrated institution of higher learning in the United States for the education of black Americans. Oberlin was the first college to put women on equal footing with men. Todd was in classes with black Americans and saw the fallacy of the racist views held by many white Americans, both in the North and the South, towards people of color.

When he was at Oberlin's seminary in 1842, Todd wrote a letter to his cousin, who favored the slavery status quo. The letter stated, "The slaves would be justifiable in rising & asserting & maintaining their liberty by force. (Although I should advise them to wait in hope of obtaining a peaceable deliverance) I don't believe any man in the world can justify the war of the American Revolution & at the same time condemn the slaves for rising to obtain their liberties. 'All men are created equal.' Is that rhetorical flourish? Or is it sober truth? If so, then the *African* has right to pursue *his* happiness, that the *American* or *European* has to seek *his*...."[9]

The Underground Railroad apparatus and its passages commenced in Tabor appropriately on July 4, 1854.[10] There was a Mississippi slaveholder heading out west with six slaves. The slaver grew tired of waiting for ferry passage across the Missouri River at the busy Nebraska City, Nebraska, crossing. He decided to go north of Nebraska City and make his crossing possibly at Council Bluffs, Iowa. However, dusk fell upon the slaveholder and despite Tabor's reputation as a hotbed of abolitionist sentiment, the slaver camped in Tabor with his three covered wagons, carriage and six enslaved humans.

Samuel Adams made contact with two of the slaves at Jesse West's well while they were drawing water for their master, and it was determined five of the six wished to escape. The five who wished freedom were a mother, father and their two children and another man. The five slaves were told where the new "depot" for the Underground Railroad was located and during the middle of the night the five made their escape.[11] A sixth female slave was thought to be so loyal to the master that the plan to flee on the Underground Railroad wasn't even presented to her, as it was believed she would tell the master about the planned escape. Ironically, John Todd advised Samuel Adams that perhaps for the safety of the conductors of this "train," this escape should be reconsidered. Adams went ahead with

George Gaston and the escape was planned.[12]

When the day broke on July 5, the slave owner, who was accustomed to having his morning breakfast started, his water for the day being drawn and his horses being taken care of at daybreak, awoke to a silent camp. Everything was at a standstill. The Mississippian didn't even ask anyone in town where his slaves had gone. He knew he would get no cooperation from the people of Tabor. The slaver went outside of town and found a number of people in sympathy with his cause, and a posse was formed to find the runaways.[13]

A general slave hunt was designed, and the posse scoured the groves, thickets and tall grass around Tabor. Special interest was given to the timbers bordering on both sides of the Nishnabota River. Every nook and every cranny that might offer a hiding place for the runaways were carefully searched.

The machinery of the Underground Railroad was in full alert. Conductors were selected. A huge cottonwood tree had fallen across the Nishnabotna River and Samuel H. Adams carried the two children across the river on top of the tree.[14] The people of Tabor referred to this cottonwood as their "railroad bridge" and felt that the tree had fallen across the river in such a manner as to be usable on the Underground Railroad.[15]

Deacon Samuel H. Adams. Given a great Massachusetts name, Adams was born in that commonwealth and came to Oberlin College and then to Tabor, Iowa. During the first Underground Railroad escape in Tabor, Adams contacted two enslaved blacks while they were passing through town with their master. An escape was planned for five in the group who wanted out of bondage. Adams personally carried two small children on this escape across the Nishnabota River over a large fallen cottonwood tree. (Todd House Museum Archives.)

The three adult runaways made their way across the river and were hidden. The group's destination would be the Underground Railroad Station in Quincy, Iowa. The slave posse continued its search for the former slaves.

John Todd and the others in Tabor employed a tactic that they would use often in cases of searches. They would have one of their members infiltrate the search posse.

The member who infiltrated the slave posse would, of course, always volunteer to search the area where he knew the runaways and their conductors were hiding. They did this in the case of the fugitive Mississippi slaves. After the "search" by the infiltrator, the conductors and their charges headed for Quincy in Adams County. On the way, they met a man who asked them where they were headed, and they told him. After this encounter, the conductors became suspicious of the man's motives and changed their route.

The conductors then took the train and, instead of going to Quincy, headed for another station house in Lewis, Iowa. Sure enough, the stranger who asked where they were headed found the slave posse and informed them the "train" was headed to Quincy. The slave posse rode off to the Adams County town only to come away empty handed again. Some pro-slavery men hassled the train around Lewis but the conductors and their passengers managed to escape.[16]

The Tabor conductors managed to get the train to eastern Iowa, where they found some Wesleyan Methodists to take the escaping slaves on their way. The runaways were next spotted in Peoria, Illinois, by John Todd's sister. His sister saw them while they were visiting a church in that city.[17] The Mississippian's slave posse harassed the "train" all the way to Detroit, Michigan, where the escapees managed to elude his grasp and take a boat and cross over into Canada.

The Mississippi slave owner had offered those in his posse or the general public $200 for the return of the slaves. He also put a reward of $50 "dead or alive," preferably dead, on the heads of the Tabor conductors who aided in the escape. It was stated by one of the men in the slave posse that the slaver intended to kill the white conductors himself if they were captured.[18] Fortunately the conductors made it back safely to Tabor, where they were well protected by their friends and neighbors.

Ironically, the slave owner had to change his plans and instead of going out to the Salt Lake City region as originally intended, he settled northeast of Glenwood, Iowa. The slaver learned that one of his neighbors, Cephas Case, had played a major part in the escape of his slaves. One day the slaver attacked Case with a black cane and serious injury was avoided only when another neighbor intervened.[19]

On another occasion, a Congregational pastor in Atchison, Kansas, sent a young slave woman north to Tabor for her freedom on the Underground Railroad. The Reverend Todd was going to an association meeting of the Southwest Iowa Congregational ministers in Council Bluffs. It was his plan to take the runaway to the meeting and give her to the Reverend

Hitchcock, who was station-master at the Underground Railroad site at Lewis, Iowa. For some unknown reason, Hitchcock was unable to make connections with Todd. It wasn't unusual for plans to be changed at the last minute on the Underground Railroad.

The reverend brought the female slave back to Tabor. Usually a trip across the prairie in broad daylight was a dangerous passage for the Underground Railroad conductor and his human cargo. The Reverend Todd and his wife noticed the runaway and Mrs. Todd were about the same size. So they devised a plan. They would have the escapee pose as Mrs. Todd and dress her in a cloak, veil and gloves to hide her true identity. Todd and the runaway took a buggy ride with no one the wiser that the reverend and his wife were out for a nice buggy tour of the region.[20]

The Reverend Todd and the people of Tabor were very active on the Underground Railroad for many years. James Gaston, cousin to George Gaston, after the

This is the best known photograph of John Todd as an elderly man. Todd once transported by buggy a black female escapee who was dressed as much as possible to look like Mrs. Todd, in hopes the casual observer would think Mr. and Mrs. Todd were on a buggy ride across the open prairies of Iowa. Most veterans of this invisible "rail line" felt the most dangerous aspect of the Underground Railroad was not harboring the fugitives in their residence or out buildings, but transporting them between stations. (Todd House Museum Archives.)

Civil War was over, took his son outside of Tabor and told him of the many trails used by the Underground Railroad outside of the town.[21] Jesse West, proprietor of the only hotel and restaurant in town, at times played an important part in these escapes.

Once, only an hour or so after an Underground Railroad train and their conductors had left Tabor, the sheriff, his deputies and various slave hunters entered the town looking for the escaped slaves. Being hungry and tired, they went to the restaurant for a good, hot meal and some rest. West was told to delay the meal for as long as possible to make sure the conductors and their train was well on their way. The party of slave hunters grew restless after an hour and no meal. West told them of all the problems he was having in securing a fine meal for such a distinguished group. Finally, after a long wait the lawmen and slave hunters were fed.

The slave posse took off behind their prey after being delayed at Jesse West's restaurant. The slavers did manage to close the gap between them and the Underground Railroad train. It was a bitterly cold night and a conductor's wife feared she would never see her husband alive again. Due to the diligence of the Underground Railway conductors and Jesse West, the train managed to shake off the slave posse and was handed off to the next station. The runaways eventually made their way to freedom in Canada.[22]

Edwin Hill was one of the conductors on this Underground Railroad escape and made it home the following morning with both of his feet badly frozen. It was feared he could lose both feet. However, a tub of snow was prepared and his feet were rubbed until the frost was all drawn out of them.[23]

In March of 1860, a very dangerous escape occurred on the Underground Railroad in Tabor. Four black men from the Cherokee Nation in what was known as Indian Territory in the present state of Oklahoma traveled hundreds of miles and appeared in the Civil Bend area in Iowa. Some of the Cherokee tribe had adopted the obnoxious institution of slavery, and this quartet wanted out of bondage. George Gaston brought them from Civil Bend to Tabor disguised in women's clothing.[24]

On a Friday night, conductors were chosen for this passage. They were Edward T. Sheldon and Newton Woodford. The conductors rode out in a sled, as there still was snow on the ground, with their load of human cargo. They stopped to rest the team of horses at Mud Creek. A house stood on a hill over Mud Creek and a young boy noticing the team down below carefully made his way unnoticed to a spot close to the sled. There he identified the true nature of the riders in the sled. The young boy went to authorities and they procured arrest warrants for the conductors.[25] The conductors were arrested in neighboring Mills County and jailed in the county seat town of Glenwood. The jailer refused to imprison the escaping black men. They were housed in a barn outside of Glenwood at an undisclosed location.[26]

An unusual trial date was set for 10:00 A.M. that Sunday morning. News reached Tabor of the wreck of their latest train on the Underground Railway. A discussion was held in Tabor to see if it would be dishonoring the Sabbath to go to the trial on a Sunday. The Reverend Todd and others decided that if an ox had fallen into a pit it would be lifted out on a

Sabbath. They reasoned how much more important it was that the two conductors and their human cargo be saved on a Sabbath. The men of Tabor went to Glenwood to give support to their railroad comrades.

During the trial, a note was handed to one of the Tabor people stating where the escapees were being kept and with the news that the slaves were to be taken back into Missouri that night. Two men from Tabor acted as scouts and sprang into action and went to the site where the escapees were located.[27]

It was a frosty, cold March night with a bright, full moon and a blanket of snow covering the ground when the Tabor men saw the runaways being loaded from the barn to a wagon. They knew the snow would make the wagon an easy vehicle to track.

The two Tabor scouts headed back to the courthouse at 9:00 P.M. just as the trial closed. Both conductors had been found not guilty. There was little time to waste on a celebration. There was more work to be done freeing the runaways from Oklahoma. The derailed Underground Railroad train had to get back on track. All the Tabor men piled into two sleds to track the wagon. It took an all night chase, but the abolitionists finally overtook the slavers as dawn broke on the Iowa prairie. Guns were pulled by both sides, but the abolitionists managed to disarm the slavers.[28] The Tabor men recaptured the human cargo in the wagon, and the derailed Underground Railroad train was once again set into motion. The former slaves from Oklahoma, now under the protection of conductors from Tabor, were now on their way to the "Queen's Dominions" and freedom as they made their way to Canada. One of these escapees came back to Tabor from Canada and made his way South to bring his wife to freedom.[29]

The Reverend John Todd and his flock from Tabor proved to be helpful allies in the cause of freedom on the Underground Railroad. John Brown also saw that Tabor's unique location and its unswerving devotion to the abolitionist cause made it a natural site for the beginnings of his offensive in Kansas against pro-slavery forces.

Brown, who had spent much of his life in Ohio, felt at home with these former residents of Oberlin. It was said that Tabor was the most congenial soil Brown had set foot upon since leaving Ohio. It was Tabor that Brown chose to be his headquarters for the training of his men to fight the pro-slavery forces in Kansas. Tabor would be the headquarters for the recruitment of the "volunteer-regulars" for whom he planned to go back East to raise twenty thousand dollars.[30]

It would be Tabor that Brown would use as a hospital area for his fighting men. At one time, John Brown's son-in-law would be recuperating from a gunshot wound; his son would be recovering from an accident and another son recuperating from an illness in Tabor. In the city park of this town,

Brown's men learned the rudimentary drills of a soldier. A firing range would be set up at the edge of town so Brown's men could learn the skills of the sharpshooter.

Other abolitionists such as James Lane and Samuel Gridley Howe would be in and out of Tabor on a regular basis. Lane would become the first United States Senator from Kansas and a power in the newly formed Republican Party for the abolishment of slavery. Dr. Howe, whose wife was Julia Ward Howe, the author of the stirring "Battle Hymn of the Republic," first saw Tabor's potential as an overland route for immigrants coming into Kansas. When pro-slavery governments issued warrants for James Lane and John Brown, they would often use Tabor as a hide out until things cooled off in Kansas and they could resurface.

Children in Tabor were also affected by the Underground Railroad activity. Young James Todd, age ten, noted that his younger sister, Louisa, who normally babysat with the Todds' youngest daughter, Flora, refused stay alone in their house for fear that the Missouri slave hunters would return to town and come knocking on the Todds' front door.[31]

During this time a young girl in Tabor went up into her bedroom and heard a noise coming from the room of her brothers. Knowing the boys

John Brown felt Tabor was the most congenial soil he had been on since leaving Ohio. He admired these staunch Oberlin style abolitionists. When warrants were sworn out for Brown's arrest by pro-slavery governments in Kansas, when things got too "hot" for him in that territory, or when Brown or his sons were sick or wounded, they would often come to Tabor for safety and rest. The town was close enough to "Bleeding Kansas" that if Brown needed to jump into that fray he could, yet it was far enough away to provide convenient security and comfort. (Kansas State Historical Society.)

were not supposed to be in their room at this time of day, she peered into the garret that was her brothers' room and was startled to see it full of runaway slaves. The next morning she awoke to find no traces of the black escapees anywhere. The former slaves had gone from the house, having taken passage on the Underground Railroad.[32]

Another time a farmer north of Tabor, Daniel Briggs, in sympathy with the Reverend Todd and his cause and who often served on the Underground Railroad, hurriedly drove up to his farm house. He had been cutting wood on a cold winter's day and his wood rack was still on his sled. He told his wife to pack him a lunch, as he had to go into Tabor immediately.

Their daughter was in Tabor going to school, and his wife feared something was wrong with their little girl; perhaps she had fallen ill. He answered that their daughter was fine but that he would not have time to see her. He said they needed to move two escaping slaves at once. One wonders if these two escaping black women had been spotted in Tabor by unfriendly people. If these two runaways had been seen there would be a great need to move them outside of Tabor for a while.

Briggs went into Tabor and brought two females runaways to his farmstead. It was necessary to keep the former slaves hidden for three days in the upstairs of their farmhouse. One of the escapees, probably not used to the claustrophobic surroundings, found the hiding to be very tiresome. She would volunteer to do housework to relieve the boredom. However, the Briggses felt it better if she kept hidden away lest someone accidentally see the hideaways. Finally it was safe to move the two former escaped slaves forward onto the Underground Railway.[33]

Maria Gaston, wife of George Gaston, would write of these times on the Underground Railroad that it "opened the way for sleepless nights, *frozen ears & toes* as some here present can testify."[34]

John Todd, George Gaston and the townspeople of Tabor would become a major cog in the Western Terminus of the Underground Railroad. To the west of Tabor and Iowa were the territories of Kansas and Nebraska. To the north, south and west were thousands of miles of lightly settled areas until the west coast was reached. Very often the rule of law in these territories was at the end of a gun or in the courtroom of Judge "Lynch." Once in Tabor the rules and laws of the United States were in full effect. Although a small village, Tabor was on the edge of what some would consider civilization. For this reason it was a very important station on the Underground Railroad. Tabor would be committed to every aspect of the Underground Railroad and the abolitionist movement from the time it was formed to the start of the Civil War. There would be more harrowing escapes on the Underground Railroad in Tabor, including one of the most famous and controversial passages pulled off by John Brown.

2

Oberlin

There have been estimates that 100,000 people escaped to freedom via the Underground Railroad. Where the Underground Railroad started and how its clandestine apparatus took shape and form are unclear. In many cases it was locally fashioned. Some slaves escaped completely unaided by anyone. Others were aided only by people of color. What became known as the Underground Railroad was a loosely formed system of station houses and conductors wishing to help slaves go from bondage to freedom.

However, one would be hard pressed to find more of a hotbed of Underground Railroad stationmasters or conductors than at Oberlin College in Oberlin, Ohio. Oberlin College in the 1830's, 1840's and 1850's became a virtual breeding ground for the Underground Railroad and abolitionist activism. There are those who say that Oberlin's activism in the Underground Railroad and other abolitionist causes was one of the primary reasons for the start of the Civil War.

When seventeen-year-old John Todd reached Oberlin, Ohio, in September of 1835,[1] the college and village were in a forested wilderness a dozen miles from Lake Erie. Todd saw devious tracks through the forest that passed for roads, and they were frequently impassable to carriages. These roads were often extremely muddy and full of water. Todd and the other students had to sometimes walk all or part of the nine and a half miles from Elyria because the road was too obstructed or there were no conveyances to take them to Oberlin.[2]

Despite these foreboding forest surroundings, John Todd and the rest of the students were on fire for the Lord. When their college studies were completed and their other work around the campus done, they were only too happy to attend any temperance meeting, help start Sunday schools in the surrounding poor communities or conduct anti-slavery lectures in the region.

John Todd pitched in like the other early students at Oberlin and helped to clear the forests and build houses and roads. The students coaxed crops out of the mediocre soils that surrounded Oberlin. James Harris Fairchild, who would have a 68 year association with Oberlin first as a student then later as its president, became a lifelong friend of John Todd. Fairchild said of his first visit to Oberlin that the happy religious character of the student body and earnest nature of the students led him to feel as if he had been "to heaven."[3]

In 1833, after a year of praying and planning, John J. Shipherd, a Presbyterian minister in Elyria, and a friend of his, Philo P. Stewart, a former missionary to the Native Americans in Mississippi, opened Oberlin Collegiate Institute. In 1850, its name would change to the more familiar Oberlin College. The name Oberlin was taken from a French pastor, John Frederick Oberlin.[4] A small book had been written about Oberlin in 1830. The book praised his work as pastor to a poverty-stricken parish in the Alsace region of France. He not only was the spiritual leader of his community, but he also helped build roads and bridges and championed public health measures. He revolutionized the local agriculture, helped promote industry and established a school system, including a type of kindergarten. Oberlin College stressed a self-denying and efficient life coupled with an overwhelming love of God and sympathy for his fellow men and women regardless of race.

Shipherd and Stewart's vision of Oberlin College was to provide the Mississippi River Valley with godly ministers and teachers. They felt this region would not only have an impact on the United States but also on the whole world. They not only wanted to establish a college but a community, or colony if you will, that would espouse the Oberlin philosophy. Families were to be gathered from different parts of the country to organize a community devoted to this philosophy. Those who wished to live in Oberlin were asked to consecrate the enterprise by subscribing to the following articles of agreement, called the Oberlin Covenant:

> Lamenting the degeneracy of the Church and the deplorable condition of our own perishing world, and ardently desirous of bringing both under the entire influence of the blessed gospel of peace; and viewing with peculiar interest the influence which the Valley of the Mississippi must exert over our nation and the nations of the earth; and having, as we trust, in answer to devout supplications been guided by the counsel of the Lord: the undersigned covenant together under the name of the Oberlin Colony, subject to the following regulations which may be amended by a concurrence of two-thirds of the colonists.

1. Providence permitting, we engage as soon as practicable to remove to the Oberlin Colony, in Russia, Lorain county, Ohio, and there to fix our residence for the express purpose of glorifying God in doing good to men to the extent of our ability.
2. We will hold and manage our estates personally, but pledge as perfect a community of interest, as though we held a community property.
3. We will hold in possession no more property than we believe we can profitably manage for God, as his faithful stewards.
4. We will by industry, economy, and Christian self-denial, obtain as much as we can above our necessary personal or family expenses, and faithfully appropriate the same for the spread of the gospel.
5. That we may have time and health for the Lord's service, we will eat only plain and wholesome food, renouncing all bad habits, and especially the smoking and chewing of tobacco, unless it is necessary as a medicine, and deny ourselves all strong and unnecessary drinks, even tea and coffee, as far as practicable, and everything expensive, that is simply calculated to gratify the palate.
6. That we may add to our time and health, money, for the service of the Lord, we will renounce all the world's expensive and unwholesome fashions of dress, particularly tight dressing and ornamental attire.
7. And yet more to increase our means of serving Him who bought us with his blood, we will observe plainness and durability in the construction of our houses, furniture, carriages, and all that appertains to us.
8. We will strive continually to show that we, as the body of Christ, are members one of another; and will while living provide for the widows, orphans, and families of the sick and needy as for ourselves.
9. We will take special pains to educate all our children thoroughly, and to train them up in body, intellect and heart for the service of the Lord.
10. We will feel that the interests of the Oberlin Institute are identified with ours, and do what we can to extend its influence to our fallen race.
11. We will make special efforts to sustain the institutions of the gospel at home and among our neighbors.
12. We will strive to maintain deep-toned and elevated personal piety, to "provoke each other to love and good works," to live together in all things as brethren, and to glorify God in our bodies and spirits which are his.

In testimony of our fixed purpose thus to do, in reliance on divine grace, we hereunto affix our names.[5]

After a few years the leaders of Oberlin felt this covenant was "too specific to serve as a general pledge of Christian purpose, and too general to be a guide to specific duty." However, many of the students in the college and townspeople of Oberlin took the covenant to heart. Many of the points of the Oberlin covenant would be ingrained in John Todd's personal beliefs and behavior. No strong drink, even tea or coffee, would be taken. Simple and unadorned design of clothing, furniture and building would be his style. When Todd's colony in Tabor was established the principal of taking care of those in need in the community would be practiced, plus many of the other points of the Oberlin covenant. Also, a personality type was inherited from the Oberlin style that praised God rather than one's own ego. John Todd was always an extremely humble man.

In a paper John Todd read at Oberlin College's Jubilee in 1883 titled the "Early Home Missionary," he stated, "Without at all disparaging the wholesale influence of godly parents, I may truly say that whatever of the aid I have been able to render in the cause of the Master, I owe, under God, to Oberlin."[6]

After a year of studies at college, John's brother, David, joined him in Ohio. David Todd started his studies at the prep school in Sheffield, also in Lorain County. David then joined John at Oberlin the next year.[7] Their close bond would continue at this unique school. The Todd brothers had grown up in a rather idyllic setting in Hanover Township near Harrisburg, Pennsylvania. Their stone house had a red water pump, and a green meadow that was picture perfect. Like most farm boys of the time, they were expected to do the many chores around their home place. Their father, James Todd, was well respected in the community and at times his views went counter to the common thinking of that era. During this period, farmers were expected to provide barrels of whiskey to harvest crews. James Todd was the first farmer in the area that banned whiskey from the harvest field. He also let his neighbors know that he was adamantly against the institution of slavery.

James Todd was a captain in the in the 2nd Regiment 1st Brigade of the Pennsylvania Militia during the War of 1812.[8] In 1814, a crisis was brewing in the newly founded nation that would affect the young Todd family. The United States had been at war with England since 1812. However, the war had been mainly a sideshow for England, which had committed most of its material and manpower to defeating Napoleon on the European continent. In the late spring of 1814, word reached America that Napoleon had fallen. The British government could now commit large numbers of Lord Wellington's battle-hardened continental troops to the United States in hopes of reuniting the rebel colonists back into the bosom of mother England.

As expected, Wellington's troops were successful in America. At Bladensburg, Maryland, the United States troops were badly beaten. The

English used a new weapon that spooked the Americans. This was the rocket. After their victory at Bladensburg, the Crown's Army then went into Washington, D.C., and sacked this nation's capital. The English then set their sights on the nation's third largest city—Baltimore, Maryland, a few miles from Washington, D.C.

Officials in Baltimore and Washington sent out appeals for militiamen to help protect their cities. At this time, most states were reluctant to send troops beyond their own state's borders. However, Pennsylvania Governor Simon Snyder authorized two brigades to go south to Baltimore to help repel the British invasion.

James Todd was thirty-five years old at this time with three small children at home. Under his command were his two younger brothers, David, age twenty-three, and Samuel, age nineteen.[9] The brothers were mustered into service on September 1, 1814, and had to hustle to get a rudimentary training and receive their arms and then go south to the Maryland city. When James Todd left his hearth and home, he had no idea who was going to harvest his crops that fall, as many of his neighbors and relations were in his Regiment. He wasn't even sure if he would have a farm or family when he came back to Hanover Township or if the British troops would overrun that whole region of the United States.

While the Todd brothers and the 2nd Regiment were making their way south on September 13 and on into the morning of the 14th, the British bombarded Fort McHenry mercilessly. Fort McHenry was the American garrison that guarded Baltimore. Rockets and cannons blasted the fort all through the night. The rockets, leaving their smoking trails with their fiery crimson heads, filled the night skies. The American commander at Fort McHenry, Lieutenant-Colonel G. Armistead, estimated the attack lasted 25 hours, and the enemy threw some 1800 shells at the American fortification.[10] Armistead had decided to fly a huge American flag "so large that the British will have no difficulty in seeing it at a distance." The American flag at Fort McHenry measured 42 by 30 feet.[11]

In the Chesapeake Bay was a Maryland lawyer who had sailed out on a truce ship to meet the British fleet to negotiate the release of an American doctor that the British had imprisoned. The lawyer secured the release of Dr. Beane, but because the lawyer and his party had heard the British discussions of the battle plan for Baltimore, they were detained on an English war vessel. At dawn's light on the 14th, the lawyer and the Americans on board were excited and stunned to see Armistead's huge American flag still flying over Ft. McHenry.

Captain James Todd and his company of men were on a hard march to Baltimore from south central Pennsylvania and reached the city on September 20, 1814.[12] Armistead's giant star spangled banner still waved over

Fort McHenry. Todd and his company of Pennsylvanians were soon incorporated into the defensive deployment around Baltimore.[13]

Francis Scott Key, the Maryland lawyer who had witnessed the bombardment of Fort McHenry, had jotted down a poem describing the event. Key's poem was combined with an English drinking song called "To Anacreon in Heaven" with the heading "Defense of Fort M'Henry." This song was printed on a handbill, and then on September 20, the day Captain Todd and his men reached Baltimore, it was published in full in the Baltimore *Patriot and Evening Advertiser*.[14] The song was an immediate hit with the people of Baltimore and undoubtedly with Todd and his fellow militiamen. After a few weeks, Key's anthem became known as "The Star Spangled Banner," and it quickly spread throughout the country, galvanizing the nation's spirit into one of unity and pride of being an American.

Captain James Todd and his company of militiamen plus many other militia forces were added to the now formidable Baltimore defenses. Rumors flew around Baltimore about a second attack on the city. However, the British sensed that these militiamen, like Captain Todd, had a resolve and weren't going to bolt and run like those around Bladensburg. Ft. McHenry's Commander Armistead and the now growing contingent of militiamen stirred by Key's lyrics in "The Star-Spangled Banner" were dug in and not about to be moved. The British had second thoughts about attacking the city again.

Soon the Crown's menace to this Maryland city passed and most of the British fleet and ground forces turned their attention to what they thought would be an easier target, New Orleans. However, Andrew Jackson and his frontiersmen waited for the English troops. After the danger to Baltimore had passed, Captain Todd and his militiamen were ordered back to Pennsylvania. The Treaty of Ghent ending the War of 1812 was signed in Ghent, Belgium, on December 24, 1814. Due to the travel time, the president of the United States, James Madison, didn't sign the treaty until February 17, 1815. Captain Todd and his brothers were separated from service 16 days after Madison signed the treaty on March 5, 1815.[15]

After being mustered out of the service, James went back to farming around Hanover Township and his operation grew. James Todd would always be called Captain Todd out of respect for his help in defending Baltimore. The future Iowa abolitionist, John Todd, was born on November 10, 1818. John Todd's father, grandfather and great-grandfather were all named James. The patriarch of the family, Hugh Todd, had migrated from Scotland to Ireland to escape British oppression and possible death; the Crown had begun executing Scottish Presbyterians. However, once in Ireland the British began excessively taxing Irish woolen products that were the lifeblood of the Scottish community like the Todds. Hugh Todd immigrated to America in 1735.

Family legend has it that Hugh Todd escaped Ireland hidden in a molasses barrel and was rolled on board the transcontinental boat. It is said that this was the reason the Todds had such a sweet disposition.[16]

In looking at the Todd family tree one is struck by how many ministers there were and how many Todds were citizen-soldiers. This clan saw its members serve in the Revolutionary War, War of 1812 and the Civil War. John's grandfather had served in the Revolutionary War in the Continental Army. Todds had fought with General George Washington, and a Todd had fought with Benedict Arnold in his campaign against Quebec. On John Todd's grandmother Wilson's side in 1690, the patriarch of that side of the family, Thomas Wilson, was awarded an 1800-acre estate in Ireland for his military bravery and deeds at the Battle of Boyne. The Wilsons also gave soldiers for the French and Indian War and Revolutionary War.

On June 4, 1774, the Todds and other residents of Hanover Township in Pennsylvania signed the following resolution expressing the sentiments of the local community concerning "the present critical state of affairs and passed resolutions." The Todds and the community's obvious loathing of the British government is evident in the following passed resolution:

(1.) That the recent action of the parliament of Great Britain is iniquitous and oppressive.
(2.) That it is the bounded duty of the inhabitants of America to oppose every measure which tends to deprive them of their just prerogatives.
(3.) That in a closer union of the colonies, lies the safeguard of the people.
(4.) That in the event of Great Britain attempting to enforce unjust laws upon us by strength of arms our cause we leaven to heaven and our rifles.[17]

Once James Todd came home after being separated from service during the War of 1812, he continued his successful farming operation. In 1807 on October 15 Todd married the former Sally Ainsworth. Three girls, Mary, Sally and Margaret, and three boys, James, John and David, were delivered to the Todd family. All six children lived to adulthood, certainly a major achievement in the early part of the 19th century.[18]

It is a mystery why the eldest son James was not sent to college, as were his younger brothers John and David. Did James not show any interest in college? Certainly in reading James' letters it is apparent that he didn't have the writing or verbal skills that his two younger brothers possessed. In reading his letters it is obvious James would have had a difficult time in college. James served honorably in the Union Army and moved to California after his parents passed away, but he never married.

Oberlin College made a great effort to keep its costs to a bare minimum, which helped the Todd family support two sons in college, a daunting proposition in any era. Oberlin charged eighteen dollars a year at a time when Harvard was seventy dollars, Yale forty dollars, Union fifty-seven dollars, and Dartmouth, "the poor man's college," charged twenty-seven dollars.[19] Room rents for students were only a few dollars a year. However, in these early years a student was never turned away from Oberlin regardless of gender or race or for the lack of tuition funds.

The founders of Oberlin thought the school could be supported by the manual labor system. The Todd brothers, along with the other male students, were expected to work four hours a day around the Oberlin campus. They worked the acres of farmland owned by Oberlin trying to grow a crop out of the less than desirable soils in that area. The male students at Oberlin milked the cows, cared for the livestock and did other chores around the campus. A sawmill was maintained by the students. The female students cooked in the kitchens and did housekeeping chores in the dormitories.

However, after a few years this system proved to be unproductive. For instance, it was less expensive to purchase Oberlin's food than to try and grow it. Gradually, the manual labor system was abandoned. After a while, many of the Oberlin students found that they could earn tuition money fanning out from Oberlin into the surrounding communities during the long three month winter vacations teaching in schools or filling pulpits. At this time, many country schools would hold classes after harvest in late fall and conclude before spring plantings, therefore a long winter break could provide Oberlin students ample opportunities for teaching appointments. In the winter of 1841 John was teaching school in Illinois, probably close to his folks in Granville, and was able to return to college in February 1842 to continue his studies at Oberlin.[20]

From the outset, Oberlin was to be open to women and even in the beginning women made up more than a third of the student body.[21] Many of the top educators in the county at the college level thought that the mixing of the sexes like this was a hazardous experiment. The thinking of the time was that women didn't have the capacity to learn as did the men, especially in the mathematics and science classes. It was thought by putting women in the same classes as men that the differences in intellect would be so overwhelming in favor of the men that woman would become humiliated. However, in 1837 four women were admitted to the freshman college class at Oberlin. In 1841 Oberlin made history when three of the four were the first women to receive a bona fide college degree ever granted to a woman in this country.[22] Oberlin's decision to allow women into the same classes as men proved to be an overwhelming success. Professor John Morgan, not an early advocate of allowing women into Oberlin, had to admit to friend Mark Hopkins that "the young ladies manifestly exert a civilizing influence on the young men."[23] Oberlin had helped to break down an ugly stereotype that women weren't as intelligent as men and that they couldn't learn as men did at the college level.

By 1835, the college was experiencing financial difficulties. After much discussion and many meetings, an unusual arrangement was made to save the newly formed institution. A charismatic revivalist, Charles Finney, would join the faculty of Oberlin College. Finney would later become the institution's second president. Also, a group of anti-slavery students from Lane Seminary in Cincinnati would join the Oberlin student body. More controversial in the agreement was the admission of black students to Oberlin.[24] This endeavor was to be underwritten by Arthur and Lewis Tappan and others.

The Tappan brothers were from New York City and desired to see the United States become a melting pot of racial harmony and to see an end to slavery. They had made a huge fortune in the dry goods business and were responsible for devising one of the first rating systems to determine commercial credit. The Tappan brothers even went so far as to advocate intermarrying of the races. Because of their forward thinking views in the 1830's, they were constantly threatened and even had a $100,000 reward on their heads for their deaths.

The brothers pledged their fortune to Oberlin only if the college would allow black students to attend. James Bradley, a former slave, was the first black student at Oberlin. Black women were also accepted into Oberlin.[25] Blacks were assimilated into the student body with no problems. The only problem Oberlin had with their diverse student body was the reaction of the uneducated and, unfortunately, the educated world around them, both local and national.

When John Todd or other students ventured outside of Oberlin to preach or discuss their views on slavery, they were often mocked and threatened, even in Ohio and other Northern states. When Oberlin students went out to teach or preach in surrounding schools or churches those institutions were called "nigger schools" or "nigger churches."[26] Because of Oberlin's stand on the equality of the races and genders and because of her activities on the Underground Railroad, when Democrats gained control of Ohio's legislative bodies on four occasions they tried to repeal Oberlin's college charter.[27] Newspapers and other publications from all over the nation, such as the *New York Observer*, wrote of the shortcomings of what they called Oberlin fanaticism.[28]

However, this attitude only strengthened John Todd's resolve to advocate the equality of all persons. He and brother David thrived at the school. In February of 1842, John would write to his cousin, Mrs. Margaret Strohm, on his view of those who opposed Oberlin's philosophy: "I do not regret that the enemies of our cause are thereby informed of our proceedings; for I am willing that the universe should know the ground we take in this matter; & our *reasons* too for pursuing the course we have insured, & which we still intend to pursue. You style the subject of Slavery a "vexed question." The discipline of it may be, & truly is a *vexing* question to tyrants & slaveholders, but to ardent lovers of liberty—to those who holds that "*all* men are created equal"—to those who possess the spirit of the gospels nothing can be more pleasing than the elucidation of those principles upon which our present prosperity is based—the "Magna Charta" of our heaven-born freedom."[29]

Many of the most radical abolitionists of the time wanted an end to slavery but many felt it would never do to let the slaves loose among the mainstream white society. Many ideas were produced at the time as to what to do with the slaves if they were all freed. A plan to send the newly freed slaves back to Africa to colonize Sierra Leone failed. The American Colonization Society had limited success in colonizing Liberia with newly freed slaves. Oberlin was one of the few beacons in the abolitionist world that advocated social and economic equality for black Americans, free or slave.

As mentioned before, Oberlin was a hotbed of Underground Railroad activity. John Todd and others who would later move to Iowa learned the tricks of the trade of the Underground Railroad at Oberlin. All the students did their part on the Underground Railroad. In 1837 one of the first Oberlin Underground Railroad escapes electrified the Oberlin student body. A former student brought four runaways through town in a wagon on their way to Canada.[30] In 1839 one of the professors at Oberlin had to discontinue his classes and go into hiding from authorities temporarily for his part in an Underground Railroad escape.[31] In 1860 Professor James Fairchild would proudly write that no former slave who made it to Oberlin was ever returned to slavery.[32]

While at Oberlin, John's brother David had a harrowing experience. He was charged in Harlan County, Kentucky, of trying to incite a slave revolt. The evidence against him was flimsy. He was from Ohio, and he did not have a good alibi for being in Kentucky. The prosecuting attorney from Kentucky figured Ohio was full of abolitionists, and that David Todd must have been up to something. In the South at this time, anyone from the North was looked upon with suspicion, especially if they were from Oberlin. David's crime could have been as innocent as talking to a black man or woman. In his summation, the prosecutor offered up no more evidence against David other than he was from Ohio.[33] It is not clear what the outcome of the trial was, but there is no confirmation that David was ever convicted of this alleged crime or had served any jail time. This experience that David had in Kentucky of being charged with trying to incite a slave revolt would have been a badge of honor at Oberlin.

John and David continued their studies at the college. John's obvious talents as a writer and orator surfaced there. John spoke at the Oberlin commencement exercises of 1841. The *Oberlin Evangelist* noted that "probably no greater interest could be excited than was felt in the address on 'The Political Economy of Slavery' by John Todd."[34] In this address John would speak on themes that he would write about later in life. One of them was what he and other abolitionists saw as the federal government consistently siding with the cause of slavery in her administrative and judicial opinions in order to placate Southern interests. Another theme Todd brought out in the speech was the stagnation of the Southern economy due to slavery. He used the example of New York state and Virginia. Virginia in 1790 had twice the population of New York but in 1841 New York had twice the population of Virginia and had greater economic worth. John also commented on the ironical condition that the country that was always touting the freedoms it had allowed slavery. He stated in his speech, "Paradoxical as it may seem our nation protests at the same time the most perfect freedom & the most object Slavery."[35]

In one of his courses with Professor John Morgan, Todd presented the class with a paper that especially impressed the professor. After John Todd had graduated from Oberlin Seminary, Morgan asked him to allow the *Oberlin Review* to print his article. In the August 1846 issue Todd's article "Christ's Last Passover" appeared. Morgan went on to praise the piece said Todd had achieved "complete success in elucidating a difficulty which has baffled some of the first minds."[36]

John made many friends at Oberlin, including James Harris Fairchild, who became Oberlin College's third president and served from 1866 to 1889. More importantly, while at Oberlin John met Martha Atkins. Miss Atkins was the ninth daughter of Quintus F. Atkins, a prominent attorney from Northern Ohio. Martha had a superb singing voice and was a tremendous asset to Oberlin's thriving music department. Martha began at Oberlin's preparatory school in the fall of 1838. In 1839, she entered Oberlin as a freshman and graduated in 1843.[37]

Even before John and Martha married, John's future father-in-law, Judge Atkins, as he was sometimes called, was impressed with the minister to be. Judge Atkins entrusted sums of money with John Todd for his son, Arthur. Arthur Atkins was the irresponsible brother of Martha. Arthur had health problems and problems with alcohol.

Judge Atkins sent Arthur to Oberlin's preparatory school, and this was as far as his formal education went. Arthur was never able to handle college course work and he never attended Oberlin College. Rather than send any money to Arthur, Judge Atkins sent the money for Arthur's living expenses and tuition to John Todd. John would then pay Arthur's bills. This way the money was sure to find its way, via John's steady hand, to its correct destination. In a letter from Oberlin dated September 20, 1842, John gives Judge Atkins an accounting of all the money the Judge has provided for Arthur's educational and living needs. John goes on to write of the trouble Arthur had gotten into: "I can only say of Arthur that he does *tolerable* well, & scarcely that. He went off one night on a "cooning" expedition without informing either Prof. Allen or myself & that too when on a former occasion he was strictly forbidden to go. The consequence is that he has been required to give the Faculty a written acknowledgement of his guilt & if deemed advisable by the [faculty], it will be read before all the members of the institution. Arthur has made the acknowledgement but it has not been read publicly yet."[38]

In this same letter, John indicates the role that he and Martha played as activists in the causes of anti-slavery and temperance at the college. He tells his future father-in-law that he attended a Liberty meeting in Elyria, Ohio, and that Martha wants to go to a Washingtonian Convention at Medina, Ohio.

Unfortunately, Arthur never quite settled down. He was frankly spoiled rotten by his nine older sisters in what was then an upper-middle class environment. He took the life as a seaman sailing in the Great Lakes region. However, during one episode in 1848, he left without bothering to tell anyone in his family where he was going. After a frantic search over many months, Martha's sister Mary found he had shipped out to New York City on the vessel *Mortimer Livingston*, then down to Apalachicola, Florida. Apalachicola then was a major port for cotton and it was

Young John Todd graduated from Oberlin College and its seminary and was completely immersed in its traditions of sacrifice and total commitment to causes, especially the abolition of slavery. After experiencing the red-hot religious and anti-slavery zeal of Oberlin College, Todd found his first pastorate at Clarksfield, Ohio, and the apathy of his congregation to be a disappointment. (Todd House Museum Archives.)

bound for London, Liverpool or Harve, France. The Atkins family believed the vessel was headed for Liverpool. Judge Atkins commented that he hoped to hear from Arthur and that he was safe and a reformed child.[39]

Martha Atkins went on to graduate from Oberlin in 1843. She then took a teaching position in Lafayette, Indiana, for a year.[40] John Todd graduated from Oberlin Seminary in 1844.[41] John Todd and Martha Atkins were united in marriage on September 10, 1844.[42]

John received handwritten ordination papers from the Lorain County Congregational Association on August 21, 1844. Later the ordination papers were printed and dated September 14, 1844.[43] John Todd's first call as a minister was to the congregation at Clarksfield, Ohio. His life's work in the ministry was about to begin. He and Martha were excited about his first pastorate.

3

First Call

After experiencing the red-hot religious fever of Oberlin, Clarksfield proved to be disappointing to the young Todd couple. In a letter to her mother shortly after Christmas in 1846, Martha wrote, "There is no particular religious interest here, still we have some hope that a discussion upon Universalism, which Mr. Todd is expecting to be drawn into, will arouse the community in some measure ... and may result in much good."

In this letter Mrs. Todd noted that the congregation had done little or nothing to help build the young couple their promised parsonage. She, however, played the part of the dutiful parson's wife and kept busy making soap, dipping candles, and taking care of the pork. She hoped to have time for some leisure reading but was sure she may be disappointed.[1]

In a letter six months later, the Todds wrote to her father and noted that there was still little work done on the parsonage. Like many of the ministers of the time, John, with the help of his wife, practiced agriculture and grew and raised most of the food his young family would eat. This greatly supplemented the small salary received by the parson from his congregation. John Todd was keeping busy planting corn and potatoes. He was also in demand as a speaker at alumni and ministerial association meetings and was engaged in formal debate on various religious matters.[2] But he took things into his own hands and began working on the parsonage. After his plantings were done he began planning siding for the dwelling.[3]

The Todds' first child, a male, was born in 1846 and in the custom of the Todd family was named James Todd. A girl followed in 1847 named Mary Louise. Another boy named after Mrs. Todd's father, Quintus, arrived while they lived in Ohio in 1849. The rest of the Todd children would be born in Iowa. Margaret came into the world in 1851. David, named after

John's beloved brother, was born 1854 but died as an infant and was buried in the Tabor, Iowa, cemetery. Flora was born in 1855, Martha in 1857 and Bertha in 1860.[4]

The flock at Clarksfield found in John Todd a man physically to be 5'6", of a slight build and carrying a light weight that he would maintain all his life. He had blue eyes and a light complexion. Like many he had dark hair in his youth that turned gray and then white as he aged. Todd moved with a quick step that was noted by all throughout his life.

John's son James would write that early in his life John Todd often wore a scowl on his face which was very noticeable because it was clean shaven. As John matured the scowl was less apparent. In his middle years he wore a short beard with his upper lip shaven. As he reached his older years the elder Todd wore a full white beard that gave him a "benignant and venerable appearance that all admired."[5]

John and Martha had a happy marriage; the trials and tribulations found on the frontier only seemed to strengthen it. However, as in all marriages, there were those little things one did that irritated the other spouse. One of those things that Martha did that seemed to irritate John was she always used poor ink or frozen ink to write her letters. When the Todds would write joint letters to Martha's folks, very often John would comment on this. John wrote from Clarksfield, Ohio, on December 29, 1846: "Martha has attempted to write you on the preceding pages of this sheet, but in consequence of using bad ink I fear you will hardly be able to decipher it. If you should be unable to read it, I trust you will be able to read what I now write."

Things moved slowly at the Clarksfield church. However, in May of 1849 thirteen souls committed themselves to the Reverend Todd's church. John had worked hard the previous winter doing evangelistic work and the fruits of those endeavors appeared to pay off in the late spring.[6]

However, it was obvious that the young couple showed signs of being restless. Even with the responsibilities of raising young children they found the religious apathy of Clarksfield stifling and were looking and talking about the possibility of moving. In addition to this restlessness, the Todds were very concerned about the direction the United States was taking with the institution of slavery seemingly becoming stronger. It seemed to them that the interests of the slave holders were being served by the politicians in Washington, D.C. The Todds wanted to see the horrible institution of slavery abolished and for America to become a true nation of equal individuals.

The wife of a minister in the 1840's had many duties and chores. Since there was little cash the wife of a preacher was expected to help grow food for the family in a garden. She was expected to make candles and soap, wash clothing by hand and a hundred other tasks. Wool had to be carded, spun and woven into cloth or knitted into socks and stockings. Most garments were hand sewn. She was also expected to attend all religious functions and help out with Sunday school and other church functions. Martha Todd had a fine singing voice and provided much music for both the church and community. Her days were filled from morning to night and recognition was very often sparse. Mrs. Martha Todd fulfilled this role with the pleasure of a true Christian.

Martha Atkins had grown up in a strong family and was surrounded by culture and refinement. Her father was a very successful attorney in Northern Ohio. He was also deeply involved in anti-slavery activities and the Underground Railroad. He was wanted as an abolitionist lecturer and in a letter it was noted that Q.F. Atkins was listed on the Central Committee of the Liberty Men of Cuyahoga County in Ohio, an obvious reference to an anti-slavery group.[7]

Martha Atkins and many of her sisters and brothers-in-law had attended Oberlin College and like her father were involved in the abolitionist movement. Her sisters and brother wrote to her father about various activities and it was obvious the family was very mobile. One very intriguing letter was written by Martha Todd's sister Bertha to their father. In this letter Bertha addressed the letter to her father the Hon. Q.F. Atkins, Wolcott, New Haven Co., Conn. The postmark was Cleveland O. however Bertha had lived in Buffalo, New York, at one time but the top of the letter states it was written at "Brooklyn Tuesday Evng July 26 [1853]:

> Your other [letter] written at Toronto came last Friday—it seems to me it takes a good while for letters to come from Canada—at least longer than it wo'd to go the same distance in our own country. Oscar & Frankie had a letter from their Father written at Toronto. We were very glad to hear that you all enjoyed your journey so well—at least you and Mr. Wade—from Mary we hear nothing—save as you speak of her I tho't you wo'd enjoy that route down the St. Lawrence—it seems to me from what I have heard of its beauties that it must be delightful—and I am glad you co'd visit it with such congenial companions. You have probably heard ere this, of this painfully exciting scene that occurred at the Falls a few days after you left—the loss of the three men over the Falls. We have had warm and very dry weather—no rain since you left until yesterday and then normal nearly all May—and some to day—we found on measuring it this morning that there was over two inches—we needed rain very much the grass in the door yard looked crisped and the corn leaves curled—the cisterns failed— and great quantities of dust to annoy us—but to night it is beautiful. Old Jack seems to enjoy his liberty very much. We have had him harnessed only once—but may oftener after Mr. Wade's horses leave which will be tomorrow or next day. Cousin Frank drives to Andover with the children where they are to remain until Mr. Wade goes for them.[8]

Was Bertha making references to the Underground Railroad? The fact that she is discussing her father's trip to Canada makes one think the references are to do with the Underground Railroad. The hundreds of lawyer Atkins' papers don't seem to indicate he had any business interests that would take him to Canada. Both Bertha and Mr. Atkins seem to be very familiar with Canada and ways to get in and out of the country. Was Mr. Atkins in Canada having taken some Underground Railroad escapees? The phrase "Old Jack seems to enjoy his liberty very much" is an odd way to talk about a horse. Is it more likely Bertha is talking about an escapee on the UGRR? Also, is the phrase "Mr. Wade's horses leave which will be tomorrow or the next day" a reference to Underground Railroad Conductor Wade and the fact that he will bring more escapees?

The Mr. Wade referred to here was Congressman Edward Wade, a well known conductor on the Underground Railroad.[9] Wade was a congressman from Northern Ohio who was a family friend and related by marriage to the Atkins family. Mrs. Todd's mother, who was an invalid, was cared for by Mrs. Edward Wade. Mrs. Wade was a sister of Mrs. Atkins. The Wades were a very well connected political family. Edward Wade's older brother was Benjamin Franklin Wade, a United States Senator from Ohio from 1851 to 1869. While in the Senate he served as president pro tempore of that body.

Even Martha Todd's sometimes troublesome brother, Arthur Atkins, noted some Underground Railroad activities in Chicago when he wrote to his mother on June 1, 1851, "There is a good deal of excitement here on act. [account] of a Fugitive Slave being claimed by its masters & the Chicago folks sure to feel inclined to turn out enmasse to the rescue I do not think they will get away with him but they may."[10]

Martha Todd's sister, Mary Atkins, was an ardent supporter of the Underground Railroad. Mary Atkins also made a name for herself as a pioneer in women's educational opportunities. Mary graduated in 1845 from Oberlin College, where she was a classmate of prominent women's rights advocate Lucy Stone. Mary became a school administrator. She became assistant principal at the Oberlin College Ladies Department after graduation. She caused quite a stir in 1848 when she became principal of the Female Department of the Woodward High School in Cincinnati, Ohio. At this time women received only a fraction of what men made, even as school teachers or school administrators. Mary caused a uproar because she received "an unusually high salary for a woman."[11]

In 1853 tragedy struck Mary as her fiancée, who was a civil engineer, went to work in Panama. While he was there he contracted a tropical disease and died. Mary became so distraught she had to go to Panama. She resigned her principal's position and traveled by herself to Central America. This was at a time when few women would undertake any kind of a journey by themselves. Once in Panama, she located her fiancée's grave and marked it with a memorial inscription.[12]

Mary then traveled over the Isthmus of Panama. At this time there was no Panama Canal and ships arriving on the Atlantic Ocean side had to unload all their cargo, which was then carried to a ship on the Pacific Ocean side. While crossing the isthmus Mary's clothes got wet and still weren't dry by the time she reached California.[13] Mary's ship docked in Benicia, California. A couple of years before Mary had arrived, Benicia had actually been the capital of California. Mary took over leadership of the Young Ladies Seminary. After a short while she became owner of the institution, which had a prominent music department.[14] Under Mary's leadership this institution prospered and she later sold it to Cyrus and Susan Mills. It became Mills College, which still exists today.

John and Martha Todd bided their time in Clarksfield. They kept themselves informed about all anti-slavery and abolitionist activities going on in the area and the nation as a whole. They tried to attend and support anything that had the promise to bring an end to slavery. All through their lives John and Martha Todd, even though in remote areas, received letters, newspapers and other information from their scattered families and from Oberlin classmates and others whose lives they had touched. From across the United States from California, Ohio, Illinois, New York and other locales, the Todds received a wide variety of correspondence of an anti-slavery nature, of current events and of a personal nature. They were well informed people for their times on not only local news but also regional and national news.

John began to hone his style and presentation as a minister. Like many who trained in Oberlin under Charles Finney, his technique of presenting a sermon was to be conversational rather than oratorical. His early sermons were written out but these were more outlines than verbatim readings. On the backs of his sermon outlines he would write the date it was given and where. This proved to be very helpful when he began preaching out West and might be called upon several times a day to sermonize at different locations.[15] However, later in his ministry John began to write out his sermons and he read them. With his white hair and beard late in his ministry many thought John's sermons were from the voice of God. The reverend had a resonate voice and many considered his sermons to be of the first order.

John Todd had a very large vocabulary. The style of the times was to be very ornate and flowery. However, that was not his style and he would always use simple, well-chosen words. John had an extremely logical mind and could see through the bluster and balderdash of most weak arguments. John's thinking process was not theoretical but concrete. He appealed to the logical mind, not the emotional heart. John would disown even widely held emotional religious beliefs if he felt they were illogical. Unlike many denominationally oriented ministers of the time, John promoted Christianity, not Congregationalism. If John was absolutely certain something was right he would convert to that thought immediately. He was not one to hold to false ideas because that was the way the denomination felt doctrine should be, or because it always had been done that way. He felt the pursuit of truth should always be the correct path even if that path was different from the one that had been taken. To John Todd slavery was illogical and the suffering it rendered on the nation and to individuals was not consistent with the teachings of Christ. He organized the first county anti-slavery society in Clarksfield.[16]

Even with the young reverend's successes in Clarksfield, he was frustrated over the lack of interest in the abolition of slavery that the town exhibited. He was frustrated over the lack of religious zeal in his pastorate. John and Martha Todd were ripe to accept a new challenge. Like many others of that generation, they would look west to see what the future held.

4

George Gaston's Trials

Young George Gaston squirmed in his hard back school bench this way and that way. He couldn't concentrate on his studies. As usual George had other matters on his mind. The young Gaston didn't hate school, but he was always thinking of ways to build houses, how to build new machinery or how to improve on machinery already in existence. His mind was fascinated with taking things apart and putting them back together to see how they worked.

Book scholarship at this time in his life didn't interest him. He grew into young manhood with much this same attitude. He did manage to finish his formal schooling and even attended Huron College in Milan, Ohio, for one term.

At age 20 in 1834 George moved with his family from New York State to near Oberlin, Ohio.[1] Although George never attended Oberlin College, he became completely immersed into Oberlin's brand of Christian sacrifice and activism. Ironically, he began to understand the importance of formal schooling after he had finished his own prescribed education. George became deathly ill with typhoid fever and the family thought he might pass away. The family had prayed over the sickbed of George. At one point he could only walk across the room with the aid of a chair. He eventually made a complete recovery. After this incident George rededicated his life to service to the cause of Christianity.[2]

He met and fell in love with an Oberlin College student named Maria Cummings.[3] They married and the Gastons set about establishing a farmstead several miles outside of Oberlin. When young George began to raise his barn, he had trouble. History books tell us that on the American frontier neighbor helped neighbor in raising their barns. What the history books don't tell is that the farmer whose barn was being raised was expected to supply a barrel of whiskey to those helping him. Gaston, being steeped in Oberlin's philosophy of temperance, refused to supply the whiskey. His neighbors refused to help him. Word was sent to a professor at Oberlin College. The professor recruited Oberlin students and they came out almost en masse. With the help of the student body and some of Oberlin's professors pitching in, they all rallied around their erstwhile friend George Gaston.

The barn was raised in only an hour and a half.[4]

After a few years of farming the young Gaston couple decided to become government farmers among the Pawnee Indians on a reservation on the plains of Nebraska. The government farmers usually tried to help the Pawnee increase their farm yields by using plows to plant crops rather than hoes, as they had done for years. By using plows and other modern techniques it was thought yields could be increased. This would help the Pawnee eliminate the times when the tribe would reach starvation situations. Gaston would receive $600 per year from the government for his duties.[5]

George also received a commission to be a Christian

Although he never attended Oberlin College, George Gaston was steeped in its traditions. Gaston thought the Missouri Valley would need ministers and teachers with the beliefs of Oberlin College. Going through Southwest Iowa on his way to becoming a government farmer and missionary to the Pawnee in Nebraska, Gaston noticed the fertile soils of Southwest Iowa. After his extremely stressful stint with the Pawnee, Gaston knew this area in Southwest Iowa was where he wanted to start his college. The Todd and Gaston group eventually settled in Tabor, Iowa, and became deeply involved in the Underground Railroad. (Todd House Museum Archives.)

missionary to the Pawnee from the American Board of Commissioners for Foreign Missions.[6] In March of 1840 George, his wife and young son made the long, arduous journey to the frontier of America. When they came to the Missouri River Gaston's love of taking things apart came in handy. George had to tear down his wagon and transport it across the muddy waterway in a ferry, actually a pompous title for this water craft that crossed the Missouri River. The "ferry" was in fact a hollowed out log propelled across the river by a large pulley con-

traption with ropes and a boatman in the log to help row. On one trip across the wide Missouri a barrel of flour was strapped to one end of the boat to provide ballast while a boatman was in the middle. Mrs. Gaston, her body swollen in its ninth month of pregnancy, sat at the other end of the boat with her two year old son. The Gaston livestock had to swim across the river.

This young family thus made it safely to Sarpy's Trading Post, now the site of Bellevue, Nebraska. The Gastons rested here for a few weeks as Maria delivered a second son to the growing family.[7] At Bellevue were Samuel Allis and the Reverend John Dunbar, who had been missionar-

Maria Cummings met George Gaston while a student at Oberlin College. Later the two married. Although a completely refined lady, Maria was incredibly tough. While nine months pregnant she crossed the Missouri River with her young son in a hollowed out log with a barrel of flour on the other end of the log to serve as ballast. When she got to the other side of the Mighty Mo' she delivered her second son. She endured the hardships of frontier life, the attacks of the Sioux on the Pawnee mission and the dangers of life as a participant on the Underground Railroad. Maria was a skilled writer and her descriptions of the happenings she witnessed were most vivid. (Todd House Museum Archives.)

ies with the Pawnee since 1834. Gaston was soon pressed into service to go to Weston, Missouri, with Dunbar to retrieve supplies for the Pawnee mission on a grueling 22 day, 175 mile journey with a team of oxen.[8]

In the Pawnees the Gastons found a people of intense magnetism and likeability. The Pawnee had some characteristics that made their lives similar to the American culture, but there were also many profound differences. The Pawnee were agriculturally inclined and were excellent hunters. Their domed earthen lodges shared some unique aspects with the sod homes built in Nebraska.

However, the Pawnee had a strong culture and belief system. The Gastons found a people who believed in spirits, ghosts, enchanted animals and magical places and they would not give up these beliefs very easily. When Pawnee leader Cha-hix-ta-ka-Lesharo, translated as White Man Chief, described a trip he had taken to Washington, D.C., it was told this way: "A dish was brought to Cha-hix-ta-ka-Lesharo containing a liquid. He was asked to take it. It was small, but 'Waugh!' he was near letting it fall, it was so heavy. A drop fell to the floor and he was asked to pick it up. It ran from him and became many drops and the more he tried to catch them, the farther they ran in every direction. A gun was brought and loaded with a bullet. He saw it pressed down with great force (Cha-hix-ta-ka-Lesharo suiting the action to the word). There was a target placed at a distance and the gun pointed toward it. He heard no sound, he saw no smoke, but looking closely at the target he saw the ball had entered the mark. That would be a good gun for his people. They could hide in the tall grass, and when the enemy came they would begin to fall, and neither seeing or hearing anything, they would run, thinking a miracle was being performed to kill them."[9]

The Pawnee were fierce warriors who often fought with their neighbors, the Sioux, Otoes and Cheyenne. As the years passed on and the Pawnee tribe dwindled in numbers due to deadly illness brought to them by the Caucasian people, the male warriors often became invaluable scouts for the United States Cavalry.

The men could have more than one wife. Respectable Pawnee women were offered to male guests by their husbands as a show of hospitality. Both men and women pierced their ears and made ornate beaded earrings. They painted their faces and used buffalo fat on their hair to make their locks look like a horn.

The United States government, as happened too often during this time, violated many of the treaty provisions they had with the Pawnee, thus making the Gastons' job even more difficult. However, Dunbar and Allis, who were often ineffectual and dishonest in their dealings with the Pawnee, would prove to be even more complicated to deal with than any Native American or even the United States government.

Dunbar, although very intelligent and a pioneer in translating the Pawnee language, had a lethargic and peculiar manner about himself. One visitor to the Pawnee Mission, a Scottish national, described Dunbar as the most "indolent, quiet, phlegmatic being I ever saw."[10]

Another time Major Clifton Wharton's 1st Dragoons were attempting to ford the Loup River and asked Dunbar, who had knowledge of the area or would be in a position to ask the Pawnee, the best place to cross this body of water. Dunbar wouldn't communicate with the major or any of the men in his command. This was, as any river crossing on an unknown body of water, a potentially lethal circumstance. Wharton and his army group spent many hours getting stuck and sinking in the river's quicksand bottom. The Pawnee, seeing the dragoon's predicament, splashed into the water and helped extricate the military men from the potentially deadly situation. The major and dragoons were appalled by Dunbar's lack of common courtesy and his cold reception to them after they made their crossing.[11]

Gaston complained to the Reverend David Green, the secretary of the American Board of Commissioners for Foreign Missions, that the seminary-trained Dunbar held no religious services for the Christians or non-Christians in the community.[12] Allis, whom Dunbar appointed as a teacher to the Pawnee, was barely literate himself. Dunbar even stated that Allis didn't have the proper educational background to teach school and when he did try the Pawnee children wouldn't come to Allis' school.[13]

After their arrival the main project for the Gastons, Dunbar and Allis was to move the Pawnee to a place 125 miles west and north of Bellevue, in the present Nebraska County of Nance, closer to the Pawnee's traditional buffalo hunting grounds on the Loup River. After the Pawnee were moved they formed villages for the four major bands of the tribe and crops were planted and earthen lodges were built. The Pawnee lodges were remarkable in construction.

John Dunbar described the building of these amazing lodges:

Six, eight, or ten posts (according to the size of the building) forked at the top, 12 or 14 feet long, are set up in a circle, and firmly fixed in the ground. Eight or ten feet from these is set up another, and larger circle of shorter, and smaller posts. The posts last set up do not rise more than 5 or 6 feet above ground and are also forked. On the posts first set up, timbers of considerable size are laid, reaching from one to another. On the outer circle of smaller and shorter posts, timbers are also laid as on the others. Numerous pieces of wood are now set up in an inclining position, enclosing the outer circle of posts, one end of each of which rests on the ground, while the other leans against the timbers laid on the outer posts. To these pieces of wood large rods are tied with slips of bark. Large posts of sufficient length are now laid on, the larger end of each resting on the timbers laid on the outer circle of posts, while the other passes over the timbers, laid on the inner posts, leaving only space enough at the top for the smoke to pass out. To these poles large rods are also tied. All these together constitute the frame of the edifice.

The covering consists of a coat of grass laid on these poles and rods. On the grass is laid earth about 12 inches deep.... The entrance to these dwellings is through a long narrow spaceway, which projects from the main building, always in this village toward the east, and it is covered with grass and earth.

Within these buildings.... In the center a circular place is dug 8 inches deep and 3 feet in diameter. This is the fireplace. The earth that is taken from this place is spatted down around it, and forms the hearth.... Mats made of rushes are spread down round the fire on which they sit.[14]

Between the Gastons and Dunbar and Allis, tension grew. It was obvious to George and Maria that Dunbar and Allis, who had been among the Pawnee for many years and yet had not established any real school or any formal religious services, were accomplishing very little. However, the two did manage to draw their salaries and increase their cattle herds during this time. Dunbar was especially adept in justifying his inaction to his superiors.

Dunbar and Allis' conduct of business with the Pawnee undoubtedly caused the Gastons much pain. George Gaston and his wife were extremely generous people who throughout their life would give away much of what they had to those in need. However, it appears Allis and Dunbar chose to profit from their association with the very poor Pawnee. Dunbar called Allis, his closest friend in the Mission, a dishonest person.

In a letter to Secretary Green, Dunbar states," It is my opinion that the less you or the board, have to do with Mr. A [Allis] and his family, as in any manner connected with it, the better. His course while connected with the Mission has been an exceedingly crooked one."[15]

Dunbar was charged with and admitted to illegally trading with the Pawnee. The Gastons must have found this activity unconscionable for a Christian minister to conduct himself in such a manner, especially among a people so much in need.

During the spring of 1844 the Pawnee were under constant attack from their bitter foes, the Sioux and Otoes, and little corn could be planted or grown. Buffalo hunting trips were not successful, as many of their fleet ponies had been stolen. The Pawnee were near starvation. Dunbar had squirreled away three to four hundred bushels of corn. However, in a calloused action, the reverend refused to share with the starving people he was sent to help.

With some kind of unconscionable reasoning, Dunbar sold the corn to the extremely destitute Pawnee at prices the reverend admits were "considered high." The reverend claims he gave back to the Pawnee much of what he had traded with them for the corn and that the Pawnee felt he had traded honestly with them. It is unclear if Dunbar actually gave back the items he traded at all, or if he gave them back after he was caught illegally trading with the Pawnee. As usual, Dunbar rationalized away his illegal activities with the starving Pawnee as being in their best interest.[16]

George Gaston was constantly pointing out Dunbar's and Allis's questionable behavior to their superiors and naturally was disliked by the two. Gaston told Dunbar he felt that what he and Allis had been doing was a disgrace to the concept of missionary work and that if it were publicly known what he and his partner had been doing, or in most cases not doing, he would be dismissed.[17]

Dunbar viewed George Gaston as an overly eager individual who was an "Oberlin" person who "retains more or less of the Oberlin peculiarities."[18] This, of course, referred to the reputation of Oberlin affiliates as activists who wanted to get things done. The two even tried to make recriminations against George Gaston. However, much to Dunbar's and Allis's dismay, the Indian Agent Miller, who they admitted was a fair man, took George Gaston's side in these disputes.

In 1843 Gaston, seeing that Dunbar and Allis were committed to a course of inaction and indifference, felt he had to take matters into his own hands. Not wishing to see another year go by with no school, he wrote to his sister Elvira and his brother-in-law Lester Platt to come and join the mission as a teacher and government farmer. The government was obliged by treaties to supply schools and teachers for the Pawnee.

Elvira Gaston Platt was an Oberlin College student who with her husband, Lester, made their way to the mission of the Pawnee at the request of her brother. Mrs. Platt would spend much of her long life working with the Pawnee and at the Industrial School for Indians in Carlisle, Pennsylvania, and with an Indian School in Genoa, Nebraska.[19]

However, disaster struck before the Platts could reach the Pawnee Mission. In late June of 1843 a large Sioux war party attacked one of the four Pawnee villages. At first they came to the village to steal the Pawnees' horses and the Pawnee went out to stop them but were badly outnumbered. The fighting became fierce, as most of the Sioux were armed with rifles and the Pawnee were not. The Sioux swooped into the Pawnee village killing mostly men. Unfortunately some children and women were killed when they tried to escape to the river. Some of the children were taken captive.

The Siouxs' main goal was to capture as many horses as possible and they took some 200 steeds. They then set fire to a score of the villages' forty-one lodges. Finally reinforcements came from another of the Pawnee villages and the Sioux retreated from Pawnee territory. In all, seventy Pawnee lost their lives and twenty-three were wounded. Many of the leading men of the

Pawnee tribe were killed that day. The battle lasted from daybreak to noon. The Sioux lost some forty in the village fight and it was told later that many had been wounded and died later.[20]

When the Platts arrived at Bellevue the devastating news reached them that a large raid by Sioux warriors had overwhelmed the Pawnee mission. Had her brother George and sister-in-law Maria been killed? Should they even go on to what might be their own deathtrap or head back to the "States"? The Platts had a difficult decision to make. It was decided that Lester would press on to the mission with the messenger who had brought the bad news of the Sioux attack.

Mrs. Platt would stay in the cabin of a blacksmith for a month

John C. Frémont, dressed in full military regalia. When Frémont stumbled into the Pawnee Mission during the fall of 1843, he looked haggard and badly in need of food. The Pawnee were only too happy to supply Frémont with food. George and Maria Gaston, George's sister Elvira and her husband Lester Platt were surprised to see the famous map maker, topographer and biographer of the frontier at the Pawnee Mission. Frémont was on one of his famous expeditions at this time. (State Historical Society of Iowa—Des Moines.)

with others until her husband returned. It would be the longest month of her life. Lester returned with six prairie schooners from the mission and she was happy to see that her brother George captained one of these magnificent wagons. She was also glad to hear that Maria was safe and sound. They loaded the schooners and headed to the unknown dangers at the mission.[21]

The Gastons and the Platts set about to help rebuild the disheartened Pawnees' village. That fall Mrs. Platt noted that John C. Frémont came into their camp during one of his famous pioneering treks across the American West mapping and making comments on this new land. Frémont had a haggard and rough look when he came into the camp. He was in need of food, which the Pawnee provied.[22] The "Pathfinder" was entertained by the Gastons and Platts. Little did the Oberlin people dream the celebrity status Frémont would obtain. He would become the Republicans' first presidential candidate in 1856. He made a respectable showing in the election, although he lost to James Buchanan. Frémont's staunch stand against slavery made him a hero to those like the Gastons and Platts who opposed this horrible institution.

In the spring of 1844 Agent Miller made his annual inspection trip to the Pawnee Mission. Red tape had delayed the appointment of the Platts as teacher and farmer and they were thinking of heading back to what they called the "States." However, Agent Miller pleaded with Lester to stay as a farmer: "For God's sake Mr. Platt do stay and help raise something for these starving Pawnees, and I am sure when the case is represented to the government, it will reward you." The Platts stayed and planted a crop in the spring at their own expense and grew and harvested it and gave it to the Pawnee. They were never compensated.[23]

Probably one of the undercurrents in the trouble between George Gaston and Dunbar and Allis were two white employees of the mission. These two Frenchmen had long lived in the West. They lived with Pawnee women without benefit of being married. George Gaston questioned the wisdom of a Christian Mission trying to be an example to the native people of the Christian way of life when their own members were not in marriages recognized by either the Christians or Pawnees.

However, there may have been another reason for Gaston's distrust of these men. One of the men was a blacksmith who was also employed by the American Fur Company. This firm had the reputation of often trading furs for alcohol, which was strictly forbidden at the mission. By doing this they greatly discounted the Pawnee out of the money the furs were really worth and made huge profits. Perhaps these men and possibly Allis were conduits for bringing alcohol onto the mission. Agent Daniel Miller was adamantly against allowing any alcohol at the mission, much to the chagrin of the American Fur Company and some of the Caucasians there.

The American Fur Company, however, showed its political muscle when it had Agent Miller sacked and in his place a drunken sot, Major Bean, took over. The benevolent outlook of Miller was replaced by Bean's anything goes attitude.[24]

Allis behavior became so obnoxious that the Indian agent finally asked him to leave the mission's property.[25] However, Allis managed to stay on the fringes of the mission and at times served as an interpreter.

Mrs. Platt finally managed to get the red tape cleared and was appointed as a government teacher to the Pawnee. Her school started slowly and the children were all volunteers. The Pawnee liked her ways and Mrs. Platt eventually had more students than she could handle.

The Pawnees were described by Mrs. Platt as magnetic people and the Gastons and Platts were attracted to them. They were amazed at how the Pawnee could read the intentions of others at an instant, even those from a culture totally alien to theirs.

La-shar-o-Pei-a-hoo-soo, known as Big Chief, called Mrs. Platt his sister and he her brother. Big Chief had been taken back to Washington, D.C., and related many stories to the Gastons and Platts. He told his story which was related by Mrs. Platt:

> He came galloping up on his little pony, dismounted and drew up his painted robe, which had lain loose above his girdle, over his right shoulder, leaving the other bare. He did this with the skill and grace known only to an Indian, and came courtesying toward me clasped my hand saying, 'This is the way women in Washington did.' On being seated in the house he continued to tell of the women he met at the seat of our government, of their dress and general appearance. He said they had coverings for their hands, but took them off and raised their hands to their heads, pretending to fix their hair, but it was done to show their rings and bracelets; and rising, he walked across the room, imitating the mincing gait of many of my sex, saying 'This is the way they walked.' How my heart sank at thought of those women whose motives for action were so plainly read by one upon whom they looked as an ignorant savage."[26]

It is doubtful that the Gastons or Platts were very successful at actually converting many Pawnee to the Christian beliefs. However, Mrs. Platt did note that the Pawnee were very respectful to their Pawnee God and that they were in general a very reverent people. They had no oaths against their God as the Caucasians did. However, much to Mrs. Platt's dismay the Pawnee picked up from the Caucasians the habit of taking God's name in vain.[27]

The Otoes and Sioux kept harassing the Pawnee. The Otoe came into the mission and decapitated an old Pawnee man and carried off his head on a spear. They then held up a mission supply train, taking all the ammunition that was meant for the Pawnee.[28]

However, it was the Sioux who proved to be the most menacing. Their war songs and war whistles made of turkey bones were recognized by the Pawnee but not always by the whites. The Sioux continued to ride into the mission and twice surrounded the mission school.

The Sioux were sniping at the Pawnee and white farmers. The Sioux warriors would line up outside the Pawnee Mission and ride at full speed up, all decked out in their fierce war garb, to the edges of the mission. Their intent was not known. Were they going to attack or merely try to intimidate those in the Mission? One time, inexplicably, the Sioux rode up full gallop complete in war regalia carrying the American flag. The meaning of this action by the Sioux was lost on those in the mission. They offered food and the opportunity to eat together with the Sioux but they were rebuffed. Instead, more Pawnee ponies and property were stolen.[29]

In May of 1846 the United States government declared war on Mexico and its meager forces of cavalry and dragoons on the American frontier was stripped to be sent south. Those at the mission were fully aware of this and the attacks and intimidations by the Sioux continued. The Sioux began to come so often in war parties that the men could do no work outside in safety.[30]

The mission school became concerned over these attacks. It was only a matter of time before the Sioux realized that the forts in the West were shells of what they had been and that the United States Army and cavalry had withdrawn from the area. It was decide to move the Mission School back 125 miles to Bellevue, Nebraska.[31]

Once back in Bellevue, Maria Gaston and Elvria Platt began feverishly to sew clothing for the Pawnee children so they could be properly clothed during the harsh Nebraska winter. Much of the children's clothing had to be abandoned on the Loup Reservation when they moved back to Bellevue.

George Gaston met Brigham Young, the great Mormon leader, in Bellevue. George told Young of their plight and he dispatch two Mormon seamstresses to help sew clothing for the Pawnee children. The Mormon leader and some of his apostles would often visit the Gastons and Platts to check on the welfare of the Pawnee children.[32]

The Gastons stayed on in Bellevue but Maria and the children came down with the ague. This was a malaria-like condition marked by chills, fever, and sweating that was common on the frontier. It was decided the Gaston family would move back to Oberlin to recover.[33] However, although confronted with much tribulation and hardship, George Gaston couldn't get this area out of his mind. Especially the Iowa side of the Missouri River with its fertile valley and unusual hills bordering the Missouri river bottoms.

The Gastons respected the culture of the Pawnee. George and Maria's sincerity and their love of the Pawnee seamed to impress these people. A decade later when the Gastons had settled into Tabor, Iowa, the Pawnee who were still on the Bellevue reservation made the 40 mile trip to visit the Gastons in Tabor. There was a genuine camaraderie between theses people from two vastly different cultures and lifetime friendships were made. The Platts also left soon after the Gastons. However, Elvira and Lester Platt would move to Southwest Iowa. The Platts would make their life's work with the Native Americans, especially the Pawnee.

The Pawnee and Sioux continued their bitter battle. On August 5, 1873, the last major battle in the United States between tribes of Native Americans was fought on that day at Massacre Canyon near the present site of Trenton, Nebraska. The Pawnee tribe, which had been decimated by European diseases, was greatly outnumbered by the Sioux.

In that battle the Pawnee lost many men, women and children. This battle so demoralized the Pawnee that they retreated from Nebraska and moved to Oklahoma. Ironically, Lester Platt's nephew, Lester Beach Platt, was with the Pawnee hunting party when they were attacked by the Sioux. Platt tried to parlay a truce between the two warring tribes but the Sioux were not interested in peace that day. The Sioux captured Platt and then whipped him. They released him after taking his clothing. L.B. Platt was badly injured by the Sioux but survived the ordeal and managed to graduate from Yale Divinity School four years later.[34]

In Oberlin George Gaston had ideas he couldn't get out of his head over the enormous area he and his family had traveled. The vastness of the Missouri Valley made a huge impression on his mind. All the settlements that would one day be in the Missouri Valley would need trained teachers and ministers for these towns and cities. Gaston knew something needed to be done, but what?

5

Settling In on the Prairies

George Gaston started a farming operation again near Oberlin. After his family recovered from their illness George's fertile mind kept thinking about the Missouri Valley. While swinging his cradle in the harvest field he formulated a plan.[1] He would take a group of pioneers to Southwest Iowa and start a colony and college like at Oberlin. As usual George and Maria prayed about this idea with much zeal. They felt God had answered their prayers and the energetic couple started to formulate a plan for this project.

George began to talk and pray about his mission around the Oberlin area. He found support from various people around this vicinity. Each week this group met and prayed and planned for nearly a year.[2] Gaston knew he would need a seminary-trained spiritual advisor for the colony. George heard about a dynamic young pastor some 15 miles away in Clarksfield, Ohio. The 29 year old preacher was John Todd.

Gaston visited the Congregational minister in the summer of 1848 and there was an instant mutual respect of each other. Almost immediately they saw in each other someone whom they could trust and respect.

After many discussions with his wife and a lot of prayer, John Todd decided to go in with Gaston and his planned colony in Iowa. John however, wanted to go to Iowa and look at this unknown territory before committing completely to the plan.

In the fall of 1848 John Todd by himself, George Gaston and his family, Josiah Hall, Samuel H. Adams and wife and Darius Matthews headed for Southwestern Iowa. Samuel H. Adams had left his home in Newbraintree, Massachusetts, to study in Oberlin under Charles G. Finney. Adams was on fire with his thirst for knowledge and he made the arduous journey from Massachusetts to Ohio to learn under Finney's direction. Finney's

47

sometimes unorthodox views had been a challenge to the conservatives in the hierarchy of the Congregational and Presbyterian churches. Adams wanted to fully understand all of the theological nuances of Finney's beliefs.[3]

However, once in Oberlin, he met George Gaston and then John Todd. Adams became excited about their idea of spreading the Gospel and Oberlin's philosophy of equality to the Missouri Valley. After much prayer Adams felt that God had sent him to Oberlin to meet Gaston and Todd. Samuel H. Adams then fell in with the Todd-Gaston group and threw himself into the project wholeheartedly.[4]

Iowa had just joined the union in 1846 but was still a wilderness in many areas. There was not one foot of rail tracks in the state at this time. Iowa was to have been admitted as a state along with Florida. It was customary at this time to admit one Northern free state along with a Southern slave state at the same time to keep the balance of power equal in the Congress and Senate of the United States. However, boundary disputes in Iowa kept the Hawkeye state from joining the union until after Texas was admitted.

The Gaston-Todd group headed out and boarded the railroad at Belleview, Ohio, and railed to Cincinnati. There they found transportation on a steamboat bound for St. Louis. The country was a house divided and many people in this middle border area where free-state bordered slave-state were very adamant about their point of view.

While a passenger on the Ohio River bound for St. Louis, the Reverend John Todd saw another traveler reading a book entitled "Fuller's Letters on Slavery." He asked if the reader would allow him to read the volume when he was finished. The reader then questioned Todd extensively on his views on slavery. The Reverend in no uncertain terms explained his views that slavery was immoral and he thought that people of color deserved equality. There was a large contingent of pro-slavery supporters on the boat. They began to gather around Todd and his adversary in this argument.

"Damn the abolitionist," "Shoot him," "Kill him," were oaths shouted at John Todd as he expressed his views. A slave holder from Louisiana waded in with his virulent comments and hollered, "The damned Abolitionist! I wish I had him! I would swap him off for a dog and then I would shoot the dog!"[5]

At this time the tension around the "debate" became too great and Todd's company, fearing some hotheaded slaver would take a shot at the Reverend, escorted him into his cabin on the steamboat. The next morning the service people on the steamer, who were mostly people of color, treated the Reverend in a most cordial manner.

While on the steamer Todd also met a young man who had a short time ago graduated from a Congregational seminary and was about to fill a pulpit in slave state Missouri. The Reverend noted the young man had a commission from the well funded American Home Missionary Society, a frequent supplier of missionaries for Congregational pulpits. In talking with the young minister he admitted that although not a pro-slavery advocate he would not speak out on the subject while in his pastorate in Missouri. This was an action that John Todd knew he could never take.

In Cairo, Illinois, the Louisiana slave owner with slave in tow disembarked and yelled at Todd, who was standing on the steamer's deck, "Ho, you abolitionist, ain't you going south with us? I'll keep you a week for nothing, till they get ready to hang you." Todd answered, "That's where they do such things. I'm not going there."[6]

Once in St. Louis Todd and his group saw a row of steamers lying at the St. Louis landing. They soon learned each boat was exceedingly accommodating with promises of leaving St. Louis at a time convenient to the passengers. The boats would blow their whistles, fire up their large boilers and rotate their large paddles, giving the impression they were about ready to start on their journey. The Reverend and company quickly found out this was all show and the steamboats would only leave when they had booked a full complement of passengers and cargo.

The Oberlin group finally secured passage on a steamer bound for St. Joseph, Missouri. As the Missouri River was very shallow in the autumn, the boat almost ran aground on several occasions. Once after reaching St. Joseph the group would be forced to take horses to the wilds of the Iowa frontier. Although the Missouri River was navigable north of this Missouri city, only steamers carrying cargo for the military and their system of forts would attempt the journey.

The 100 mile trip north of St. Joseph would be completed and the group made it across the Iowa border to a spot that would be called Civil Bend on the Missouri river. They reached the home of Lester and Elvira Platt, who had moved to this area after leaving the Pawnee Mission in Bellevue, Nebraska. John Todd noted that after the long trip it was nice to feel the gracious and friendliness of the Platt family. Todd also met the Platts' neighbors Dr. Ira Blanchard and family, and Miss Abbie Walton, who had been a missionary to the Kaw and Delaware Indians in Kansas.[7]

Todd and George Gaston and the others in the group noted the luxurious soil and dreamed of the corn these Missouri bottoms could produce. Lester Platt and Ira Blanchard would escort the group around the region to look at various locations for settlement. It was finally agreed that the area known as Civil Bend was where the group would start their college and colony. John Todd would head back to Ohio for his wife and family and any other Oberlin pioneers who wished to come to Southwest Iowa to settle.

Unfortunately, before John Todd and Josiah Hall headed back to Ohio, an issue came up. North of Civil Bend in what would become Council

Bluffs, Iowa, was the town known as Kanesville, a large community of the Church of Jesus Christ of Latter Day Saints, more commonly known in the area as Mormons. At that time many in the Midwest were uncertain about the doctrines and intentions of the Mormon Church. Some in the little community around Civil Bend and that part of Southwest Iowa feared the Mormons would become too powerful and have political pull in their community. A public meeting was held at the Wabousa Indian Agency which 40 to 50 people in the area attended. Many in attendance at this meeting were actually squatters and had no legal rights to the land they were living on.[8] Those in attendance wanted Todd and Hall to take a petition, which most everyone in the area signed, to create a new county in that district of Southwest Iowa. The idea was that Todd and Hall would carry the petition on their ride through Iowa and present it to the first member of the Iowa legislature that they found.[9]

John and Josiah Hall would ride 1,000 miles on horseback back to Ohio. They would often sleep under the stars with their horses' tails tied to each other so they wouldn't wander off on the vast Iowa prairies. They accepted the hospitality of an elder in a Mormon settlement after several nights of sleeping on the open prairie. At Fairfield, Iowa, Todd and Hall found a member of the Iowa legislature, a blacksmith named Baker. They presented the petition to him but heard nothing. Years later Todd found out that the blacksmith thought Todd and Hall were in fact Mormons and he felt their petition was some sort of elaborate ruse. The blacksmith never presented their petition to the Iowa legislature.[10]

Was John Todd, who promoted racial harmony, bigoted towards Mormons? At the time there were many wild rumors and gossip about the Mormons and their religion. Undoubtedly John and others were probably influenced by this. As always John would, with his very logical mind, be the first to dismiss any rumor or gossip that had been proven to be not true. The aspect of polygamy certainly would have troubled Todd and others in his community. It is interesting to note that when John Todd originally wrote of this incident in "Reminiscences" in 1877 he said, "Wherever good soil, timber, & water were found together. The Mormons had the sway, &, exhibiting as they did many of the traits which rendered them so odious in Missouri & Illinois, The Gentiles ... were adverse to Mormon rule." However, John later omitted this section when talking of this time, even though much of the "Reminiscences" of 1877 were printed into his book, *Early Settlement and Growth of Western Iowa or Reminisces* word for word. In his book John seemed to have nothing but respect for the Mormons when he wrote on page 30, "As there were thousands of Mormons who, dissatisfied with their treatment in Nauvoo (Illinois), had decided to make Salt Lake valley their home, persons were sent in advance to look out a practical route, build bridges, and prepare the way. Sixteen months or more before, the mass of them passed over this road on their way from Illinois to Utah. In order to avoid famine in that wild and uncultivated region, many of them stopped temporarily by the way, so that the first settlers along the road, in the Missouri valley, and along the way by groves and streams, were chiefly Mormons." Todd goes on in his book to tell of acts of kindness paid to him in Mormon settlements on his way back to Ohio. John's son James would later teach at a Mormon settlement in Southwest Iowa at Manti in the 1860's.[11]

Todd and Hall continued their journey back to Ohio. While riding through Illinois John was able to visit his father, brother and sister in Granville. They took a much needed rest before heading back to the Buckeye state. He was glad to see his family members again. After resting in Illinois they again began their journey back to Ohio. Finally Todd made it back to Clarksfield. Despite the long trip John excitedly told Martha they should move to Iowa. The dutiful parson's wife agreed. However, John would stay on for 18 more months in Clarksfield, fulfilling his duties as its pastor.

John Todd held a public meeting in Oberlin to talk of the college and colony they proposed in Southwest Iowa. He found some support and a few others said they would join him, but there was a problem. In a letter dated January 29, 1849, to his father-in-law, attorney Q.F. Atkins, Todd tells of the great difficulties in recruiting colonists to go to Iowa. Many potential colonists were having a hard time raising capital to go to the Hawkeye State. The would-be colonists were not able to sell their property or farms for what they were worth because everyone was leaving for the gold fields in California. Farms and personal property were selling for pennies on the dollar because of the California gold fever. Gold fever was on the verge of scuttling the whole Oberlin colony project in Iowa.[12]

In 1848 gold had been found at Sutter's Mill in California. At the time the area was part of Mexico. The Treaty of Guadalupe Hidalgo ended the Mexican War and ceded California to the United States. News of the gold strike began to be reported throughout the nation during the summer of 1848, and Northern Ohio as well as the rest of the United States suddenly had gold fever. Sometimes whole towns would disappear overnight as everyone left for California. This gold fever exodus in Ohio depressed land and prices for personal goods.

In the spring of 1849 the church at Clarksfield, which at times had been neglectful in supporting Todd as their pastor, feared losing him to the Iowa colony. They offered him a permanent position as pastor and said they would support him and his young family to the best of their ability. The old question of taking the safe course as opposed to the unknown course crossed the young preacher's mind. At a time when the whole Iowa project was in doubt the young preacher told of his unwillingness to take the Clarksfield installation. He finally agreed to it but only with the provision that either party could cease the relation by giving three month's notice.[13]

While John was in Ohio a major event would occur back in Iowa during the spring of 1849 that would have a profound effect on the Todds and the rest of the Oberlin group. Heavy snows and then torrential rains would cause the Missouri River to flood the area around Civil Bend, and this would cause an intense problem for the colony.[14]

Buffalo fish came out of the river banks into the heavy grass onto the lowlands. The few residents of the area would drive out into the lowland water and get wagon-boxes full of fish. They caught these buffalo fish with their bare hands or speared them with pitchforks or homemade spears. Some of these fish were very large, weighing twenty-five pounds or more. The fish were used mainly for hog feed. However, when the water receded, ague and fevers struck.[15]

By the spring of 1850 John Todd had convinced enough colonists to make the trek to Iowa and had given the required three month's notice and resigned from the Clarksfield pastorate. George Gaston and the others back in Iowa most urgently requested that John be sure and recruit a schoolteacher for the colony. John did and her name was Miss Rachel Tucker. Miss Tucker would write in her diary, "Saw Brother Todd today, have made up my mind to go with him. O! what grace do I need to sustain me in the trial of parting with my friends and leaving Oberlin.... The very thought of leaving my friends and bursting asunder the ties that bind me to home and country is like taking a right arm, but my Savior has given me grace sufficient for me."[16]

John forwarded his household goods with the group making their way to Iowa. The Reverend then took his wife and children to Cleveland, Ohio, for a final reunion with the large Atkins family contingent. Todd then went for a visit to his boyhood home in Pennsylvania. He traveled onto New York City and went south to the seat of the American government in Washington, D.C. He observed the august legislators of the time, such as Daniel Webster and Henry Clay. He stood by the side of President Zachary Taylor in the White House only a short time before Taylor would die.

Todd returned to Cleveland for the long journey to the frontier of the nation. He left with wife and family and teacher Rachel Tucker who had also joined them in Cleveland. Leaving by steamer from the city on Lake Erie, the pastor noted the "calm bosom of Lake Erie." They passed through Chicago, then an insignificant village. While in Chicago they tried to find Martha's errant brother Arthur, but just missed her unstable sibling. They then sent out by canal and wagon to Granville, Illinois. There the Reverend would see his father, Captain James Todd, for the last time. They traveled to St. Louis and then onto Southwest Iowa. The Reverend Todd observed,

"We found that a long and tiresome journey prepares the emigrant to be content with necessary privations and hardships of a frontier settlement."[17]

Although the Reverend had been gone from the settlement for some 20 months there had been much activity by its few members. Many acres of land had been broken by plow. A house for the Todds had been erected, though it still needed doors and a floor. A kiln had been started for bricks. A shingle factory had begun and thousands of shingles had been made. A school house and a steam sawmill had been framed. The boiler for the sawmill had already been ordered. Since lumber was oftentimes difficult to obtain, a sawmill would be indispensable. On the spiritual front a union church had been started and a temperance society had been founded.

However, as July of 1850 heated up the Reverend and all the others in the colony soon found an unbearable enemy in their midst. It was so small yet so annoying. The mosquito! Mosquito bars in the house were a necessity and mosquito smoke on the outside during dusk was absolutely needed. The children were constantly crying out in the night due to bites from this insect. It was difficult to go out during the day and breathe without getting a mouthful of mosquitoes. The usual prairie breezes kept them down in the tall grasses on some days but, on a calm afternoon they would rise in the millions to cast a haze over the sun. The floods from 1849 caused perfect breeding grounds for these invaders. Wherever there were mosquitoes the ague appeared. The fever associated with the ague attacked those in the colony. One time while John Todd was preaching at Civil Bend he was seized by the ague and had to shorten the sermon.[18]

The colony prevailed and carried on till the first killing frost. However, another malevolent force threatened the small settlement. Asiatic cholera took its deadly toll on some of the people of the area. There was no lumber at that time for coffins for the victims of this outbreak, so boards from one of George Gaston's upper room floors were used.[19] Then an even more dangerous enemy reared its ugly head—bigotry.

At this time the Missouri River made two bends on the Iowa side of this body of water. The lower bend was across from where Old Fort Kearney was situated on the Nebraska side of the river and at the present site of Nebraska City, Nebraska. This area became known as the "Devil's Bend" because the people in the area were hard drinkers who found an easier way to make a living than farming and that was by selling whiskey to both whites and Native Americans. They were a disagreeable, cantankerous lot. Lester and Elvira Platt and Dr. Ira Blanchard, then George Gaston and his group and later the Reverend John Todd settled into the area of the upper river bend. The upper bend area, because it was being settled by sober, upright people, became known as "Civil Bend."[20] Although the local post office was named "Gaston" after George, the area's nickname of Civil Bend stuck.

In 1849 a log school house was erected and Mrs. Platt served as school-teacher. The Platts' house was very close to the schoolhouse.[21] Those at Civil Bend, even though they burdened the whole cost of the school, invited any-one from the Devil's Bend or surrounding vicinity to attend at no cost. Dur-ing the fall of 1850 the Garners, a black family that had known Dr. Ira Blanchard, was welcomed into the Civil Bend area. Their children were encouraged to attend the new school.

On New Year's Eve of that year someone burnt down the schoolhouse. All the books, Bibles and other related school items were also destroyed. This was the only building in the area that could be used as a schoolhouse, church or meeting area. It was believed that the arsonist came from either the Devil's Bend area or was from slave state Missouri, whose border was only a dozen miles from Civil Bend. Elvira Platt said she could see the fleeing arsonists run into the forest.[22]

The Oberlin group showed they were resilient and wouldn't let bigotry or prejudice deter them in their mission. They sent off for more books and school supplies and in forty-one days—on February 10, 1851—they started up their school again in a rented house.[23]

Flooding on the Missouri River began again in 1851 and the summer was made intolerable by the high waters and the insects that followed. The Reverend Todd began his duties as a circuit preacher. He went north of Kanesville (later Council Bluffs) and south into Missouri. The Reverend began to notice that in the high ground to the east of their settlement the effects of the insects and flooding was negligible. However, since timber was very scarce in that area, it was thought not to be a good locale.

Toward the latter part of the summer the water began to dry up, but as the water retreated malarial fever struck up and down that part of the Missouri river. Quinine was taken to abate the outbreak but supplies ran out and none could be found in St. Josesph, Missouri, or Kanesville, Iowa, the closest towns that would have those supplies. Dr. Blanchard came to the rescue of the small colony. He had read in a medical journal that chloride of sodium, common salt, would sometimes arrest malaria. After trial and error it was determined three teaspoons were a recommended dose and the disease was halted.[24]

After the outbreak of malaria it was decided that the colony would have to move to higher ground. A spot was picked in the hill area east of Civil Bend, but it lacked timber near the proposed site of the village. The town would be called Tabor and timber claims would be made outside of town to supply the new village with necessary wood. So during the spring of 1852 most of the colony would move to Tabor with the notable excep-tions Dr. Blanchard and the Platts.

The Loess Hills area east of Civil Bend where Tabor was established was a unique series of windblown deposits of loose soil. Although loess soil is common around the globe, its formation into hills is very unusual and found only in a couple of spots around the world.

Houses were built and the people were moving in. The Congregational church was formed. Prayer meetings and concerts were held on a regular basis for the ending of slavery. These meetings were held until President Lincoln issued the Emancipation Proclamation.[25]

The move from Civil Bend to Tabor was not without problems. A cow the Reverend Todd owned decided she liked the grazing better at Civil Bend than Tabor. The cow proceeded with other bovine in the parson's herd and made the 20 mile hike to their former home. The Parson, upon waking, went looking for them on foot since he had no horse. Sure enough, he found his herd in their former grazing pasture. He drove them back the twenty miles to their new home by nightfall.

After the move to Tabor more people joined the colony, including George Gaston's cousin James. Fifteen year old Julia Matthews came into Tabor at its infancy. Miss Matthews enjoyed the hospitality and welcome accorded newcomers to the town. She also noted that most of those coming into the town were friends or related to those already in the village and many were from the Oberlin, Ohio, vicinity.[26] However, there were hardships to endure. The Parson recalls he was near destitution when a widow lady for no apparent reason, except maybe an answered prayer, gave the preacher fifty cents. Since the Todds had no other money at this time, this cash was immediately put to good use purchasing some milled corn, which was the primary source of their diet for many days.

The Tabor colony kept in contact with Oberlin. The Reverend didn't have a horse to ride and when it was necessary to ride his circuit a horse would have to be borrowed. George Gaston wrote back to friends in Oberlin and money was raised for a horse named "Queen" for the Reverend.

The pioneers in Tabor went about the mundane business of organizing the town and its local government. Public meetings were held to lay out the town and the important town square. A schoolhouse had to be built and of course a church was to be constructed.[27] A stone quarry was established on Plum Creek three miles southwest of Tabor and the citizens in town served on its board. The profits and benefits of the quarry were apparently shared by all.[28] George Gaston operated a much needed mill that milled both flour and lumber.[29]

A Washington Temperance Society was formed in the town for the purpose of promoting temperance, and of course this hotbed of abolitionist fever held meetings and passed resolutions denouncing slavery. On September 2, 1853, John Todd, Jesse West and W.J. Gates were appointed to a committee to prepare an expression of sentiment in relation to slavery, temperance and mission boards. The committee adopted these resolutions:

I. Believing that the gospel breathes peace on earth and good will to men ... we regard American slavery as essentially hostile to the principles of Christianity, and all who in any way uphold it ... occupying a position inconsistent with Christian benevolence.

II. Cursed as our country is with the institution of slavery ... we believe the time has come to treat the holding of men as slaves as we would any other flagrant sin.

III. In obedience to the divine injunction, remember them that are in bonds and bound with them, we feel constrained to bear testimony in every proper way against this giant sin of our land. Consequently, we will not admit slave-holders or apologists for slavery to the privileges of the church. Nor will we patronize mission boards that support churches in which slaveholding is not treated as a disciplinable offense.

IV. We cordially concur in the principles of the American Reform Book and Tract Society, and also in the American Missionary Association and believe them worthy of the confidence of the Christian world.

V. Resolved, that this church will admit no persons as members who make, vend, use or provide intoxicating liquors as a beverage.[30]

Resolutions III & IV were obviously a slap in the face to the American Home Missionary Society, which supported ministers and churches in areas where slavery was permitted. Also, the processing of corn into corn liquor was much more lucrative to farmers than selling it on the open market. However, John Todd and the elders of Tabor prohibited this in resolution V.

One anti-slavery demonstration that the people of Tabor tried to hold in the county seat town of Sidney on September 15, 1855, almost ended in bloodshed. Sidney was in the middle of Fremont County, much of which was pro-slavery or in many cases just in favor of the slavery status quo. In 1854 the Kansas-Nebraska Act had opened these two territories to settlement. The thought was that Nebraska would not allow slavery but Kansas would allow slavery in its territory. To abolitionists like John Todd this was unacceptable. It was thought to be necessary to hold an anti-slavery meeting in Sidney to show the town's support in keeping Kansas a free territory.

Almost everyone in Tabor descended en masse upon Sidney singing anti-slavery and temperance songs. Everyone was in a spirited mood as they traveled the fifteen miles south to the seat of Fremont County. Sidney was full of people from all over the county, mainly gathered around the courthouse. The Tabor people went to the courthouse but this building was occupied by a pro-slavery paramilitary group. The Tabor group then proceeded to the schoolhouse to hold their meeting. However, they were denied the use of the schoolhouse. After a round of negotiations the key to the building was produced and the anti-slavery meeting proceeded.

However, the courthouse crowd of pro-slavery sympathizers made their

This was the residence of the Reverend Todd and his family in Tabor. It was the third house built in the town, and was made of native lumber, as there was no pine available. The siding was made from cottonwood. Additions were made to the original house most notably in 1868. The Reverend Todd helped in the construction of this dwelling. It reflected the Oberlin philosophy of simple shelter, dress and manners. The house had many people staying there at various times; students from the Tabor Literary Institute, visiting ministers, visiting abolitionists such as John Brown, James Lane and Dr. S.G. Howe to name a few and, of course, those traveling on the Jim Lane Trail and the Underground Railroad. Oswald Garrison Villard, author of "John Brown Fifty Years After," one of the most respected biographies of Brown, visited the house in 1904. Slated for destruction in 1969, it was purchased by former United States Congressman Otha Wearin, a graduate of Tabor College. The house was then purchased by the Tabor Historical Society and they have maintained the residence as the Todd House Museum ever since. The house is on the National Historical Register and is recognized by the National Park Service as an Underground Railroad station on their "Network to Freedom" program and by the State Historical Society of Iowa as one of four verifiable UGRR stations in Iowa. (Todd House Museum Archives.)

way to the schoolhouse and they mingled with the anti-slavery Taborites. At the meeting anti-slavery resolutions and speeches were attempted but the pro-slavery crowd would drown them out with drunken oaths. Rocks and stones were thrown against the building.

John Todd spoke eloquently on the evils of slavery. However, the pro-slavery group outnumbered the Tabor people and under the guise of democratic action began to pass sham pro-slavery resolutions. These sham resolutions were published in the newspaper in Nebraska City.[31]

The only thing that seemed to quiet the intoxicated pro-slavery mob was when the Tabor women started singing their songs. Even the most inebriated marveled at what they called the "angel voices" of the Tabor women. Fortunately, the leader of the pro-slavery group got so drunk he wasn't able to lead his minions in what had been planned as a barrage of eggs and brickbats or even worse. The presence of so many Tabor women and their voices also helped keep the situation from becoming violent.[32]

After their meeting the Tabor people managed to leave in an orderly fashion. Mrs. George Gaston noted that the seed of freedom had been planted and that in later years anti-slavery speeches were made in Sidney without the speechmakers being mobbed. John Todd noted that ironically, the leader of the pro-slavery crowd later joined the Union Army during the Civil War and lost his life in its great cause to end slavery.[33]

Frontier ministers often received their remuneration from missionary societies since most of the pioneers moving west would not have the means to support a church and pastor until they were more established. Most of these frontier ministers were encouraged to begin new churches all over the region they were in and try to conduct as many Sunday services as possible. John Todd did this traveling a circuit of some 100 by 40 miles. John Todd began to search out communities that didn't have a church or regular preaching. He was not always able to conduct services every Sunday at each location, but he did his best. Some of these locations are no longer in existence. His circuit at that time was Linden, Missouri, California City (later Florence) on the Iowa side, Trader's Point, Stutsman's Mill on the West Nishnabota, Cutler's camp on Silver Creek, High Creek and Honey Creek.[34]

At this time most of the frontier Congregational pastors in Iowa were supported by the American Home Missionary Society. However, it was thought by many at Yale and Andover, the leading Congregational centers of learning, that those who graduated from Oberlin College were too radical. Oberlin allowed women and blacks in the same classrooms as white men! How scandalous!! Oberlin's extreme position on the immediate abolition of slavery, the equality of the races and their impatience with the interests of the slave holders in the South made them outcasts even amongst the most liberal Congregationalists in the East. The American Home Missionary Society would not support Oberlin pastors. So John Todd received support from the not-as-well-funded American Missionary Association based in New York City.[35]

John Todd and American Missionary Association President George

Whipple corresponded often. In one of the early letters from the A.M.A. Whipple wasn't sure if John and his band of pioneers were located in Missouri or Iowa. The letter was addressed to Atchison County, Missouri or Gaston, Fremont County, Iowa. On the envelope of the letter Whipple asks John plaintively, "Tell us whether you live in Iowa or Missouri?"[36]

John Todd and George Gaston and the others in the village of Tabor now began to set up a city government at their new site. However, they would be forced to encounter many new trials and as always the issues of the Underground Railroad and slavery would loom over the young village.

As the town began to take shape these first settlers had much to do: putting up barns, planting and harvesting crops, and building sheds and fences for livestock such as cattle, sheep and horses. The livestock had to be fed and the unpredictable nature of calving was sometimes made that an all night affair. The woman's touch was always in evidence as shade trees and flowering ornamental shrubs began to take root. Lilies, irises and other blooming perennials began to flower around Tabor. Yards began to take shape and the appropriate flowers and shrubs were planted around the doorsteps.

The village began to grow. However, even though life on the prairie could be merciless for frontier towns like Tabor, John Todd and the residents of the town savored holidays and the fun they could provide in the harsh environment. The Fourth of July provided time for a pageant. A large platform and some board seats were built. A grand marshal for the celebration would be appointed. A comely young lass would be named Miss Columbia or the Goddess of Liberty. The younger ladies would be selected to represent the states. Loren Hume, who grew up in the George Gaston home, even reported that one year the cannon that was hidden in the Reverend Todd's barn was taken out and fired.[37]

Although many events were taken seriously among these abolitionists, James Gaston showed humor was important. Just before he was to be married James rode by the George Gaston home imitating a horse in a halter. He was obviously making a comment on the state of bachelorhood and his upcoming nuptials.[38]

6

Race, Politics and Land

The Iowa into which John Todd and George Gaston and their families settled was far different from Oberlin or even Ohio for that matter. When Iowa was admitted to the Union in 1846 it was the westernmost state in the United States at that time. Iowa was the first free state to be admitted out of the territories that had formed the Louisiana Purchase. However, many have called Iowa in the early 1850's the most racist state north of the Mason-Dixon line. Iowa was different from other states in the North in that she had a long border with a slave state that had no natural hindrances, such as a river that might impede an escaping slave's journey to freedom. Many in Iowa at this time had a racist mentality and were afraid of a massive slave exodus across the long, unprotected southern border of Iowa with its neighboring slave state Missouri.

The first senators from Iowa, Augustus Caesar Dodge and George Wallace Jones, and her congressional legislators often voted like their counterparts from Alabama and Mississippi on matters of slavery and race. Also, compounding the race and slavery problem in Tabor and Fremont County was their physical closeness to slave state Missouri.

Many of the slaves that came through Tabor came from Missouri. While not a state with a large slave population, Missouri had 114,931 slaves in 1860. For comparison, Virginia had the largest slave population of all those states that allowed this odious institution, with 490,865 enslaved humans in 1860. Missouri, however, was an important state among those that allowed slavery. She had the second highest free population among the slave states only behind Virginia. Her population of free persons was almost that of Massachusetts. Her influence in the Senate and Congress was considerable. Missouri's major city, St. Louis, was the third largest city in a state that allowed

60

slavery. In Western Missouri around the area which would include Kansas City slavery proved to be very popular.

Iowa certainly didn't put out the welcome mat for black Americans either free or slave. Iowa was only too happy to return runaway slaves. Free blacks and mulattos were required 20 days after settling in the state to file with the county clerk a court-attested certificate of freedom. Blacks and mulattos were required to post a bond of $500 just to live in the state of Iowa.[1] The census of 1850 showed only 333 blacks in the state of Iowa and even though white emigrants were streaming into the state in the 1850's the black population decreased, as a census in 1856 showed. That census tallied only 271 blacks in the Hawkeye state. It was said blacks in Iowa were not very free; they were just "north of slavery."

Many Iowa citizens were afraid that any free blacks coming into the state might become welfare cases. John Todd found this posting of a bond by blacks just to live in Iowa to be entirely consistent with the racist sentiment of the times in the Hawkeye state.[2] Slave-owners routinely brought their slaves into Iowa when passing through the state or visiting, much to the horror of abolitionists like Todd. United States government workers such as surveyors that hailed from southern states thought nothing of bringing their entourage of slaves with them on work assignments in free states like Iowa.

The Reverend John Todd had spoken out against slavery and what he felt was just as evil: the glorification of the Anglo-Saxon race. He noted in a sermon entitled "Oppression" that "prejudice ... has long excluded colored persons from educational facilities—from honorable competition in business ... from testimony [in] courts of justice ... access to the Scriptures & knowledge of the way of salvation." John went on to preach that God will "hear the cry of this very class, & assures us that He [will] execute judgment for all that are oppressed." John Todd wished that America would have "an appreciation of the golden rule" when it came to the treatment of other races. Todd saw not only slavery but the unequal treatment of the races as a shame for Christians. Four years before the start of the Civil War, John Todd predicted that because of these attitudes of racism by those professing to be Christians, "What doom awaits our country!"[3]

Todd would later write about this time, "We were a nation of oppressors—The true idea of impartial freedom announced by our fathers was kept under by law & government patronage until it influenced legislation, gagged the bar & the pulpit—Silenced clubs, & benevolent societies—expurgated our literature—muzzled the press, & threatened the overthrow of Freedom. Some [abolitionists and their societies] would not bow to the Moloch of Slavery."[4]

Among abolitionists in Iowa and elsewhere was the feeling that slavery was evil and it should be ended. However, most abolitionists of the time felt equality for blacks or any other people of color was out of the question. They had no desire to incorporate people of color into the daily lives of white citizens. To let people of color vote or hold office, testify in court or to have any equal footing in opportunities open to those of the white race was not an option to most of the population in the state or even to many of the supposed liberal abolitionists. Even in Grinnell, Iowa, one of the most liberal points in the state, when L.F. Parker and Josiah B. Grinnell tried to enroll black students into the school system there occurred an uprising among the townspeople. The school had to be temporarily closed down.[5]

Many of the most liberal abolitionists in the early 1850s felt the freed slaves should be sent back to Africa. If that wasn't possible then the newly freed slaves could be put on their own island in the Caribbean. Another preference sought for the freed slaves if emancipation came about was to put them on reservations, as was being done to the tribesmen of the aboriginal people of America.

James Brooks, the president of Tabor College, noted that when the Reverend Todd or the citizens of Tabor read scripture such as "Inasmuch as ye have done it unto one of the least of these, my brethren, ye have done it unto me," They did not see the word "white" before "brethren."[6] Unfortunately, at this time very few people in Iowa or the United States of America, North or South, believed people of color should be treated with Christian charity.

To most of the early inhabitants of Iowa the state was for "whites only." The people and the legislature had little desire to debate this question. It was a forgone conclusion. Prejudice and the thought of racial superiority were written into the state's constitution and its laws.

Augustus Caesar Dodge, Iowa's most prominent United States senator, was in fact a racist of the worst kind and he despised abolitionists like John Todd. Dodge felt that abolitionists were trying to destroy the Constitution and inevitably the Union. Like many of his time Dodge felt that since the constitution approved slavery then it must be holy and sacrosanct.[7] Dodge fully and wholeheartedly supported the Fugitive Slave laws. Dodge bragged that never in a single instant when slave owners had brought suit in Iowa for damages relating to those who had harbored or secreted escapees on the Underground Railroad had juries in Iowa not awarded compensation to the slave owners. Dodge liked to cite the case of *Ruel Daggs vs. Elihu Frasier.*[8]

Daggs v. Frasier et al. was a well known case among those in the Underground Railroad community. It told of the dangers of their work. The community of Salem was a well-known Quaker stop on the line of freedom. Nine slaves of a Missourian named Ruel Daggs escaped to Salem, Iowa. Daggs and a group of his cohorts invaded the town with warrants to search houses. The slave hunters came up empty handed. However, several of those involved in the escapes of his human chattel were arrested. Later four of the slaves were captured and returned to Daggs. A trial was held in 1850 in Burlington, Iowa, in which a jury awarded Daggs $2,900 for the five slaves who managed to escape. Thus the underground conductors were held liable for a large amount of money for that time.[9]

Dodge detested the Underground Railroad conductors and abolitionists, of whom he said, "While they will move heaven and earth to induce Negroes to run away from a home at which they are well fed and provided for, the very instant the Negro gets into a free State their sympathy for him ceases, until an opportunity is afforded them to interfere between him and his lawful owner."[10] Dodge with his racist mind had special venom for what he called "political abolitionists." He believed, "Behind these are those grave and momentous questions of equality, amalgamation, and superiority between Caucasian and the African races." Dodge's biographer said the senator felt that these abolitionists were seeking not only to establish the equality of the African race but even its superiority over the Caucasian. Their doctrines would induce flat-nosed, black-skinned, and woolly-headed senators and representative into the halls of Congress. Furthermore, they were seeking to break down and destroy all distinctions between the two races in respect to suffrage, office, marriage, and other relations in life. Dodge was quoted as saying, "And knowing these things to be their ulterior and cherished purpose, and believing as I most sincerely do, that the practical enforcement of their doctrines will degrade and debase my own race, and sound the death-knell to the Union, I here and everywhere [advocate] war upon abolitionism, in all its Protean shapes and guises."[11] Dodge even had the ridiculous notion that because of the abolitionists and the Underground Railroad agitated the slave owners, the slave owners had to curtail much of the liberty they would like to grant to their slaves.[12] Unfortunately, much of Iowa at this time felt as did their senator about race relations.

John Todd, George Gaston and the rest of Tabor began working on one of their most cherished dreams—that of starting a college in Tabor modeled after their beloved Oberlin College in Ohio, one that would incorporate Oberlin's ideas of racial equality. However, John Todd and the others had to face the reality that they didn't have the finances to begin a college. So instead the Tabor Literary Institute was formed as a forerunner to Tabor College. John Todd wrote up the articles of incorporation for the new institution on October 5, 1853.

Prominently written into the articles was the statement that "neither race nor sex shall be made a condition of admission to the privileges of the College."[13] This was included even though the Iowa legislature had passed a law, although never enforced, that excluded blacks from not only its educational institutions but the entire Hawkeye state in 1851.[14]

Although most of the Native Americans such as the Pottawattamies, who had lived in Fremont County, had been removed from Iowa by the time Tabor was settled, occasional bands of what was referred to then as Indians would hunt and camp around the town. These bands of tribesmen were welcomed around Tabor. Many times these Native Americans were looking for food and would be fed by the residents. One child in Tabor would later describe being frightened by the "Indians." She reported that one day a tribesman walked into their kitchen while her mother was frying doughnuts. The mother had the man sit by the stove, as it was a very cold day. The Native American man noticing the little girl clinging to her mother's skirts and her fear of him, gave out a hearty laugh.[15]

Some members of the Pawnee tribe had remained around Bellevue, Nebraska, and when George Gaston moved into Tabor some of them would come and visit their old friend. One of the Pawnee children had even attended school in Tabor. However, when the United States government removed the Pawnee to Okalahoma, then known as Indian Territory, this child went with his family to the Oklahoma territory.[16]

However, not all race relations were positive. John Todd reported an attack by Native Americans on a white settlement a few miles North of Tabor. Regrettably, some of the Native Americans were killed in the attack. The attackers had been supplied alcohol by white traders and assaulted a home in which shots were fired at the retreating assailants. Todd saw alcohol as the "apt tool of Satan for the destruction of mankind, whether he be white, or red, black, brown, or yellow."[17]

The Western frontier would often become the battleground for the nation on the question of slavery. The Compromise of 1820 allowed Missouri to enter the Union as a slave state and Maine as a free state devoid of slavery. One of the most important provisions of that compromise was to not allow slavery north of the Southern border of Missouri, with the exception of that state. The Western expansion of the United States always provided the question of which territories would be allowed to include slavery within its borders. This question was always controversial and the nation began to become polarized North and South. Whether a newly admitted state was to be pro-slavery or anti-slavery was the question of the day.

In 1850 the nation again faced another major crisis with the expansion of slavery as its major fracturing point. A series of bills were passed that became known as the Compromise of 1850. Abolitionists like John Todd applauded the measures of the Compromise of 1850 that prohibited slave-trading in the District of Columbia and the admission of California as a free state. However, the pro-slavery faction in Congress got as their part of the bargain the harsh Fugitive Slave Act.

This act proved to be immensely unpopular with the anti-slavery movement in the United States. The act provided that slaves could be chased into free states like Iowa and that anyone assisting the runaway slaves were subject to fines and jail time. It created a force of commissioners whose duties were to recapture runaway slaves. These commissioners could compel anyone, even abolitionists like John Todd, to help pursue and apprehend any runaway slave. Those who refused to cooperate could be fined and imprisoned.

Any marshal or deputy marshal who refused to help in the location or the arrest of a runaway slave was subjected to stiff fines. If a marshal captured a runaway slave and that slave escaped from the marshal's custody, that police officer was also subject to stiff fines. There was no statute of limitations on this act, so a slave who had escaped years ago and lived as a free person could be captured and taken back into bondage. No arrested black person was allowed even to testify in their own behalf. [18] Some abolitionists thought that one of the main purposes of the Fugitive Slave Act was to break the back of the Underground Railroad. [19]

As if the Fugitive Slave Act wasn't enough to make the abolitionists of Tabor's blood boil, the Kansas-Nebraska Act of 1854 surely did. This act hit close to home. It provided that the next door territories of Kansas and Nebraska would be formed. The question of slavery, of course, came to the forefront. Since the Compromise of 1820 forbade any slavery north of the Southern border of Missouri, the United States Senate had to do back-flips to appease the slavery interests in the United States.

Stephen Douglas, who would later contest Abraham Lincoln in the famed Lincoln-Douglas debates, chaired the Senate Committee on Territories. It was Douglas's opinion that the question of slavery should be left to the settlers of the territories. This policy became known as "popular sovereignty." Douglas, with an eye towards geography, knew Kansas would be settled by many from neighboring Missouri and they would vote in a pro-slavery constitution. He also reasoned that Nebraska would be settled mainly by those from free state Iowa and presumably would vote in an anti-slavery constitution. So the balance of power between slave states and free states could be accomplished in the Senate and Congress. Thus Douglas and others wishing to placate the Democrats in their Southern wing felt they could hold their political party together.

This bill infuriated John Todd. He felt it was just another example of the appeasement of the slave-holding interests in the United States. Todd would speak later of this time that "slavery [interests] had been petted ... like a spoiled child."[20]

Things only got worse with the Dred Scott decision. Scott was a slave who with the support of his master petitioned the St. Louis Circuit Court for his freedom. The basis for his petition was that he had resided in the

free states of Illinois and Wisconsin thus he should be considered a free person. Scott's case was a political hot-potato. If it was ruled that Scott in fact should be free because he had resided in free states, then there would be a rush north by many of those who were enslaved for their own freedom. Many in the South felt that if the court ruled in favor of Dred Scott, then the South would be in economic and social ruin.

After an eleven year legal odyssey the United States Supreme Court dropped a bombshell. They ruled that Dred Scott and any free blacks or slaves had no rights in the United States. Also, the decision stated that Congress had no right to prevent the spread of slavery.[21]

This ruling infuriated abolitionists like John Todd. It became crystal clear that the Underground Railroad and other means were the only way to fight slavery and the out of control Supreme Court and Congress. The passage of these unfortunate laws only sealed the resolve of the people of Tabor. The people of Tabor were law abiding citizens; however, they felt they were answering God's higher law in helping runaway slaves find freedom. They definitely were of the mind that racism and slavery were unchristian and those that practiced these vices would be punished in the next world.

What also helped to exacerbate the problems of slavery in the United States in the 1850's was the office of the presidency. In 1852 Franklin Pierce from New Hampshire was elected president. John Todd and many abolitionists felt this was a positive sign to the slowing down of the expansion of slavery and possibly the end to the institution by having a New Englander elected president.

However, Pierce's presidency from 1852 to 1856 proved to be a disaster. Franklin Pierce supported the Kansas-Nebraska Act that abolitionists like John Todd despised. The territory of Kansas splintered into two factions. The pro-slavery crowd had as their capital Lecompton, Kansas. The anti-slavery people viewed Topeka as their capital. Pierce saw the Lecompton

Opposite: Abolitionists were very buoyed when New Englander Franklin Pierce was nominated to the Presidency in 1852. Very few people in the country knew who Franklin Pierce was or his views. However, Pierce's handlers had positioned him as a Northerner who was pro-slavery to pacify the slave interests of the Democratic Party in the South. Pierce appointed pro-slavery men to positions of power in the territory of Kansas and sent in Federal troops to back up a pro-slavery constitution. Jefferson Davis, the future president of the Confederacy, was a close advisor to Pierce and their wives were best friends. By the time of the presidential election of 1856 Pierce had tried to appease so many people, in what was probably an impossible situation, everyone was mad at him. Even though he was the sitting president his own political party didn't nominate him for the election of 1856. (State Historical Society of Iowa—Des Moines.)

community as the legitimate government of Kansas. He viewed the Topeka citizens as rebels. The president wielded enormous power in these territories through the appointment of many top governmental positions. If the president appointed pro-slavery people to positions of power this of course had huge consequences as to the political outcome in these territories. Many Midwesterners accused Pierce of allowing Missouri's pro-slavery senator, David Rice Atchison, of having a free reign in dictating policy in Kansas.[22]

Shortly before his presidency the Pierces had suffered a tragedy. A beloved son had died when a rail train the Pierces were traveling on derailed. Mrs. Pierce never recovered from this heartbreak. When they took possession of the White House Mrs. Pierce rarely was seen. She hardly ever performed the duties of the first lady. One of the few friends she had at this time was Mrs. Jefferson Davis.[23]

Jefferson Davis was Pierce's secretary of war and closest advisor. Jefferson Davis, of course, went on to become the president of the Confederate States of America and for many he represented all of the horrible abuses of the institution of slavery. Some historians feel that the great influence of the slave holding interests in the United States was in part due to the closeness of the Davises to the Pierces. At every turn, to the abolitionists like John Todd, Pierce always seemed to side with the slave-holding states. In all fairness to Franklin Pierce, he tried to appease all the wings of the Democratic Party, which was slowly falling apart over the question of slavery. It seemed as if everyone in the Democratic Party disliked Pierce's polices. The Democratic Party, even though it had an incumbent in the office of the presidency, didn't even nominate Pierce for that office in the election of 1856.

In the election of 1856 James Buchanan was elected President. Buchanan never saw the importance of the question of slavery expansion in the western states. He spent most of the next four years trying to avoid an outbreak of the Civil War, giving little leadership to the country. To most abolitionists it seemed as if Buchanan sided repeatedly with the southern states in his effort to avoid an all-out civil war.

Considering this void of leadership in the highest posts of the adminis-

Opposite: President James Buchanan. The presidential election of 1856 proved to be of little satisfaction to abolitionists in Tabor. Again another Northerner, James Buchanan, was elected to the presidency but John Todd felt Buchanan sided with the pro-slavery interests at all times. All Buchanan seemed to want was to not have the impending Civil War break out during his presidency. Buchanan also failed to see the importance of the expansion of slavery into Kansas as it related to the anti-slavery and pro-slavery positions. (State Historical Society of Iowa—Des Moines.)

tration and legislative and judicial branches of government, the abolitionists in Tabor saw their only course of action was to continue their activities on the Underground Railroad and to support the flow of anti-slavery emigrants into Kansas. So these activities continued.

Although Fremont County was filled with many slavery sympathizers this county was listed by Wilbur Siebert in his book as having more people involved in the Underground Railroad than any other county in Iowa. Also Mills County, the county north of Tabor, had many in that region involved with Tabor's activities in helping escaping slaves.[24]

The abolitionists, especially in areas like Boston and Ohio, were very active in producing books, newspaper and magazine articles and propaganda pamphlets demonizing the South and the institution of slavery. John Todd and the rest of Tabor read these and of course they managed to increase their resolve against slavery. The fact that slavery broke up families split mothers from their children and the fact that slaves were treated in such a harsh manner and not allowed to read the Bible or hear the religious messages of the day seamed to be extraordinarily unchristian.

Even in Kansas there arose some that wished to exclude all blacks from the territory whether they be slave or free. This they thought would end the question of the expansion of slavery. Some even offered the idiotic idea that blacks would wish to come to Kansas as slaves only. However, John Todd knew slavery had to be stopped in Kansas if this terrible institution was to ever be stamped out from the fabric of this country.

However, despite the lofty calling of the Underground Railroad and the need to end slavery, it still fell upon the citizens of Tabor to earn their daily bread. Many long hours had to be devoted to this endeavor, as life on the frontier prairie was often tough and primitive and always unforgiving. Also, the mundane chore of establishing a city government fell to the citizens of Tabor.

On May 15, 1854 a meeting was held in George Gaston's house to lay out the village of Tabor. By chance John Todd's father-in-law, Q.F. Atkins, was in town and attended the meeting. At the time he had traveled from Cleveland, Ohio. It was agreed at this meeting that a schoolhouse would be built on subscription. A committee of three that included John Todd, Jonas Jones and J.S. Smith were appointed to plat out the town.[25] During this time when Q.F. Atkins was in Tabor he wrote a letter to the *Cleveland Morning Leader* for publication. In this letter he noted the "snails-pace which marks the transmission of letters, newspapers, and Telegraphic dispatches to this particular locality."

Atkins took much interest, as did many in the United States, to the land in and around Tabor and all of Southwest Iowa. Atkins continued his narrative to the folks back in the Cleveland:

There is much here to attract the attention of every intelligent, unprejudiced observer. The soil is unexceptionable,—taking it as a whole the best I ever saw. The face of the country, as far as I have passed over it, may be called beautiful—lovely ... it is emphatically—"Rolling prairie." I know of no better way to describe it, than by the hypothesis that, it was once (when in a semi-liquid state,) put in motion by the breathe of the Almighty; and when huge waves had attained a base varying ... they were fixed in their present position, by the same Omnipotent hand which had lifted them up, and so they remain even unto this day. The grade of ascent and descent in passing over these swells, is, in most cases easy; and about the same on each side.... There are many wells dug in this country, of various depths—from 12, to 65 or 70 feet—which have not been stoned or walled up,—unless it be some few, as high as the water rises in them—, which contrary all the experiences I have had in well-digging in New England, Ohio, and elsewhere, yet stand with their earth walls as smooth and firm, as when they where first opened. And what is quite remarkable, the earth in which these wells have been seen here, is so easily removed, that Mr. Adams ... tells me, that these men will open a well 60 feet deep in two days.[26]

Atkins purchased land around Tabor, as did John Todd's brother. Land speculation was rampant in the United States and many saw the area around Tabor a tantalizing prospect for wealth. Many of the letters the Todd family received from family members mention land deals or proposed land sales. Many of John Todd's relatives trusted him in handling these business matters. John, as he did with so many other things, had a good head for business.

However, in a letter to his father-in-law in 1854, John mentioned one of the major problems of land around Tabor. While the land is of the best quality and water reasonably plentiful, timber is not. Timber claims were hard to come by. All the good timber claims have been made around Tabor and John wrote, "A scarcity of timber is the chief difficulty with which this country has to contend, & it is a serious difficulty."[27]

When John Todd's father passed away on December 11, 1851, the Todd siblings divided his small estate.[28] It was evident from a family letter that John desperately needed the money from his share of the estate.[29] At this time John received little from his flock, as they had no money and he was not receiving support from any of the missionary societies at this time. His brothers were only too happy to comply and even offered their share of their father's estate if necessary to him. However, the estate took some time to distribute the money. Although intellectually the younger Todd brothers, John or David, would have been better suited to be executors of their father's estate, out of respect for their older brother James they let him be executor of the estate, even though younger brother David often directed his efforts.[30] Brother David, not married, and although on the slim salary of a minister, had enough money left over after the estate was settled to speculate $200 on land around Tabor.[31]

John sold David's property for a profit several years later. However, when his father-in-law wanted to sell his land during the winter of 1856–57, John advised against it, as there was little demand for farmland during the wintertime.[32]

Later that spring in April of 1857, John wrote to his father-in-law that demand for farmland again was up and this would be a better time to sell. The land was sold by John but the problems of buying and selling land on the frontier prairie were no easy matter, as his letters attest. John had hand sewed the ten twenty-dollar gold pieces for the land that his father-in-law had sold into the money belt of Timothy Dwight Ladd, who was returning to Ohio and meeting Mr. Atkins. Apparently Mr. Ladd or the bank he did business with exchanged the gold pieces for paper money. This did not make Mr. Atkins or John Todd very happy, as the paper money was often worth less than the gold pieces.[33]

However, John did start receiving a little money from the American Missionary Association in 1853.[34] This was to support himself and his work until his flock could became solvent enough to do so. Within a year the church in Tabor was able to fully support its minister. John duly reported in March of 1854 that he would not need the support of the American Missionary Association. S.L. Jocelyn and George Whipple from the society wrote to Todd that they were surprised that the church in Tabor was able to support him so quickly. They wrote, "We wish now to say that we hope that if you are not sustained, that you would renew the application, as we need all the true men we can secure in Iowa, and in all the West...."[35]

By 1856 the Congregational Church in Tabor had paid back all the money the American Missionary Association had advanced Todd. This was unusual in that many churches never did this. The church was also starting to send extra money to the A.M.A. so they could help other frontier ministers and churches. In a letter in 1856 Whipple told Todd he would like to quote from some of the Reverend's correspondence in the newsletter of the organization, the American Missionary. Whipple also wanted to use the Tabor Church as an example of the good works the society was doing. Whipple wrote, "It seems to be due the donors of the Association that they should receive this reward for their donations, to see that some, at best, of the churches that have shown their liberality are early beginning to make pecuniary return for the acct given them."[36]

The thoughts of the Underground Railroad or making sure Kansas came into the Union as a free state were never far from John Todd's mind. These lofty ideals sometimes clashed with the hardscrabble life on the frontier. As the decade of the 1850's was marching on, the politics of Iowa showed a ray of hope. Jonas Jones remarked in a letter to Q.F. Atkins that he hoped racist Iowa United States Senator Augustus Caesar Dodge would be replaced in that body.[37] Dodge was replaced in 1855 by a man, James Harlan, more in tune with the sentiments of Tabor. But there was much work ahead in the Hawkeye state by John Todd and the rest of Tabor's Underground Railroad.

7

Routes to Freedom

John Todd, George Gaston, Samuel H. Adams and most of the founders of Tabor all came from Oberlin and cut their Underground Railroad teeth at the feet of Oberlin's masters. John Todd once stated, "Of all the thousands of Oberlin students, I never knew one who studied there long, who did not go out from there a thorough abolitionist."[1]

No one is certain where the term Underground Railroad came from or when it started. There were slaves who had escaped bondage almost as soon as they were brought to the colonies in the 1620's. George Washington once noted that there were many people who would just as soon help escaping slaves as help apprehend them and return them to their masters.

However, one important year in the history of the Underground Railroad would have to be 1833. William Lloyd Garrison headed the New England Anti-Slavery Society, Margaretta Forten formed the Female Anti-Slavery Society in Philadelphia and various other northern cities organized groups to prevent the return of fugitive slaves to their Southern homes of enslavement. Southern slave posses would go into Northern cities, capture fugitives and free blacks, take them south where they had no rights and sell them into slavery even if they were not fugitives. Every black, even if they were free, were fair game to be sold back into slavery by unscrupulous whites. Northern blacks were forming organizations to help keep blacks safe from being kidnapped and forced back into slavery. Many of these groups became associated with the Underground Railroad.

The most important event of 1833 was that the British Parliament passed its Emancipation Act banning slavery and the slave trade, not only in the British Isles but also in her empire and dominions. This meant, of course, that Canada could become a safe haven for escaping blacks. Once in Canada a black American—free or slave—had no fears of being returned to bondage.

It is interesting to note that when Britain banned slavery, many pro-slavery opponents in the United States used this as an argument against abolitionists in America. Since there was still a lot of resentment against Britain in America at this time, painting the abolitionists as being pro–British to some weakened the abolitionists' position. John Todd's cousin used this very point when they were having a discussion on slavery via the mail. She stated that because Todd was advocating the abolishment of slavery, then he must be "in league with the British."[2]

It would seem that since Canada became a safe haven for blacks in the mid–1830s, they were assured a safe place to go where American slave laws couldn't touch them. One newly freed black said in Canada he was "not known for the color of his skin, but the government knows me as a man."

Places like Oberlin were willing to openly flout the slave laws and the return of runaways. Although slaves had been escaping bondage from colonial times, it would seem these influences would put the Underground Railroad into a forward motion in the 1830's. At this time, of course, the overland railroads were beginning to lay metal tracks all over the North and South. It was natural that the Underground Railroad co-opted many of the terms used by the "overland railroad." Terms such as conductor, depot, passengers, stationmaster, derailment, routes, cargoes and packages were all code words used by the Underground Railroad.

One unfortunate by-product of the term "Underground Railroad" is the fact that so many people believe that the escaping slaves did in fact travel underground via a system of tunnels. The "underground" in Underground Railroad pertains to the fact that the whole operation was out of sight and out of the watchful eyes of authorities. It had nothing to do with being physically underground. Tabor has had its share of fanciful tales of the town being honeycombed with underground tunnels. George Gaston's granddaughter, Etta M. Gaston, put those rumors to rest when she stated that "never was there a tunnel between Father Todd's and my grandfather's G.B. Gaston's house or anywhere else for helping slaves away."[3]

There just would have been no need for John Todd or George Gaston or the rest of Tabor to tunnel under the town to hide runaways. When the escapees were in Tabor and needed to be hidden, they would be put in attics or basements. There were no references of any kind in the Todd or Gaston writings of tunnels. However, attics, basements and out buildings were mentioned as hiding places when that necessity presented itself.[4]

The notion that some Underground Railroad towns were honeycombed with tunnels was hardly unique to Tabor. Some people in these Underground Railroad towns would swear they even had seen these tunnels. The answer was probably they had seen some kind of storm or storage cellar, as children, and it was mistaken over time as a tunnel. One of the more persistent myths about underground tunnels that circulated about the Underground Railroad occurred in the Cleveland and Oberlin, Ohio, area. It was rumored that St. John's Episcopal Church in Cleveland had a tunnel or tunnels underneath its structure that were used to advance or hide escaping slaves. The Western Reserve Historical Society conducted two separate investigations that concluded no such tunnels ever existed. In 1993 Byron D. Fruehling made on-site investigations of seventeen Ohio houses that reputedly had some kind of tunnel used for hiding fugitive slaves during the Underground Railroad period. Fruehling concluded there were no subterranean hiding places at these houses. He did believe fugitive slaves had been hidden at these locations in these houses in such quarters as attics and spare rooms and also in outbuildings such as barns.[5]

Many of the slaves who came to Tabor escaped bondage in Missouri, Arkansas, Oklahoma or elsewhere. Many escapees went west out of Missouri, north out of Arkansas or north out of Oklahoma into Kansas and looked for sympathizers black or white. They found these sympathizers in the Kansas towns of Lawrence, Quindaro, Sumner, Clinton, Oskaloosa and Holton, among others.[6] The escapees headed north through Nebraska and usually crossed the Missouri River in Nebraska City, Nebraska, Wyoming, Nebraska, or other busy crossings. There was another landing situated one-half mile north of Nebraska City on the Iowa side near a hotel named Eastport House. However, very often pro-slavery bounty hunters or others would monitor these landing points hoping to catch escaping slaves disembarking from the ferry. Once the runaways had crossed the Missouri River at Nebraska City or elsewhere, they would proceed to either Civil Bend or Tabor.

At Civil Bend the escapees would be hidden by the Platt family, Doc Blanchard or others sympathizers. The "train" would then proceed to Tabor or possibly Lewis or Quincy, Iowa. There were a few free blacks, such as the Garner family and John Williamson, in the Civil Bend and the Tabor area that unquestionably played a part in hiding or helping escaping slaves make it across the Nebraska City crossing. Williamson was described as part black and part Native American. He showed considerable business acumen and had ample opportunity to aid escapees. Williamson traded eggs and butter and other goods and commodities traveling between Nebraska City on the Nebraska side of the river and then proceeding via the ferry or boat to the Iowa side of the river. Thus Williamson had a perfect cover for moving escaping slaves from the Nebraska side of the river to the Iowa side of the river and then helping them on to Civil Bend or Tabor.[7]

The other more obvious route a runaway might use would be to come straight north out of Western Missouri. In this route the runaways would go to Tabor, Civil Bend or possibly Amity, a small village some 40 miles to the southeast of Tabor. This village lies some 3 miles inside the Iowa line near the Missouri border. Amity was known as a "Stop and Start," as the escapees from slavery could stop there and rest before starting on their Underground Railroad journey.[8]

The name of Amity was already in use so the locals had to name their post office "College Springs," the name by which it is now known. Amity somewhat mirrored Tabor in that a group of people from Knox College in Galesburg, Illinois, wanted to come west to provide educational opportunities and put an end to slavery while building a college that espoused these points of view. Galesburg was a hotbed of Underground Railroad activity and even one of the experts on this subject, Wilbur Siebert, believed that this town was the most important station in Illinois. What John Todd found compelling about the colony at Amity was the fact that it was nondenominational. John felt that the religious denominations in American had as their focus the idea of keeping their membership rolls and their collection plates full. Todd felt they did not spend enough time saving souls or trying to put an end to slavery or poverty.

In the fall of 1858, John Todd traveled to Amity with his wife and B.F. Gardner. They were treated very well and the small community was busy preparing for winter. People were moving into the community and Todd noted hastily built homes and even some tents were in use. A comet put on a splendid show with its tail reaching from the horizon to its zenith, a sight many in the small community would never forget. John helped with revival meetings at night and undoubtedly passed on Underground Railroad and abolitionist information while he was in Amity.[9]

From Amity escaping fugitives could go north to Montgomery County, Iowa. The Reverend William W. Merritt was the stationmaster at his farm in Montgomery County.[10] From Montgomery County fugitive slaves could head east along the Underground Railroad.

This route straight north out of Missouri was used by some escapees, but many felt it was safer to get into Kansas as soon as possible. For instance, a slave from the Kansas City area would have to travel around 160 miles straight north to Tabor through Northwest Missouri. Along the whole 160 mile route they could be harassed the entire way by slave hunters or slave posses. Many counties in slave states such as Missouri had regular slave hunting patrols to make sure runaways were captured quickly after escape. In many cases in Missouri, depending upon where the slave resided, the runaway could traverse only a few miles over into Kansas and have a somewhat safer journey. If the escapee found the right party they could be protected by the Underground Railroad in Kansas.

If a runaway was caught in a slave state such as Missouri their punishment was harsh according to the slave codes. Any white person or free black helping a runaway in a slave state was subjected to extravagant fines, hard labor and jail time. In a slave state any white person could stop a black person—free or slave—and ask for their papers. If their papers weren't to the liking of the white person, regardless if the black was not a slave, the black person could be taken to jail where they sat without benefit of an attorney or access to a trial by jury. A white person could claim oral ownership of a jailed black escapee before a judge and the black person would be bound over. The only argument over ownership would be with another white person. Unfortunately, most of the time it didn't matter to the judicial system in slave states if a black person was in fact a free man or woman. The only legal question of importance was which white person owned the black person. Blacks had no say in the matter.

Slave states like Missouri not only had local law officials searching for runaways, slave patrols and bounty hunters were always on the lookout for escapees. Dogs were also trained to track any runaways. The bounty hunters and posses often didn't care if they snared free blacks in their dragnets. Any black person on the move in a slave state was assumed to be an escaped slave.

A male slave in good physical condition during the 1850's was thought to be worth around $1,000. Many rewards for runaways on the Underground Railroad would be for around $100. This proved to be a great financial incentive for men to join a slave posse. The areas of Western Iowa, Western Missouri and the territories of Kansas and Nebraska were starved for cash. Most of the residents of this area were subsistence farmers who saw very little hard or paper money during the year. A reward of $100 or a part of the reward, if to be shared, was more than enough monetary incentive to bring out a large slave posse.

Most of the escapees walked to freedom. They usually traveled at night to avoid contact with anyone. The North Star and the Big Dipper became the Holy Grail to many of these escapees as they followed these astrological stars to freedom. The Big Dipper was often referred to as the drinking gourd. They followed the North Star many times never knowing who was friend or foe and without maps or compass. Unfortunately, some white people would pretend to befriend the escaping slaves only to turn them in for the cash rewards or to sell them back into slavery at their earliest convenience.

One such escaping slave was making his way through Kansas on his way to Iowa. He became suspicious of the way his supposed Underground Railroad benefactor was acting. His supposed benefactor was in fact planning to sell the escapee in Missouri and back into slavery. The fugitive managed to escape from this ersatz Underground Railroad conductor and made his way to the Sac and Fox reservation south of the Nemaha River in

Nebraska. There he found no sanctuary, as the Native Americans also planned to sell the black man back into Missouri for the monetary gain. Fortunately, an abolitionist intervened and disguised the black man as a Native American and got him off the reservation and on his way to the Underground Railroad.[11]

In January of 1859 a large group of escaping slaves consisting of eleven or twelve were captured around Holton, Kansas, while on their way to Iowa. A Dr. John Doy was put on trial for aiding these escaping slaves. It was also charged that Doy not only aided these slaves in their escape but enticed them to do so. After two trails Doy was convicted and sentenced to five years in the Missouri penitentiary. Ironically, Doy became an escapee from the legal system when abolitionists broke him out of jail in St. Joseph, Missouri, and took him to safety in Kansas.[12]

There were more violent incidents for those on the way to Tabor. Just south of Nebraska City on the Missouri River was a town named after slave owner Richard Brown. Brownsville was known as a proslavery town and was to be avoided by those trying to make it to Tabor.

During the autumn of 1857 three armed black men seeking freedom in Tabor were spotted south of Brownsville. A four man slave posse hunted the men down in some willows south of town. A gun battle broke out between the two factions. One of the slave posse was killed and one of the black men was badly wounded. The wounded black man was taken to a hotel in Brownsville where surgeons amputated his injured arm. Proslavery men wanted to take the injured black runaway to Missouri for some cruel punishment for having the audacity to shoot and kill a white man. Nonetheless, the injured man stood trial. Incredibly, considering the racist attitude of the time toward black on white violence no matter what the justification, the black runaway was acquitted of all charges.

The two black escapees took the horses of their pursuers and obtained more firearms. They made their way onto Iowa soil but were again found by a slave posse. Another gun battle broke out. This time another of the runaways was wounded and both were captured.[13]

While Missouri or Arkansas didn't have the number of plantations or slaves that states like Mississippi or Alabama had, it nevertheless used slave labor in many of its agricultural products such as corn, rice, livestock, wheat and hemp. Female slaves often worked doing the domestic chores around the houses of their white masters. However, many times these female slaves worked right alongside their male counterpart, expected to do the same type of backbreaking work. Cotton may have been king in the Deep South but the bales of cotton had to be tied by ropes made of hemp. Prior to the start of the Civil War, Missouri was the leading hemp grower in the slave holding states due largely to the demand of Deep South cotton plantations.

The area around Kansas City was a major hemp growing region. Jo Shelby from Waverly, Missouri, just east of Kansas City, had the largest hemp factory in the state. In a slave state like Missouri there were few large plantation settings. However, slaves would work in large factories like Jo Shelby's. Slaves also toiled as agricultural workers, miners, teamsters, craftsmen, domestics, stevedores on loading docks or as day laborers plus a myriad of other occupations.

John Todd and other Underground Railroad conductors knew that even in a free state like Iowa they were subject to fines and even jail time if caught aiding runaways. Also, civil suits could be brought against "conductors" for "stealing property" and could force restitution. Todd and others in Tabor were well aware of the risk they were taking. Newspapers in Ohio, which some in town received, and elsewhere in the United States told of lawsuits, convictions and jail times that were given to conductors on the Underground Railroad.

What motivated the folks like John Todd to take these risks? Todd's own natural sympathetic nature undoubtedly played a major part in his risk taking. The time spent at Oberlin also was a major factor. The book *Uncle Tom's Cabin* by Harriet Beecher Stowe published in 1852 was a reason in keeping the resolve of the abolitionists in focus. *Uncle Tom's Cabin* electrified the Northern abolitionists with its portrayal of the ugliness of slavery and the righteousness of the cause of the escaping slave.

John Todd and the other residents of Tabor wrote to fellow abolitionists and articles were passed back and forth from newspapers and magazines that promoted the abolitionists' cause. When John was still in his pastorate at Clarksfield, Ohio, while he was chairman and secretary of the Huron County Anti-Slavery Society he would collect anti-slavery articles.[14] This practice stayed with him while in Iowa. If these letters or articles didn't directly mention the Underground Railroad, they would imply that this was a justifiable institution. Also, the American Reform Tract and Book Society published many anti-slavery pamphlets that helped the abolitionist see the horrors of slavery. Tracts were published on subject matter such as slave auctions, slave auctions that broke up families and slave auctions in Washington, D.C., within sight of the nation's capital. Other pamphlets were on the subject of how righteous men should use their vote to end slavery in the United States. One tract was titled "Is it Expedient to Introduce Slavery into Kansas—A Tract for the Times." These tracts and pamphlets were widely read and circulated in Tabor and helped to keep the Underground Railroad sentiments at a high pitch.[15]

Anti-slavery and abolitionist meetings were held in Tabor and in the immediate area such as the seat of Fremont County—Sidney, Iowa.[16] These meetings kept this subject on the plate of public discourse even for those

SALE OF A FAMILY OF SLAVES IN WASHINGTON CITY.

A TRACT FOR SABBATH SCHOOLS.

Slaves are people held as property. They are bought and sold, as if they were cows or horses. Some of them are black, some yellow, and some white. In Washington city, where the President of the United States resides, where Congress meets, and the great men of the nation resort, there has been in times past one of the greatest slave markets in the world. One specimen of the sales of who didn't read the abolitionist material that the residents of Tabor kept up on. Even out of town anti-slavery rallies were well attended by Tabor and Civil Bend people.

The runaway slaves, of course, risked even more than the white participants in the Underground Railroad. Their lives were on the line and the potential for them to be killed on purpose or by accident was great. There were no criminal penalties if an enraged owner killed one of his slaves after being returned from an attempted escape. The possibility of a brutal beating was a distinct threat if caught and returned to bondage. Slaves who were captured were often crippled or body parts dismembered to prevent future escapes. The escapees who made their way north on the Underground Railroad were undoubtedly some of the bravest individuals in American history. Their courage and valor is a model for not only the people of the United States but also the world. They embody what sacrifices human beings will make to be free. Their hunger for freedom is a testament to the wish by all human beings for liberty, as expressed in the American Declaration of Independence.

Once the escapees made their way to Tabor the town's Underground Railroad apparatus would shift into high gear. Conductors would be chosen to forward the "human cargo" on their journey northward to Canada. Usually the conductors were chosen upon the basis of who had the time to perform these duties, which sometimes could consume several days. If there were slave or bounty hunters, county law enforcement officials or a slave posse in the area, special care would be taken to ensure the runaways could proceed on their long journey to the "Queen's Dominions." Special tactics would be employed to impede any slave hunters from derailing the cargo on the Underground Railroad. These tactics included infiltrating slave posses with Tabor people to insure hiding places wouldn't be discovered. Jesse West and his restaurant and hotel would be called upon to hold up slave hunters when they stopped for meals or rest. West was always very imaginative in delaying slave posses or sheriffs bent on capturing runaways in town. Also,

Opposite: **A woodcut from a tract by the American Reform Tract and Book Society shows a black family being sold at a slave auction in Washington city (Washington, D.C.). Abolitionists like John Todd were infuriated that "in the land of the free" slaves were being sold close to the nation's capital. The family in this woodcut was purportedly sold to different slave owners, breaking up the strongest bond known to man— the family unit. There was a major war of propaganda going on in the United States between the pro-slavery and anti-slavery sides and the American Tract and Book Society supplied much of the anti-slavery propaganda. This tract was used by children and distributed mostly through Sunday schools. The complete text appears in the appendix. (Todd House Museum Archives.)**

as Tabor is near the boundary line of Fremont and Mills counties, if confronted by the sheriff from Fremont County the Underground Railroad conductors from Tabor would claim they were in Mills County and thus the law official didn't have the authority to inspect their cargo or arrest them. If they were stopped in Mills County they would claim they were in Fremont County and the sheriff couldn't interfere with them. The law officials would comply and let the "train" and its unseen cargo proceed. Thus the Tabor conductors sometimes avoided being apprehended by local law officers.[17]

Transporting the "passengers" was probably the most complicated and hazardous activity on the Underground Railroad. Because of this traveling at night was the recommended time of passage. When traveling at night, even with experienced conductors, notable landmarks that were clear to the eye during the day time could become obscured by the night darkness. Ravines, gullies and rivers could become death traps. Poor weather conditions, including rain swelling streams and rivers and snow and cold weather, could greatly impede advancement on the rail line of freedom. Surprisingly, many of the accounts of escapees coming into Tabor occurred during the wintertime.

Winter may seem a poor time to attempt an escape with the inherent dangers posed by temperatures and snow. However, since many slaves were engaged by their masters in agricultural pursuits, winter might have been the only time an escape attempt could be made. During the mid-1800s wintertime was usually considered downtime for many slaves or farm workers. Planting, harvesting, cultivating and other chores occupied most of the hours of the slaves engaged in agriculture. Their labor wasn't as critical as it was in other times of the year. Consequently they weren't watched as closely. Most slaves wanted to escape but had little opportunity to do so. Wintertime sometimes provided a small window of opportunity to leave a life of human bondage. When an escape was made during the winter, very often the slaves weren't missed right away and their chances of a clean getaway more likely. Also, on the other side, sometimes it was harder to pursue runaways during the extreme cold or high snow drifts of wintertime.

However, fleeing during winter could be very dangerous. It is unknown how many escapees lost their lives due to exposure or hypothermia. During the winter of 1856–1857 John Todd wrote to his father-in-law that during January days went by with the thermometer below zero much of the time, including a low of minus 28 on the 18th of January 1857. Todd went on to report that the snow was at the top of the fence posts a good deal of the time. Several area people had frozen to death, including one Tabor man who went out to cut wood and became disoriented and froze to death within two miles of his home. This harsh winter of 1857 lasted into April.[18]

However, an examination of newspaper ads run in Missouri newspapers for runaway slaves point out that June, August, September and October were the most popular months for escapes. Apparently July, with its extreme hot weather, was not a well-liked month for escape.[19]

Two of the more notable features that these advertisements of runaway slaves in Missouri newspaper revealed was the fact that in the late 1850's larger groups of slaves were escaping than had in earlier times. Also, there seemed to be more violence connected with these escapes between hunted and hunters.[20]

To the conductors in Tabor the Nishnabotna River was both a blessing and a curse. The Nishnabotna has two branches, the West and East. The West branch, which was closest to Tabor and was a little wider, was the first major obstacle in an escape on the Underground Railroad. The river's bottom lands and banks provided great hiding places for the conductors and their "cargo." Usually when a slave posse was chasing a train they could hide down by the "Nishna" river bottoms. The Reverend Todd's people would often have one of their own infiltrate the posse and that person would assign himself to look on the Nishnabotna River bottoms for hiding places.

The river could be a curse because it had to be crossed a couple of times. The West and East branches both had to be negotiated. If the train was headed to the station in Lewis, Iowa, there was a ferry to take the train and its cargo across the East branch of the Nishnabotna. So that route had fewer river crossings. There were creeks to cross—the Walnut, Silver and others—but these were not as daunting as the Nishnabotna unless the creeks were swelled by flooding waters. However, the Nishnabotna had a well earned reputation as being a river only too willing to pour over its own banks, making crossings and fording difficult. If the train was headed to the station in Quincy, Iowa, both branches of the Nishnabotna had to be crossed, as did the Nodaway River.

Very often the "train" had to avoid main roads, as slave bounty hunters or posses would be more likely to travel on them. Roads passable during normal times became impassable during high water or winter snow. Almost all the roads were dirt and untreated, making them questionable even during the best weather conditions. Special places like the cottonwood tree bridge across the Nishnabotna River would be kept secret so as to make the train more likely to avoid capture. Other special hiding places were kept as secret as possible. As happened with the Reverend Todd's companion, sometimes fugitives were disguised and transported by carriage. If possible wagons were used by conductors on the Underground Railroad. Some of those wagons had false bottoms to hide their cargos. Whatever the manner of conveyance, the key was to draw as little attention to oneself as possible. Often times exploits performed on the Underground Railroad or routes

The Nishnabotna River was one of the major obstacles as the Underground Railroad trains left Tabor and moved east. It had two branches, East and West. Its thick underbrush provided great cover and multiple hiding places for Underground Railroad trains and their "conductors" and "passengers." However, it was prone to overflow, causing delays. Oftentimes, the same crossing points couldn't be used as posses or bounty hunters or unsympathetic eyes could watch these points and cause a crash of a "train." The Nishnabotna seen here in the winter time, with its plush vegetation gone, could be friend or foe. The question that always arose over rivers like this during the winter time, "Was the ice thick enough to support a person, a wagon?" An incorrect assumption could cause death or severe injury. If a night crossing of the Nishnabotna was attempted, familiar landmarks often changed shapes on cloudy and moonless nights. (Todd House Museum Archives.)

taken were not talked about or advertised for fear of jeopardizing future escapes.

Once the escapees were transported to the next stationhouse, usually they were hidden in attics or basements. Sometimes these stationhouses had trap doors or other hiding places. It was very popular at this time to build houses with trap doors or small hidden closets or small rooms. The literature of the times told of castles and mansions being built with secret passages and hidden rooms providing hiding places for the very wealthy. If you were building a cabin or modest house the least you could do is add a trap door or a "secret closet." The importance of these hiding places has probably been overly exaggerated on the Underground Railroad. A half dozen or even two or three escapees would be very hard pressed to hide in most of these rather diminutive "secret hiding places." An attic or basement or sometimes the children's sleeping rooms would be more likely temporary hiding places. If fugitives could not be hidden in the house they would be taken to barns, haylofts or other farm outbuildings such as hog houses. Sometimes escaping babies, to be kept out of sight, would be temporarily stuffed into a grain sack. Larger adults could be hidden in a hay mound or on a hay wagon. If you were in an area where the hay pile could be examined by unwanted individuals, a large, menacing dog could be put by the hay stack to keep the curious at bay.

It would have been difficult for one stationhouse to communicate with another. The United States mail was often too slow to be of any real or consistent use and the mail service was at times unreliable. There weren't a lot of telegraph lines in Iowa at this time for use as a means of communication.. Much of the time the stationmasters had no idea when a "train" was arriving at their "depot." The stationmaster and conductors always had to be on guard for new arrivals and for any potential dangers.

However, there were times when communication could be done under the cover of normal business practices that would cause little suspicion. As mentioned before, John Williamson in his business as a tradesman working between the Nebraska and Iowa sides of the Missouri River had a perfect cover for transmitting communication and bringing runaway slaves to the stationhouse in Tabor. In another example, Josiah B. Grinnell, from Grinnell, Iowa, and "Uncle Tom" Mitchell from Central Iowa had knowledge of the sheep trade. They used this knowledge to convey a message of some escapees' movement. Since the mails were too slow they sent a messenger with a note telling of some escapees that were coming on the Underground Railroad: "Dear Grinnell: Uncle Tom says if the roads are not too bad you can look for those fleeces of wool by to-morrow. Send them on to test the market and price, and no back charges. Yours, "Hub."[21]

John Todd in his work as a Congregational minister could pass information on at district meetings in Council Bluffs, Iowa, with other Congregational ministers, such as the Reverend George B. Hitchcock, the stationmaster at the Hitchcock House in Lewis, Iowa. Todd even mentions trying to forward an escapee at one of these Congregational District meetings. Todd also mentions one of these district meetings occurring in Lewis. John discusses in a letter holding revivals in the area and spending almost two weeks helping the Reverend Hitchcock with a revival. What a perfect opportunity to not only initially bring escapees to Lewis, but to also pass communications and plan strategy for future forwarding of their human cargo on the Underground Railroad.[22]

In Eastern Iowa in 1859 the United States mail was at that time considered reliable enough to pass a message of an incoming "train." From Low Moor, Iowa, G.W. Weston sent a letter to the stationmaster in Clinton, Iowa, C. B. Campbell, that read,"

> Mr. C.B.C.   Low Moor, May 6, 1859
>   Dear Sir—By tomorrow evening's mail, you will receive two volumes of the "Irrepressible Conflict" bound in *black*. After perusal, please forward, and oblige.
>   Yours truly, G.W.W.[23]

However, the other side also had advantages. One of the leading citizens of Nebraska City, then the center of commerce in the area, was a slave owner. He had a general store in Nebraska City and also had stores in Sidney and Glenwood, Iowa. He regularly had messengers and freight moving between his various stores. So he had ample opportunities to help slave posses, provide communications, and provide assistance in hunting for runaway slaves, which he was only too happy to provide.

Once the "train" would leave Tabor it would usually advance to Quincy, Iowa, or to

The Reverend George Hitchcock and the rest of the Underground Railroad apparatus in Lewis, Iowa, worked very well together with the Tabor and Civil Bend conductors. Their cooperation undoubtedly helped to execute numerous escapes. The Reverend Todd thought a lot of Hitchcock, and they held a religious revival together in Lewis. Hitchcock was a Congregational minister, as was Todd. Many of the UGRR stations had religious connections such as Congregationalists, Quakers or Friends, Wesleyan Methodists and Reformed Presbyterians. (Hitchcock House, Lewis, Iowa.)

the Hitchcock House in Lewis, Iowa. However, in some instances the runaways were escorted clear across the Hawkeye state, such as the case of the Mississippi runaways who were taken almost from the western border of Iowa to the eastern border by Tabor conductors in 1854.

The Reverend Hitchcock had come west after he had suffered a severe illness while attending Illinois College. He moved to eastern Iowa when an accident caused him partial blindness. He recovered enough in 1853 so he was able to move to Lewis, in Cass County. He started the Congregational Church there and became a link on the Underground Railroad.[24]

In 1856 Hitchcock built a stately stone house that would serve as a stationhouse. The house was large and impressive for the times. The notable sandstone structure must have given the escaping slaves a feeling of security when they were safely within its walls.[25] Another house that was used in Lewis as a stationhouse was that of Oliver Mills. The Mills house was of incredi-

Hitchcock House, Lewis Iowa. In 1856, the Reverend George Hitchcock built an impressive limestone house. This notable structure must have given the escaping slaves very much a sense of security on the way to their long journey. The sandstone was quarried nearby and then hauled by ox teams to the Nishnabotna River. Then it was floated across the river on a raft and then with great effort hauled up the steep hill and set in place. (Hitchcock House, Lewis, Iowa.)

ble construction, it had only one
door and it was two inches thick
and its walls were eighteen
inches thick.[26]

Once the escapees made
their way from Southwest Iowa
their direction was often determined by circumstances. One of
the most important circumstances was if a slave posse was
on their trail. The Underground
Railroad system on the Western
Frontier in Iowa was unorgan-
ized. Routes often had to be
changed so law enforcement or
slave hunters would not for sure
know where to look. Many of the
underground stations in Iowa
were centered in towns with a
strong religious community. The
Congregational Church and the
Quaker or Society of Friends
churches were also very support-
ive of Underground Railroad
activities. Wesleyan Methodists
and Reformed Presbyterian
churches also provided aid and
comfort to escapees.[27]

After leaving Southwest

Oliver Mills also had an Underground
Railroad station house in Lewis, Iowa.
At the time, his house had only one
door to it. The door was two inches
thick and the walls to the house were
18 inches thick. The Hitchcock House
was the next transfer station most
often used by the conductors at Tabor
and Civil Bend. (Hitchcock House,
Lewis, Iowa.)

Iowa the escapees would usually travel east towards the Des Moines area.
Along the way were many potential stops such as in Adair, Stuart (Summit
Grove), Earlham and Winterset for the escapees and their conductors. The
Jordan House in West Des Moines was used often as a stopping place. Once
leaving the Des Moines area, trains would find stations in Newton, Grinnell
and Iowa City on their way to Davenport and the crossing of the Mississippi
River.[28] There were dozens of Underground Railroad stations in Iowa; many
of their names have been lost to the mists of time. Some station houses'
importance has been enhanced beyond reality by various local legends. Unfortunately, the history of the Underground Railroad, because of its illegal
nature, was often left to the oral traditions of an area. Oftentimes oral traditions can provide very accurate information to an area's history but regrettably, sometimes the historian is left trying to judge the voracity of someone

long dead. Wilbur Siebert, in his remarkable study of the Underground Railroad in the United States, noted the lack of written materials such as diaries and letters by those keeping station houses and aiding escapees.

Escapees and their conductors would often find routes that would have to be changed due to the swelling of streams and rivers or the approach of a slave posse. Sometimes days were lost due to weather conditions such as winter storms. Waiting until a river froze over to provide easier crossing often consumed much time. Sometimes escapees would avoid the comfort of a stationhouse to forage on their own, thus not taking the chance of contacting anyone for fear of being turned in.

The food and shelter of the various stationhouses in Iowa often varied. Most, however, did their best to provide for the escapees. Folk legends claim certain individuals were the "President" of the Underground Railroad on the Iowa frontier but in fact most of the conductors and others engaged in this activity didn't know each other. In many cases to keep the work of the Underground Railroad viable it was best that individuals from one area didn't know the names of others occupied in this clandestine business. If you didn't know the names of your fellow Underground Railroad companions in the next stationhouse, you couldn't testify against them in criminal or civil courts.

In the Southeast part of the Hawkeye state those that escaped bondage on the Underground Railroad came north out of Missouri into the waiting arms of several communities like Salem, Cincinnati and Denmark. From these and other communities the escapees would be sent on their way to freedom. Most of the Underground Railroad activity was centered in the bottom half of Iowa in counties closest to slave state Missouri's border. Salem was a Quaker community deeply involved in the Underground Railroad. The Lewelling house in Salem was an important station in giving aid to those seeking freedom from their horrible bondage in Missouri.[29]

In Cincinnati, Iowa, J.H. B. Armstrong was very active in seeking freedom for escaping slaves. Armstrong helped two escapees known as John and Archie escape bondage in Missouri. What made this an unusual incident is that Archie sent a letter once he was safe and sound in Canada. It was very unusual that conductors ever heard from their "passengers" once they were sent along the Underground Railroad.[30]

Even free blacks in slave states often grew tired of the continuous harassment by slave patrols and slave posses every time they tried to move about. They also sought escape on the Underground Railroad. One such free black man with the interesting name of Davy Crockett escaped out of Missouri into Appanoose County in Iowa. He eventually found his way to the Armstrong station in Cincinnati. Crockett was forwarded on the Underground Railroad by Armstrong and others.[31]

Denmark was a small community in Lee County involved in the Underground Railroad. Deacon Theron Trowbridge of the Congregational Church there was a noted conductor. Denmark was the site of the first Congregational Church in Iowa. The church and Pastor Asa Turner were deeply committed to helping runaway slaves.[32] It is interesting to note that Trowbridge and the Reverend Turner were from Galesburg, Illinois, as were the residents of Amity, Iowa. It is reported that one time a young black female escapee from slavery showed up at the Deacon Trowbridge's door crying and in an incredible state of stress. She had been forced to abandon her baby when she fled slavery in Kahoka, Missouri. Trowbridge supposedly said, "Any

mother is entitled to keep her baby." Trowbridge strapped on his gun and mounted a fine horse and rode towards Kahoka. Two days later he returned with the baby for its excited mother.[33] Denmark's people valued John Todd's counsel and when they wanted to start an academy there in the 1860's they asked John for his advice.[34]

John Todd and George Gaston and the others involved in the Underground Railroad in Tabor found out that most of their instruction on running the Tabor branch of the railroad came from on-the-job training. They had to be nimble and flexible in their thought and actions. Many escapes were routine, while others took much planning and thought. However, almost all had an element of danger.

Pastor Asa Turner of Denmark, Iowa. In the Southeastern part of the state of Iowa, Pastor Asa Turner and Deacon Trowbridge ran an Underground Railroad station at Denmark. Both Turner and Trowbridge were from Galesburg, Illinois, a well known hot bed of Underground Railroad activities in that state. When Denmark wanted to start an academy they asked John Todd for his advice. (State Historical Society of Iowa—Des Moines.)

8

Difficult Journeys

"Whom God made free, no man shall chain"
We said; & o'er the dangerous track,
No hunted fugitive ever went back.
The oppressor's threats were all in vain,
And when the Lord's good time drew near,
He saw his humble children's woe,
And he rang aloud in every ear,
His mandate, "Let my people go."
Excerpt from poem of Arabella E. Smith
Read in Tabor, October 11, 1877

The Tabor Underground Railroad apparatus was running at full steam. To the casual observer it would look as if George Gaston and his wife Maria were on a ride to Civil Bend to visit his sister Elvira. However, as usual on such visits, the Gastons would inquire if there were any extra passengers to take back to Tabor. They were directed to the house of Dr. Ira Blanchard. Blanchard had at his house two males trying to escape the bonds of slavery. After much discussion on how to advance these gentlemen on the Underground Railroad during the daylight hours, it was decided to dress them as much as possible as females. Mrs. Gaston and Mrs. Platt took off as much of their clothing as possible, including their coats and veils and anything else that would aid the disguise. The party then went back to Tabor with two extra members.[1]

Once safely in Tabor there was a hand-off. James Gaston and Edwin S. Hill were then dispatched as conductors for this new "cargo." On their way to the next station on the Underground Railroad James Gaston and Hill were stopped by the slave owner looking for his two runaways. The female

91

disguises must have been very convincing. The slave owner didn't recognize them in their new outfits. Gaston and Hill and the two runaways were successful in reaching the next station without further interruption.[2]

Many of the proponents of slavery in the 1850's liked to point out that if they could have Kansas as a slave state then Nebraska could be a free state. John Todd countered this argument with the reality that some of the leading citizens of nearby Nebraska City, Nebraska, openly owned slaves, as it was not illegal in that territory until shortly before the start of the Civil War. Steven Friel Nuckolls[3] and Alexander Majors, of the famed freighting company of Russell, Majors and Waddell, were two of the wealthiest citizens of Nebraska City and owned almost a dozen slaves between themselves. Nuckolls, who was known by his initials, S.F., was a representative to the Nebraska Territorial legislature. He had even voted against the prohibition against slavery in Nebraska and even voted not to allow free blacks to live in the state.[4] As late as 1860 the sheriff in Otoe County, of which Nebraska City was the seat, offered for auction at a sheriff's sale one "negro male" and one "negro female."[5] John Todd found this kind of action in a supposed free territory to be unconscionable.

S.F. Nuckolls was an incredible business mogul in the emerging Nebraska territory. Nuckolls was the leading merchant in the area, owning mercantile stores in various communities. He owned the only bank in Nebraska that survived the panic of 1857 and he was the president of a rail line. He also owned stock in many different companies.[6] However, he owned five slaves and was a racist of the worst kind. In November of 1858 two of Nuckolls female slaves wanted to escape his bonds. John Williamson brought the two escaping females across the river to Doc Blanchard's place in Civil Bend. Blanchard then proceeded north to Tabor with the two escapees.

It was decided it was too dangerous to move the two in broad daylight. The Reverend Todd thought they needed to be moved at nightfall at the first opportunity. The people of Tabor knew Nuckolls would probably be after them as soon as possible. As soon as Nuckolls discovered his chattel to be gone, he was furious. He had a store in Glenwood, Iowa, managed by his brother and he also had two brothers-in-law in Sidney, Iowa. Messengers were dispatched to these places telling his relatives to acquire a posse and go on an active search for the two runaways in and around Tabor and Civil Bend. The slaver Nuckolls knew well of their reputations as stations on the Underground Railroad and had the advantage of knowing where his slaves would probably be taken for their next stop. The bridges on the Nishnabotna River and Silver Creek were especially watched by the Nuckolls slave posse.

The conductors moving their "cargo" in a covered wagon left on a moonless, cloudy and misty night that made for miserable conditions for the "train" as it pulled out of Tabor. Deacon Origen Cummings had to lead the way with a lantern so the wagon could make its way. The "train" crossed the bridges on the Nishnabota and Silver Creek before Nuckolls men could man their posts.[7]

The pro-slavery *Nebraska City News* on November 29, 1858, was only too pleased to hurl insults at the abolitionists in Tabor and Civil Bend for their part in the escape of the Nuckolls slaves. The paper stated in that edition, "Quite a sensation was created in town yesterday morning by the fact being known that two female servants had been enticed away from our townsman, S.F. Nuckolls, by some vile, white livered abolitionist. Many of our citizens are out in search of the runaways. Mr. Nuckolls offers a reward of $200.00 for their apprehension and delivery to him in Nebraska City. They will doubtless be found in some abolitionist hole."

The *Fremont Herald*, the only newspaper in Fremont County at the time, sheds some interesting light on this escape. The *Herald*, which claimed to be neutral in politics and independent, was in fact pro-slavery in its outlook. In its December 4, 1858, edition the *Herald* tells of the escape. It adds some interesting facts. According to its account the escaping slaves "are supposed to have been controlled by outside influences, as the home and treatment they had with Mr. Nuckolls could be no incentive to change their situation; and we have no doubt but before now they have found that they left a home, the comforts of which they will never find away from the premises of Mr. N. We learn that Mr. Nuckolls had promised them their freedom in a year and a half with property amounting to several thousand dollars."

The females, one of whom was named Eliza, in fact got away and made her way to Chicago. Nuckolls got it into his head that his slaves were still in the Civil Bend area. Nuckolls went to Civil Bend with some thugs and without warrants or any other proper legal authority began searching the houses in a most barbaric manner.

Reuben Williams was a farmer in Civil Bend. He loudly protested Nuckolls' illegal search of his property and the slaver rode up and hit Williams with a blunt instrument that disabled him.[8] Williams lived in the house formally occupied by George Gaston when he moved from the Civil Bend area to Tabor.[9] The Nuckolls mob descended on other houses in the Civil Bend area, including that of James W. Smith.[10]

Henry Garner, a young black man who lived in the Civil Bend area, was set upon by Nuckolls and fourteen of his henchmen. They choked and beat young Garner. They then stripped him of his clothing and then tied him to a tree, where he was beaten to an inch of his life. From his neck to his waist Garner had cuts, bruises and lacerations of a most serious kind. Joseph Garner, Jr., brother to Henry, was also choked and hung by his neck.[11]

neck.[11] Word was sent out from Civil Bend and the proper authorities arrested Nuckolls and ended his reign of terror. Trial was to be set for the next day and Nuckolls was allowed to return to Nebraska City, as two of his men were kept in Civil Bend to assure his return.[12] The people of Civil Bend sent a messenger to Tabor asking for a company of men to come down and insure the trial was a fair one. It was feared that Nuckolls would bring a mob from the more populous Nebraska City seeking revenge.[13]

Two years earlier the citizens of Tabor felt the need to arm themselves with a militia-like group to protect themselves. At the urging of Gaston and Todd the people of Tabor rallied around their friends in Civil Bend and the militia group was once again mustered in at full force. Each able bodied man in Tabor was issued a musket or rifle from the Kansas aid committee supply that was being stored in town, along with 12 rounds of cartridges.[14] The next morning Tabor was abuzz with the news. The Tabor men armed themselves and headed to Civil Bend. It was a very cold December day when they set off. Gray clouds obscured the sky and flakes of snow fell across the Iowa farmland. When the Tabor men got to Civil Bend they learned that ice on the Missouri River was flowing so swiftly as to make a crossing unsafe. Nuckolls was unable to come to trial. The trial date was delayed several times.[15]

After some time Nuckolls found out that Eliza and her companion were in fact in Chicago. He set out for that Illinois city. The two females had disappeared into the black community of this city along Lake Michigan. Nuckolls, with his considerable wealth, was able to ascertain the escapees' whereabouts. One day Eliza was walking along Clark and Van Buren streets in Chicago and Nuckolls came along with a carriage and forced her into it. Eliza cried out and a passerby heard her pleas and intervened. The authorities came and Eliza, Nuckolls and an accomplice of the Nebraska City slaver were arrested.

Nuckolls and his comrade produced warrants that Eliza was an escaped slave and should be returned to Nebraska. A mob soon appeared of blacks and abolitionists who were incensed that these two interlopers were attempting to kidnap someone they considered to be a citizen of their city. They mobbed the scene and managed to hustle Eliza out of the area.

Nuckolls heard the Chicago crowd yell, "Hang the Slaver Man! Throw him in the lake!" A contingent of Chicago police broke up the throng and Nuckolls was spirited to safety.[16] Nuckolls made his way back to Nebraska and found Henry Garner had filed suit against him for $10,000 in Fremont County in Iowa.[17] Reuben Williams also sued Nuckolls and won a judgment of $8,000 against the slaver. Williams built a large new barn with the proceeds from his suit.

Henry Garner took advantage of a new law passed in 1857 that said blacks had the same standing as whites in Iowa courts and could testify against them. Henry Garner, Green Garner and Thomas Reid, all black men, testified against Nuckolls and his men. There were many threats yelled at these three and the lawyers in the case. The scene in the crowded courtroom at times seemed as if it could get out of control and many racists vowed they would interrupt the proceedings. What made it an even more tense trial was the fact that Nuckolls was one of the richest men in the whole region. The magistrate in this case was Judge Sears. Although a Democrat, Sears was up to the challenge. In his superb addresses to the courtroom he left no doubt that he felt the majesty of the law was important and that everyone, regardless of the color of their skin, was entitled to their day in court. Sears was firm, fearless and unmoved. The trial proceeded without any interruptions.[18]

Nuckolls went on to prosper with his business dealings. He moved out to Colorado in the early 1860's and had a mining operation. In 1864 he moved to New York City, where he made a fortune in mining speculation. Nuckolls became a member of the Forty-first Congress as a Democrat from the Wyoming territory.[19]

The Reverend Todd couldn't help but note that when Nuckolls lived in Colorado he came to visit friends briefly in Nebraska City. During this stay Reuben Williams' barn was burnt to the ground. Todd thought that it was very suspicious that the barn was torched when Nuckolls was in the vicinity.[20]

It is also interesting to note that the Nebraska City newspaper called these two escaping slaves "servants." Why would Nuckolls take 50 men to look for two escaping "servants"? Nuckolls was an extremely wealthy man for his time. The loss of these two female slaves would have been of very little monetary consequence to him. One of the most disgusting aspects of slavery at this time was the fact that some very wealthy men like Nuckolls would buy attractive young female slaves and make them nothing more than "sexual slaves." These women would be dressed in the latest clothes, fed well and given respectable housing. It is probable that these two unfortunate female slaves were used by Nuckolls for his own personal gratification.

The fact that they were promised their freedom and property would suggest this was their situation. Later two of Nuckolls' male slaves ran away and Nuckolls made no effort to go find them. Fortunately, John Williamson was able to conduct them to their freedom. Also of interest in this case was the attitude of the *Fremont Herald*. Its outlook seemed to be that the girls were well fed and clothed, so they should look to Nuckolls as their benefactor. Unfortunately, this was the attitude of many of the apologists for slavery.

At this time the freighting firm of Russell, Majors, and Waddell was one of the largest of such concerns in the United States. Alexander Majors lived in Nebraska City with his family and six enslaved humans. These included two women in their forties, a young woman in her twenties, a girl and boy of fourteen and another young boy of twelve.[21]

Even for that time Majors was worth over a million dollars but had large liabilities. He was away from home a lot and this probably made the escape of his slaves easier. The last week of June in 1860 all of his slaves escaped. Later that year things didn't get any better for Majors, as in December the family's huge residence burnt to the ground.[22] The six Majors slaves never were recovered. They made their successful escape on the Underground Railroad.

There were, however, people in Nebraska City and vicinity who supported the Underground Railroad. Unfortunately they were not as prominent as Nuckolls and Majors and regrettably, like so many others who risked their lives and property, their names are lost in the mists of history.

Local traditions in Nebraska and Tabor tell of one or possibly more groups of fifteen to twenty escapees making their way out of the Nebraska territory to the Underground Railroad in Iowa. This would corroborate the story of the young girl in Tabor seeing a roomful of many escapees one day in her brothers' bedroom.

Alice Lockwood Minick was a small child living with her family south of Nebraska City during the Underground Railroad days. She also told of what must have been a large group escaping on the Underground Railroad when she related, "It was there I received my initiation into the order under promise to keep still. I had gone to the Russell home to visit a daughter; she was going to the cave to get vegetables for the meal and invited me to go with her. On entering the cave, I found myself in the midst of colored people of all sizes, men, women and children. All I could see was red lips, white teeth, eyes, and black faces; frightened is no name for the sensation I experienced. Should I run, scream or fall down? The more frightened I became the more they showed their white teeth. I begged the girl to help me away, for I could not rise on my feet. These were the first colored people I had ever met, and to a northern child it was an experience. This was early in the operation of the Nebraska line, for in the next two years I overcame all my fears of colored people."[23]

To advance the runaway slaves from Tabor or Civil Bend many times the train had to come across the wide Missouri River. Bringing escapees across the Missouri River at Nebraska City or other points such as at the Wyoming crossings were at times difficult. John Kagi, one of John Brown's closest lieutenants, had a difficult encounter trying to get runaways across the river.

Kagi was a tragic figure in that he had so much potential. He was bright and extremely articulate. He had just started a legal career when he felt it was more important to join the struggle to free slaves. He found Brown in Kansas and hitched his wagon to this troubled star. Kagi was killed in 1859 when Brown and his men tried to forcibly occupy the federal arsenal at Harper's Ferry, Virginia. When the eyes of the nation were focused on "Bleeding Kansas," Kagi was the eyes and ears for many of those in the Eastern States. He was, in addition to being a fighter in Brown's and other Kansas Free State armies, a correspondent at various times for the *Chicago Tribune, Cleveland Leader, New York Tribune, Kansas Tribune, New York Evening Post* and the *National Era* of Washington, D.C.[24]

Three escaping slaves from the Topeka, Kansas, area shepherded by Doc Blanchard were brought into Nebraska City in a wagon with a false bottom. John H. Kagi then took charge of the operation and negotiated the band through some pro-slavery neighborhoods in Nebraska City. It is presumed that Blanchard didn't take the group through Nebraska City because his actions on the Underground Railroad were too well known there. The wagon was stopped but its true contents were never discovered. Kagi then proceeded with his "train" to the Wyoming crossing north of Nebraska City. Kagi's group would cross the Missouri River at Wyoming to Lambert's Landing on the Iowa side of the river. The ferryman refused to go, as the river was full of large blocks of floating ice. Legend has it that Kagi pulled a gun on the ferryman and told him to make a choice—either the ice or his pistol. The ferryman decided the ice blocks were better odds than Kagi's weapon. The three escapees, the ferryman and Kagi made it across the river but because the ferryman had to avoid the ice floes, they had drifted a half a mile from the proper landing site. Kagi then took the escapees to Doc Blanchard's place in Civil Bend.[25]

Kagi's sister Barbara was married to Allen Mayhew. The Mayhew cabin in Nebraska City has been the subject of much folklore on its role in the Underground Railroad in the area. Kagi's father, Abe, also bought some 80 acres on Camp Creek south of Nebraska City.[26] These two locations would, among others in the Nebraska City area, be logical places to hide escaping slaves before taking them across the Missouri River to Tabor or Civil Bend.

Doc Blanchard, when runaways found their way to Civil Bend, usually proceeded with his Underground Railroad "cargo" north to Tabor. Blanchard was a very interesting fellow who had settled in Civil Bend before Gaston and Todd. Even after Todd and the others left Civil Bend they and Blanchard were in contact all of the time concerning the Underground Railroad and other matters.

Blanchard was very friendly with James Lane and the two thought of ways to bring escapees out of Kansas to Civil Bend then on to Todd, Gaston and the others in Tabor. A false bottomed wagon was fashioned and runaways were brought up this way on occasion. An escaping slave had made his way to Nebraska City, Nebraska. He was hungry and decided to expose himself and make it across the river where he had heard the residents of Civil Bend were friendly towards blacks. The runaway hid in the timbers around Civil Bend. The former slave came out from the forest and told a Mr. Ricketts that he was lost and hungry. Ricketts took him to his house and fed him corn bread, meat and potatoes, a fine feast for a hungry man. Ricketts told the runaway slave that he would have to take him to the jus-

tice of the peace. Ricketts saw the trepidation on the former slave's face and then Ricketts went on to tell him the nature of Doc Blanchard, the justice of the peace. Relief was seen and a short trip to Blanchard's home was done. Blanchard then forwarded the runaway onto Tabor and to freedom.[27]

It is not certain the extent of Blanchard's medical training. In the 1850 federal census Blanchard is listed as a physician. Todd and others in the area felt Blanchard was a healer of the first order, having saved the community from an outbreak of malaria fever when supplies of quinine ran out.

Blanchard was from Ohio, one of the first residents in Fremont County and was involved in many of the beginning incidents

Doctor Ira Blanchard was a very interesting fellow. John Todd had a lot of confidence in him as a physician; however, the extent of his medical training was unknown. No one ever questioned his commitment to the Underground Railroad or the abolitionists cause. He was physically a very courageous man. Apparently, Blanchard ran afoul of the law as a young man and possibly even did jail time. Blanchard opened-up a mission school for Native Americans in Kansas. However, a problem that was to dog him all his life surfaced. He was accused of having sexual relations with a woman to which he was not married. The Baptist Board in Boston that sponsored his mission fired him and he came north to Civil Bend where local gossip also had him involved in sexual misadventures. However, his rescue of the Garners from the slave pens in St. Louis, Missouri, and the subsequent journey home, proved without a doubt Blanchard's incredible courage. (Kansas State Historical Society.)

of that area. As justice of the peace, his house was used as a place where voting was done in the township. Blanchard formed the first temperance society in the county. There is a curious letter that John Todd wrote to his father-in-law, who was a lawyer, about Blanchard. In the letter the Reverend Todd writes to Atkins about Blanchard and apparently had been acquainted with him in Ohio. Todd wrote in 1854, "Dr. I.D. Blanchard of Civil Bend has a fleet horse, with which he caught three deer last winter in one day by running them down on a fair race in the open prairie. By the way, do you remember the circumstances respecting his crime committed, I think in Ashtabula, in his earlier years. He purloined money from a merchant there I believe. Can you tell how much it was that was taken, & the circumstances connected with it. A more full acquaintance with him increases my curiosity to know, nor is it idle curiosity."[28] It has been rumored that Blanchard had even spent prison time in Ohio for this crime.

Had Blanchard come west to reinvent himself after some youthful error in judgment? Is the fact that he started a temperance society so soon after his arrival in Fremont County an indication that at one time he had serious problems with alcohol? Many times recovering alcoholics are very zealous about reforming others from this affliction by means of temperance. It is interesting to note that Todd apparently had knowledge of Blanchard when he was younger but still was confident in his abilities and training as a physician. Todd and George Gaston and the rest of the Underground Railroad movement in Iowa and Kansas had always considered Blanchard to be one of the best conductors on the Underground Railroad and his commitment to the cause of the abolition was second to none. Blanchard was always willing to back his convictions with his incredible physical courage.

Blanchard had founded the Delaware Baptist Mission in Wyandotte County, near the present town of Edwardsville, Kansas, in 1837.[29] The Delawares had been shipped to the territory of Kansas from back East in the mid–1830's.However, a problem that was to follow Blanchard all his life occurred. He was accused of having sexual relations with a woman who was not his wife. In 1848 the Baptist Mission Board in Boston dismissed Blanchard from the mission.[30] He came north to the Civil Bend area and established a home. He became one of the leading citizens of the area. The Garner family Blanchard had known at the mission in Kansas came north to Civil Bend. Because the Garners were black Blanchard and George Gaston had to post bond for them just so the Garners could live in the Hawkeye state, as was regulated by Iowa law of the time.

However, Blanchard got into trouble again. The Union Church in Civil Bend suspended him from its membership in 1853 or 1854.[31] The reason was not clear. But it would be very unusual for a frontier church such as this to suspend such a prominent member of its small church number. Local legend has it that Blanchard had a sexual affair with another married female church member. Rumors of sexual misadventures accompanied Doc Blanchard most of his life. However, John Todd felt the dismissal of Blanchard was a power play by some in the Union Church to overrule Blanchard and the majority in the church.[32] Was Todd's loyalty to his friend blinding him to the truth? In 1863 Blanchard was one of the founding members of the Missionary Baptist Church in that area.[33] The contacts between Blanchard and the Reverend Todd were not always to do with Underground Railroad duties. In 1852 John Todd performed the marriage ceremony for Blanchard's 15 year-old-daughter, Lydia.[34]

John Williamson had married into the Garner family when the Reverend Todd wedded him to a Garner sister, Betsy.[35] Loren Hume, a nephew to George Gaston who was orphaned and adopted by the Gaston family, stated that the Williamson and Garner wedding was one of the most magnificent and solemn he had ever witnessed. Williamson cut a striking figure being part Cherokee and part black. Betsy Garner was said to have had a fiery temper and they made a remarkable couple.[36]

Blanchard, Williamson and Henry and Maria Garner were players in one of the most dangerous race incidents that happened in Western Iowa. John Williamson the commodity trader and Henry Garner and his sister Maria were traveling north to Omaha in 1860. During their journey to Omaha a carriage pulled up alongside of them. Jacob Hurd, who had a long record of pro-slavery criminal activities in Kansas, N.B. Beck and Joe Wildey overpowered Williamson and the Garners. Henry Garner was dealt a savage blow to his cheekbone that broke it. The group was hustled off to Missouri. One wonders if Williamson and the Garners were kidnapped because of the role they played in helping escapees on the Underground Railroad and their role in suing S.F. Nuckolls.

As they made their way to eastern Missouri Williamson managed to escape. However, as Williamson was making his way back to Iowa he was recaptured by those who thought he was a runaway slave. Despite his protestations that he was a free black man, Williamson was put in a temporary jail in Rockport, Missouri. Williamson had the officials in Rockport write to Williamson's friends in Council Bluffs and $75 was raised to free him from bondage. The city marshal of Council Bluffs and the sheriff of Pottawattamie County came down and secured Williamson's release and took him back to Iowa.[37]

The Garner brother and sister were taken to a slave pen in St. Louis. They were put up for sale. No protestations they made were listened to, as blacks had no standing in the courts or anywhere in the state. Blanchard heard about the kidnappings and dropped everything and enlisted the aid of George Gaston. Together they headed into Missouri not sure which direction to take.

The two rescuers headed for St. Joseph, Missouri, and found information that indeed the Garners had been taken to St. Louis. Gaston was not able to continue on but had to go back to Tabor. Gaston however, financed the rest of the search for Blanchard, who made his way to St. Louis alone. Once in that city on the Mississippi River the doctor ascertained that the Garners were located in that city's barbaric slave pens. The physician pleaded his case before the warden of the slave pens. The warden, not sure of what to make of this situation but with Solomon-like wisdom, ordered the Garner brother and sister to be presented before the warden and Dr. Blanchard.

Henry Garner not having received proper medical attention for his broken cheek bone, was totally despondent with fear that relief would never come to the pair. He didn't even look up. However, his sister Maria looked and saw Doc Blanchard. She was overcome by joy. Maria proclaimed, "Oh! Dr. Blanchard! Where did you come from?!"[38]

The evidence was indisputable. After some legal procedures the Garners left the slave pens free again. Blanchard and the Garners left St. Louis on the steamship *Warsaw* to head back to Iowa.[39] However, the trip would not be an easy one.

On the way back upstream from St. Louis on the Missouri River to St. Joseph also were Hurd, Beck and Wildey, the men accused of kidnapping the Garners. They were held in custody by law enforcement officers. At various stops the steamship would load and unload cargo and passengers. Word would then leak out about the Garners and Blanchard. Then pro-slavery crowds would arrive at the steamship loading docks and would loudly curse Blanchard and the Garners and demand the release of the kidnappers. Hurd especially was looked upon by the pro-slavery crowd as a hero. At St. Joseph a large crowd boldly pronounced they were going to release the kidnappers, but a party heading for the gold fields in Colorado stated they would stand by Blanchard and the law officers.[40]

Then things even got dicier. The steamship made its way north out of St. Joseph, Missouri and headed for Hamburg, Iowa. Hamburg is an Iowa town located on the Missouri River and is extremely close to the Missouri border. The steamboat landing for Hamburg was actually in Missouri a mile away from the Iowa border. The Missouri police officers from St. Louis had as their job the task of bringing Hurd, Beck and Wildey to the border to hand them over to Iowa authorities for trial. Hurd especially maintained that if he was taken into Iowa that he would be hung immediately. Many in the pro-slavery crowd that had followed the steamboat to Hamburg wanted to make sure Hurd and his accomplices were not taken into the Hawkeye state. The Missouri officers told Blanchard they had no authority to take the prisoners out of the state of Missouri. Woodward, the head Missouri police officer, and Blanchard devised a plan where Woodward and his fellow officers would hold Hurd and his gang in Missouri while Blanchard went into Iowa and had a justice of the peace swear out warrants for the trio of badmen. As Blanchard went to get the Iowa warrants and bring the Garners back into Iowa, things went from bad to worse for the Missouri officers.[41]

The officers proceeded to a farmhouse on the Missouri side of the border and a mob of some 50 pro-slavery men began to follow them demanding that Hurd and his men be set free and saying they would not let them be taken into Iowa. One of the leaders of the mob was a man named Durst who had known Hurd in Kansas and they began speaking in some unintelligible language, possibly a Native American dialect they had learned on the frontier.

Blanchard returned with the warrants and with three Iowa peace officers, but this was hardly enough to keep the crowd at bay. These groups, the pro-slavery mob, prisoners and police officers proceeded to the Iowa line for the exchange. The mob declared that if Hurd was touched there would be bloodshed. Blanchard had to pull a gun to keep the mob at bay. The mob members even said they would hand Hurd over if they could take Blanchard.

A stalemate occurred. It was then decided to take the prisoners and peace officers to Rockport, Missouri, some 21 miles away until the Iowans could bring down enough force to overcome the mob. Since there was no jail in Rockport to accommodate everyone, once the parties got there, incredibly the peace officers and prisoners were chained together![42]

The crowd in Rockport seemed to favor the pro-slavery prisoners and were adamant in their hatred of Blanchard. An attorney, J.A. Harvey, arrived from Iowa promising the force necessary to take control of the prisoners. However, the local sheriff, probably with an eye to his reelection chances, said he would, then he said he wouldn't take the prisoners to Iowa. Woodward said since there was no jail in Rockport he would take the prisoners back to St. Joseph to sort things out until Iowa officers could take over the situation.

Once in St. Joseph it was discovered Hurd had four warrants for his arrest on other matters. The officers arrested him on these warrants, thus finding an agreeable compromise out of the situation of having to take Hurd to Iowa.[43] The other kidnappers were transported to Council Bluffs and were jailed but managed to escape before their trial.[44]

The Garners and Blanchard finally made their way safely back to Civil Bend. As usual, many in the region were deeply divided on the question of slavery. In many quarters there was much hatred for those that chose to help their fellow human beings out of bondage.

Undoubtedly, the Garner family, John Williamson, and other blacks in Southwest Iowa continued to be active in the Underground Railway, as they had before with Blanchard, Todd and George Gaston. Unfortunately, documentation is woefully thin. It would in all probability have been difficult for the blacks in Southwest Iowa to help transport those on the Underground Railroad, as this incident of the kidnapping of Williamson and Garner would testify. It was extremely difficult for even free blacks to travel in the area with the abundance of unscrupulous slave posses and slave bounty hunters in the area.

The Missouri River crossing at Nebraska City offered opportunities for blacks to escape bondage. America was on the move in the decade of the 1850s. Thousands upon thousands were going to California, Oregon, Utah, Washington, Colorado and other points out West. The river crossings at Nebraska City and nearby points were very busy in this decade. A river crossing was a chaotic affair with chances to make an escape. Slave owners thought nothing of bringing their chattel with them on their treks to the Western United States.

In all probability, this is how Thomas Reed (or Reid) made his way from Kentucky to freedom in Southwest Iowa, and it could be how Williamson, who was born in Arkansas, obtained his freedom. Reed threw his lot in with John Williamson.

Williamson probably aided another man in his escape from slavery. The census of 1860 finds John Williamson, Thomas Reed and another man named Henry Garner living together in Council Bluffs. What makes this interesting is that there already is a Henry Garner living in Civil Bend with Doc Blanchard. That Henry Garner states he is originally from Missouri and is a black man with $600 of personal property. The Henry Garner in Council Bluffs describes himself in the census as being a mulatto, not a black man, and having only $100 of personal property. The Council Bluffs Garner says his birthplace is unknown. But then he has the marshal doing the census cross out unknown and put in N.C. as the place of birth. Does N.C. stand for Nebraska City? Did he consider Nebraska City as his birthplace in freedom? It is probable that this Henry Garner was a runaway slave and had a forged document stating he was a free black man named Henry Garner, and this document was probably secured by Williamson.

9

The Jim Lane Trail

As winter was releasing Iowa from its icy grip in March of 1856, John Todd sent a letter to his father-in-law, Q.F. Atkins, about Kansas. The whole nation had its eyes on this territory and how the question of slavery would play out. Todd wrote, "From Kansas we hear nothing.... We have been in great suspense in relation to the fate of the brave spirits of Kansas for some time. At one time a collision between the armed forces of freedom & slavery seemed inevitable.... Hoping only in God, we have not ceased to pray that truth & righteousness may prevail."[1]

Little did the Reverend Todd realize the role he and the town of Tabor would play in Kansas's struggle to rid itself of the blight of slavery. During the late spring of 1856, Samuel Gridley Howe came to Tabor looking for a route that anti-slavery emigrants could take into Kansas. Howe, whose wife was Julia Ward Howe, writer of the great anthem "Battle Hymn of The Republic," was one of the leading abolitionists in the country.

Howe had led a storied life. Graduating from Harvard Medical School, he became surgeon-in-chief for the Greek Navy in their struggle for independence from Turkey. Later Howe became head of the famous Perkins School for the Blind in Boston when he became deeply involved in the abolitionist movement. He traveled far and wide for the abolitionist cause. While Howe was in the Tabor area the Reverend Todd acted as his guide.[2]

Violence in Kansas had many calling it "Bleeding Kansas." This territory was becoming the surrogate battleground for the Northern and Southern states on the question of human bondage. Would slavery be contained in the states that allowed it or would it be permitted to expand to new territories like Kansas? Abolitionists like John Todd knew if slavery was to be completely abolished from the Union it would first have to be limited to the states that allowed this awful institution. The expansion of slavery to Kansas would be a severe setback to the abolitionist cause.

Pro-slavery and anti-slavery factions were fighting and trying to gain control of the Kansas territory. The United States' tightrope dance over this vexing problem was coming to a head. Each side tried to flood the territory with partisans who would vote for a constitution that would mirror their particular beliefs, either for slavery or against slavery. The route into the Kansas territory from the Eastern States or from Middle America that most abolitionist emigrants took was to acquire passage on a steamboat in St. Louis, Missouri. The abolitionists would then proceed west on the Missouri River and go into Western Missouri. They would then disembark in the Kansas City area and then go overland into neighboring Kansas.

However, in 1856, slavery proponents along the Missouri river were throwing abolitionists off steamboats and seizing their property. If a steamboat passenger had an accent from a state where slavery wasn't allowed, that person was assumed to be an abolitionist and forced to disembark from the riverboat.[3] Cargo to free-state towns dwindled to almost nothing. A new route would have to be found so that anti-slavery men and their families could emigrate into Kansas to throw the balance of power to the anti-slavery movement. Howe and a group of men found Tabor and knew this town of ardent abolitionists was a perfect stop on their new trail into Kansas. It was noted that on the overland route Tabor was far enough from Kansas to be free from that disorder; yet it was close enough and stable enough to provide much needed aid and comfort to those going into the fray in the territory.

Ironically for Howe, this new route would be commonly known as the Jim Lane Trail. Howe despised Lane. In a letter Howe wrote from Tabor in July of 1856 to his old friend, Massachusetts United States Senator Charles Sumner, Howe commented on the fact that Lane would bring the first emigrants into Kansas on the trail, "The men are ready for a fight, pity that such a man as Lane is at the head. We shall do all we can to keep a bit in his mouth."[4]

It is of interest to note that Senator Sumner, when this letter was written to him from Tabor, was recovering from a severe beating that he had taken in the United States Senate Chamber. In May of 1856 Sumner had given a strong anti-slavery speech called "The Crime against Kansas." In the speech Sumner had singled out and insulted fellow senator and slaveholder Andrew Pickens Butler of South Carolina. Butler was not in the Senate chamber to defend himself. Two days later Butler's nephew, Preston S. Brooks, severely attacked Sumner in the Senate chamber with his cane. It would take Senator Sumner more than three years to recover from this unprecedented assault.

Jim Lane had been in and out of Tabor often in 1856. Lane was a former lieutenant governor of Indiana, a congressman from Southern Indiana and he had been a colonel during the Mexican War and was considered a war-hero.[5] Lane would become the first United States senator from Kansas. He was a spellbinding orator and able politician at best. At worst he could be a charlatan and opportunist. Nicknamed the "Grim Chieftain," Lane would have incredible highs as when he nominated Abraham Lincoln for re-election at the Republican National Convention in 1864. He would also have incredible lows as when he assumed the command of military units during the Civil War while still a United States senator and was accused of blessing military atrocities in Missouri.

James H. Lane has been called the man the historians forgot. His influence on national politics and on the politics of the Midwest in the 1850s and '60s was immense, but because of his sometimes erratic behavior and his eventual suicide, he has largely been swept into the dustbin of history. After studying law in his father's office, as was the custom of the times, Lane became an attorney in Indiana. Lane learned well from his father, who was the Democratic political boss of southern Indiana. Jim followed his father into politics and became a state legislator, a United States congressman and then lieutenant governor of Indiana. He later joined the army during the Mexican War, attaining the considerable rank of colonel, and was thought of as a war hero because of his exploits during that conflict.

Lane came barging into Kansas in the spring of 1855. His six foot frame and eyes that looked like black diamonds when he spoke excitedly caught the attention of the people right away. He was perpetual motion. Albert D. Richardson, a writer for the influential *New York Tribune* and an admirer of Lane, once wrote: "For years he controlled the politics of Kansas, even when penniless ... he manipulated men like water. He had a sinister face, plain to ugliness, but he could talk away his face in twenty minutes."[6]

He was a divorced man in an era when that was political suicide. He also had a penchant for trying to seduce other men's wives. He used his considerable oratory skills to confuse and confound the many bill collectors who came his way. Until he became a Senator he was always in a state of being short of cash. Lane challenged United States Senator Stephen Douglas to a duel and in 1858 he killed his neighbor in a dispute over a boundary line. Jim Lane was about as opposite from the men of Tabor as could be, except in his desire to end slavery in the United States and in Kansas in particular.

In June of 1856 Jim Lane started assembling men for a wagon train caravan across Iowa. The governor of Iowa, James Grimes, was very pro-active in the Kansas situation. Grimes let some of the men in Lane's group take 1500 weapons from the state arsenal.[7] The story goes that Grimes told Lane's men he couldn't give them the weapons from the state arsenal but he would

James H. Lane was one of the most fascinating characters on the frontier. He was often in and out of Tabor and Civil Bend. The pro-slavery
governments of Kansas issued warrants for him. They saw Lane and his
desire for the abolition of slavery in Kansas as being a detriment to the
development of Kansas. Lane was one of the most wanted men by the
pro-slavery elements in Kansas. Tabor and Civil Bend became convenient
hiding places for Lane when things were too dangerous for him in Kansas.
Lane would sometimes come into Tabor, with his flare for the dramatic,
disguised in some sort of costume. (Kansas State Historical Society.)

leave the keys to the arsenal on his desk. They took the keys, which had
been put out in plain sight, and then went and took the weapons from the
state armory. Grimes felt that since Lane had Iowans in his group they had
every right to protect themselves from pro-slavery partisans in Kansas.

Lane's men would have to be ready to go into the cauldron of fire in
Kansas. Lane's wagon train started in the area of Iowa City, then still the
capital city of Iowa. Iowa City was also then the end of the rail head and
men hoping to be anti-slavery settlers in Kansas came into the area via the

railroad by wagons or
on foot. Lane had been
recruiting men from
Iowa, Illinois, Indiana
and states in the New
England and New York
area. He had also been
raising money for this
venture.[8]

In July Lane and
his wagon train left
eastern Iowa and made
their way west. They
would mark their trail
by placing poles in tall
prairie grass or by pil-
ing stones one on top
of each other. These
stones became known
as Lane's chimneys.[9]

At this time even
though Iowa had been
a state for a decade,
there were few maps of
the state. Knowledge of

James W. Grimes represented the new kind of politician who was being
elected in Iowa. Grimes was governor from 1854 to 1858. He was then
named a United States senator in 1859. His views coincided more with
John Todd rather than racist Iowa Senator Augustus Caesar Dodge. When
Jim Lane's men came to visit Grimes, on their way to "Bleeding Kansas,"
Grimes let Lane's men take 1500 weapons from the Iowa state arsenal.
Grimes felt since Lane had Iowans in his group that they had a right
to defend themselves in Kansas. (State Historical Society of Iowa—Des
Moines.)

the geography of many areas was often sketchy and the new lands at times seemed peculiar. Lane and his group were, of course, moving east to west. Later some moving west to east on the Underground Railroad used Lane's markings, the stone chimneys and tall poles in the prairie grass, as road guides to make their way out of the Hawkeye state and on their way to the ultimate freedom that Canada provided.

As the wagon train made its way through Winterset, Iowa, Lane met an enthusiastic 16-year-old Thomas Henry Tibbles, who after the fashion of the time, and as Lane had done, was clerking and reading law in a law office. The young Tibbles was excited about the carnival atmosphere of Lane's caravan, and the fact that some of the men in Lane's group sported the new and novel Sharps rifle. Asked what they were doing, the men replied that they were going to Kansas to help free the Negroes. That was all Tibbles needed to hear. After getting reluctant permission from his parents Tibbles was off for an adventure. He was only too eager to join, and the Grim Chieftain gave the young lad a hearty welcome.[10]

Thus Tibbles, an intriguing personality in his own right, began his career as a social activist and advocate for human rights. Later in life he became a writer for some of the leading newspapers in the Midwest. Tibbles was involved in the famous case of *Standing Bear v. Crook* in which the court ruled that indeed Native Americans were legally persons and, therefore, had rights as set forth by the laws of the land.[11] Another high point of Tibbles' career came when he ran as vice presidential candidate for the Populist Party in the presidential election of 1904. Tibbles, a fine writer with a unique experience, however, had the madding habit of always self-aggrandizing his role in the various episodes he participated in on the American frontier.

On his trek across Iowa, Lane kept recruiting and trying to raise money. He claims to have made seventy-two speeches while crossing Iowa.[12] Lane's exploits as an orator were legendary. He had stood before boisterous mobs that were one step away from lynching him for his unpopular beliefs. But within a half an hour Lane would have them laughing and admiring him for his heroics in the Mexican War. Lane could play on a crowd's emotions. He could make them laugh; he could make them cry. He could be incredibly crude and vulgar or unbelievably refined. He could make them feel scorn, anger, tears or wild enthusiasm.[13]

At this time one of Lane's favorite lines in his oratory was to read the pro-slavery statutes that had been passed in Kansas. He pointed out crudely, and by modern standards offensively, how slavery's heavy hand skewers the laws of the nation. Lane would proclaim, "If a person kidnaps a white child the utmost penalty is six months in jail—if a 'nigger' baby, the penalty is death.... To kidnap a white child into slavery, six months in jail—to kidnap a 'nigger' into freedom, death!"[14]

As Jim Lane's caravan made its way from Winterset to Western Iowa, the Grim Chieftain made his way to Tabor. Once in Tabor, Lane's emigrants to Kansas were treated royally. Lane gave a speech at the local schoolhouse. John Todd noted that Lane bought a fine cream colored horse in this town that he rode throughout the troubles in Kansas.

The Reverend Todd noted that some of the settler-soldiers in Lane's group were complaining that they had not been given Sharps rifles as they had been promised. The Sharps rifle was a modern weapon for that time that had become almost synonymous with the anti-slavery movement. They were sometimes called Beecher's Bibles. Some of these settler-soldiers had been promised they would receive the Sharps rifles when they got to Albany, New York. When they didn't receive them there, they were promised they would receive them when they got to Cleveland, Ohio. When Cleveland produced no Sharps for the men, then it was at Chicago the men were told they would receive the weapon. When Chicago didn't give the men this rifle they were told Tabor would produce the magic arms. When these men got to Tabor they still were not given the Sharps. These settler-soldiers began to complain rather loudly about not receiving the weapon. Lane, as usual, was up to the task of keeping this group intact. He mounted a cannon carriage and spoke, "Comrades—a good soldier always grumbles. I know you have borne much already, since you left your homes. You have not always been fed on dainties, nor have you slept on down. You have endured with fortitude the perils, inconveniences, and privations of the way as good soldiers. Now you want Sharps rifles. Well, let me tell you, a Sharps rifle is a good weapon to use on an enemy at a distance, but it is good for nothing in a close encounter. If you come into a close fight (and I hope to God you may), a Sharps rifle is worthless. It is far inferior to a weapon with a bayonet. If I had my choice of arms, I would arm no more than one in ten with a Sharps rifle. As the arms you want are not here, I hope you will conclude to go on and see us through."[15] Todd reported no defections among Lane's men. Knowing Lane, one could almost bet that the rifles he received from the Iowa arsenal had bayonets on them and this is why he touted that weapon. Also, since Lane mentioned one Sharps rifle for every ten men, you could bet that this was the ratio he had amongst his men.

Some have estimated that Lane had almost 1,200 settler-soldiers with him. This would have been a tremendous burden on Tabor to feed and in some cases even clothe this many men. Tabor at this time only consisted of a couple of hundred people. After their bellies had been sated, their gun powder reserves filled and other supplies given freely to the anti-slavery forces, Lane and his group left Tabor to cross the Missouri River. The crossing of this mighty river proved difficult, as there was only one flatboat to accommodate the emigrants in Lane's troop. It took three days for everyone to cross the Missouri River on this single flatboat and get into Nebraska.[16]

One emigrant quickly forgot the decorum that Lane's company had shown in Tabor. Tibbles reported that across the Missouri River in Nebraska City. Native American women stood with baskets of corn all roasted and ready for eating. Each woman held a small wooden bowl in which coins were to be placed for payment of the corn. However, the women were not familiar with the value of the coins. The emigrants would put whatever amount they wanted into the bowls and take as much corn as they desired. One emigrant took unfair advantage of this situation and took a dozen full ears of corn and threw 25 cents into the makeshift till, then took as his change 50 cents.

This action outraged Tibbles. According to his account he knocked the offending emigrant down and hammered him until he agreed to put into the wooden bowl one dollar and take no corn.[17] The Lane train then proceed to Abraham Kagi's farm south of Nebraska City. This was obviously a popular rendezvous point for the Underground Railroad and Lane's people.[18]

Since the start of the Lane's emigrant train into Kansas, many newspapers all over the country, North and South, East and West, were confused by what was its real purpose. The abolitionists maintained that Lane's caravan contained only yeomen farmers wanting just to settle in Kansas to make it a free state devoid of the horrible institution of slavery. Many proslavery newspapers and politicians portrayed the emigrants as soldiers invading Kansas. Often the Grim Chieftain's wagon train was referred as "Lane's Army of the North."

Everyone, both North and South, was well aware of Lane's exploits in the Mexican War. If they weren't aware of Lane's exploits he was sure to inform them. The fact that Lane in his many speeches and orations used military terminology and the defiant stance he took left no one in doubt that he was spoiling for a fight. Also, the Sharps rifles, the abolitionists' favorite weapon, that his men carried were proof to many that Lane's emigrant train had military intentions. The July 1, 1856, edition of the New York Weekly Times reported that Lane was in Council Bluffs, Iowa, with a thousand buffalo hunters. This was a wildly inaccurate account but indicative of many of the newspaper reports of the time.

There was much talk of Lane's invasion of Kansas. Wild rumors and speculations put the total number of his men in the thousands. Even abolitionist leaders like Samuel Gridley Howe became alarmed at the sometimes negative press Lane's emigrant train was receiving for its military bearing and attitude. Howe and others wanted Lane to be removed from command of the Kansas convoy. This they felt would rid the emigrant train of what Howe called "the disadvantage of the military aspect which that [Lane's] presence gave it."[19]

While "Lane's Army" had made it across the Missouri River to Nebraska City, Jim Lane was still on the Iowa side. Lane was at Doc Blanchard's house near the old Civil Bend settlement in a dismal mood and on the verge of tears. Lane's enemies in Kansas had put United States marshals on his trail for treason against the proslavery government in Kansas. Howe had gotten his wishes and Lane was ordered by the National Kansas Committee to give up command of his wagon train of emigrants.

Then Sam Walker rode to Blanchard's and gave Lane a letter that stated some of the abolitionists in Kansas didn't want him to come either. Not to be deterred, Lane looked at Walker and said, "Walker, if you say the people of Kansas don't want me, it's all right, and I'll blow my brains out. I can never go back to the states and look the people in the face and tell them that as soon as I had got these Kansas friends of mine fairly into danger I had to abandon them. I can't do it. No matter what I say in my defense no one will believe it. I'll blow my brains out and end the thing right here."[20]

This was classic Jim Lane. Backed into a corner he didn't want to be in, he made an end run. Sam Walker was taken aback. Walker had been sent north to find Lane and to get him to relinquish the command of his "army." Walker had not been sent to Civil Bend to watch Lane blow his brains out. Walker convinced Lane to put himself under Walker's "orders." Lane would need to disguise himself until the proper time. So instead of relieving Lane of his command, Walker insured the Grim Chieftain that he would escort him into Kansas. Doc Blanchard sponged on silver nitrate to blacken Lane's salt and pepper beard. Mrs. Blanchard found some old clothes that they hoped would disguise Lane's appearance.

Walker and Lane made their way to Lawrence, Kansas, although not with Lane's "army." This, however, did not stop the Grim Chieftain. After the men of Lawrence had won a skirmish outside of the town against proslavery men, Lane proudly announced that he and his "Army of the North" had arrived in Kansas and had their first victory.[21]

Lane was a prominent figure in the pageant played out in Kansas. He became a prime target for assassination because of his high profile and inflammatory personality. Even in Tabor, the Reverend Todd told of Jim Lane dressing "incog" to hide his whereabouts and true identity.[22] This was to thwart any possible assassination attempt. In 1857 Lane felt his life was in danger to the point he traveled with two bodyguards. One of his bodyguards was a tall, rawboned youth who had won recognition for his abilities with firearms at shooting matches in Kansas. The youth's name was James Butler Hickok. He later would become better known by his sobriquet "Wild Bill" Hickok.[23]

Lane continued to move in and out of Tabor. Once after an incident in which a pro-slavery newspaper, the *Nebraska City News*, was attacked by Lane's partisans for an anti-Lane article, the Grim Chieftain called off his men and they made their way to Tabor. In the Lane group were some men of low character and morals. Once outside of Tabor Lane stopped with his troops. He pleaded with them to act with the utmost decorum. He told them keep in mind the high religious and moral principles that the people of Tabor lived by. He told them the people of Tabor would give them what they wanted so there was no need to steal anything. It is said that when Lane's men were in Tabor they spoke no profanity, which was often their custom, and they stole no chickens.[24]

Different abolitionist societies and organizations began sending men through Iowa and Tabor to settle in Kansas. A.D. Searl was sent to Tabor by the National Kansas Committee to coordinate the emigrants' trips into the Kansas Territory. Searl was also in Tabor to coordinate the supplies held in that town for the emigrants. The route was becoming known as the "Jim Lane Trail." Col. Shaler W. Eldridge, funded by the National Kansas Committee, came through Tabor in October of 1856 and was far better outfitted and organized than was Lane's "Army of the North." The Eldridge group also had a distinct military purpose and they spent two days in Tabor refitting before setting out for Kansas.

However, their trip to this territory didn't go as planned. The Eldridge group was armed for a fight and even had a cannon amongst their wagon train. The government in the Kansas territory was pro-slavery and didn't want this group of free-state men to cross into their state from Nebraska. The pro-slavery government called for United States troops to position themselves just inside the Kansas border and stop the Eldridge train.

Eldridge heard of these troops and had his men hide most of their weapons. They even buried their cannon in Nebraska soil. There were seven women from one family on his caravan. They assigned these women to different wagons to give the appearance of peaceable families going to settle in Kansas. Once the Eldridge caravan crossed into Kansas it was descended upon by 300 federal troops and a deputy United States marshal. The wagons were searched and any weapons not claimed as personal property were confiscated. They were all detained and given the choice of being arrested or escorted under surveillance. The Eldridge group chose to be arrested, as then the government had to pay for their transportation and meals as they went into the territory to settle.[25] The group took some time to secure their release.

From Milwaukee came a group headed by Edmund Ross. Ross had worked in the newspaper business in Milwaukee, Wisconsin. In 1854 while working in a newspaper office, Ross heard a ruckus on the street below.

Slavers were trying to capture a fugitive slave. Ross joined the mob and helped to free the runaway.[26] The die had been cast in his life.

He led a group down into Iowa across the Jim Lane Trail. Ross came into Tabor with an outfit that had 24 head of oxen, six large covered wagons, a cow, an extra horse and team and a smaller covered wagon.[27] The Ross group went into Kansas and settled where the former newspaper man became involved in politics and business in the new territory.

Ross led an interesting life. After United States Senator Jim Lane committed suicide in 1866 the governor of Kansas named Ross to Lane's Senate seat. Ross became embroiled in the impeachment of President Andrew Johnson. He cast what many believe was the deciding vote not to impeach Johnson even though his Republican party was against the Democrat Johnson. John F. Kennedy, in his Pulitzer Prize winning book, *Profiles in Courage*, singled out Ross' vote as a profile in courage.[28]

The free state emigrants coming into Kansas were always in danger of having their weapons confiscated by deputy marshals who traveled with U.S. troops. The status quo pro-slavery territorial Governor Geary thought he could diffuse the situation in Kansas by disarming the free state forces as the came into the territory. Of course Lane and the others would have no part of it.[29]

Earlier during the summer of 1856 Eldridge was commissioned by a committee in Kansas to head north to Tabor to get much needed lead for bullets. Eldridge met up with A.D. Searl. After reaching Tabor the two started for Council Bluffs where it was believed a large amount of lead could be found. They got all the lead they could find from every hamlet on the way to Council Bluffs. Once in the Bluffs they found, contrary to what they had been told, that lead was hard to find. Eldridge finally obtained fifteen hundred pounds of lead pipe to cast into bullets. While the teamster Eldridge had hired was loading the lead, a pro-slavery crowd surrounded the wagon. Seeing the mob the teamster quit the project and Eldridge was summoned. The mob asserted that the lead would not leave Council Bluffs. Eldridge told the crowd what he thought of them.

Dramatically, an older Quaker man wearing a broad-brimmed hat stepped forward and announced he would take the load. He announced to the mob that if any of them wanted the lead he was taking the load to Tabor. The mob parted as he left. It took two days for him to reach Tabor. Once in town the Quaker was offered payment, which he refused. He also offered to take any such load in the future.[30]

Thomas W. Higginson, a leading Boston abolitionist and officer in the National Kansas Aid Society, was carrying a large sum in a money belt through the no-man's land between Kansas and Tabor. He made it to Tabor in one piece and with his money intact. As he was heading back into

Kansas with the money the men of Tabor decided to provide an escort for Higginson.

A.D. Searl noted in a letter from Tabor that some of the pro-slavery ruffians even operated as far north as Plattsmouth, Nebraska. An old bachelor had headed to Kansas to settle the area. He became alarmed at the violence in the territory and left five crates full of plow chains and other property with a free state man in Plattsmouth until the violence abated in the territory. Pro-slavery "law and order" men from Plattsmouth, fearing that the crates held rifles for the free state forces in Kansas, illegally opened the crates to see what the contents of them were.[31]

Most of the emigrants coming through Tabor were poorly funded and equipped. John Todd noted in a letter to his mother-in-law on September 12, 1856, that the emigrants "come in a destitute condition—poorly armed & without money or provisions almost."[32] The resources of Tabor were often stretched to the limits. The town turned no one away even though these events often turned the local citizen's lives upside down and their pockets inside out. Todd wrote, "Chicago, in the time of excitement, agreed to raise 500 men & 15,000 dollars, but where is it & what has it amounted to?"

When battles occurred in Kansas between the anti-slavery and pro-slavery forces, often the injured and wounded were brought to Tabor for care. As the wagon trains of emigrants bound for Kansas continued to pass through Tabor, Mrs. George Gaston wrote a descriptive account of this time:

> That summer and autumn [of 1856] our houses, before too full, were much overfilled and our comforts shared with those passing to and from Kansas to secure it to *Freedom*. When houses would hold no more, woodsheds were temporized for bedrooms, where the sick and dying were cared for. Barns also were fixed for sleeping rooms. Every place where a bed could be put or a blanket thrown down was at once so occupied. There were comers and goers all times of day or night—meals at all hours—many free hotels, perhaps entertaining angels unawares. *After* battles they were here for rest—*before* for preparation. General Lane once stayed three weeks secretly while it was reported abroad that he was back in Indiana for recruits and supplies, which came ere long, consisting of all kinds of provisions, Sharps rifles, powder, and lead. A canon [sic] packed in corn made its way through enemy's lines, and ammunition of all kinds, in clothing, and kitchen furniture, etc., etc. Our cellars contained barrels of powder and boxes of rifles. Often our chairs, tables, beds and such places were covered with what weapons every one carried about him, so that if one *needed* and got time to rest a little in the day time, we had to remove the Kansas furniture, or rest with loaded revolvers, cartridge boxes and bowie knives piled around them, and boxes of swords under the bed. Were not our houses overfilled?[33]

The National Kansas Committee and the Massachusetts Kansas Committee sent weapons and other equipment to Tabor. Sometimes the people of Tabor had difficult decisions to make. Should these supplies be given to the often ill-armed and ill-equipped emigrants going through Tabor? Or should this cargo be forwarded to the emigrants already in Kansas?

On September 12, 1856, John Todd wrote to his mother-in-law that a band of emigrants were holed up in Tabor for almost three weeks They were unable to move into Kansas until a larger force of men could be organized. Todd reported that pro-slavery partisans had blocked Kansas by land and only large parties of abolitionists dared venture into the territory. Todd also told of some $20,000 worth of provisions that needed to be moved into Kansas, but more men were needed to escort such a large amount of goods lest they be captured by pro-slavery Missourians.[34]

It was thought only an armed escort could get goods and emigrants through to Kansas because of armed "border ruffians" from Missouri blocking the route into Kansas. A call was sent out in Southwestern Iowa for volunteers to help take goods and emigrants through. Although the area had very few permanent residents many responded, including the Reverend Todd. Eventually some 200 men answered the call to be armed escorts into Kansas.

The Underground Railroad stationmaster at Lewis, Iowa, the Reverend George Hitchcock's son, Leang Afa Hitchcock, answered the call. (Hitchcock named his son after an early Chinese convert to Christianity.) The escorts camped within a mile of Tabor.[35] There was a bunch of young men in the party who treated the whole exercise as a lark rather than a serious mission. These young men fired their guns in the air and brandished their weapons in a menacing manner.

One young man playfully pointed a supposedly unloaded pistol at Leang Afa Hitchcock and pulled the trigger. The pistol turned out to be loaded and the discharge killed the minister's son almost instantly. The group of escorts was of course in shock. The body of young Hitchcock was prepared and taken by wagon to Lewis. The Reverend Todd rode via horseback all night so he could tell the Reverend Hitchcock and his family the terrible news before their son's body got to their place. The family, needless to say, was heartbroken.[36] Shortly after the Reverend Todd returned to Tabor from Lewis it was learned that the escort would not be needed. The way into Kansas was now clear and the emigrants and supplies could go forward.[37]

Some of the men who had volunteered to be escorts decided to go into Kansas anyway. By September of 1856 the Reverend Todd observed that not nearly enough men had passed through Tabor on their way to Kansas to turn the tide. Todd knew it would take thousands to settle the territory and clear out the pro-slavery faction. Tabor, with little help from the outside world, found the finances of its local citizens often taxed to the breaking point.

The Reverend was often perplexed because as he read the newspapers from the East he heard of money and men being raised for expeditions into Kansas. But where were the money and men going? He had seen some men but almost no money passing through Tabor. He knew Lane and his "Army of the North" needed reinforcements.[38] Where would they come from? Even on the eve of the Civil War, George Gaston was still contributing to those in need on their way to Kansas. He provided them twenty-five sacks of flour, fifty bushels of meal and a large lot of clothing.[39]

Lane became a powerhouse in the politics of the Midwest. He became the first United States senator from Kansas. When the Civil War broke out Lane formed the "Frontier Guards" to help guard the White House and keep Lincoln safe, as rumors of kidnapping and assassination attempts were rife in the capital of this country. Lincoln viewed Lane's support in the Civil War as critical.

Lane went back to Kansas and organized the Third, Fourth and Fifth Kansas volunteers. They became known as Lane's brigade. Lane also formed the First Kansas Colored Volunteers. While he was a sitting United States senator Lane was named a brigadier general by Lincoln. This action was illegal but Lincoln went along with Lane's subterfuge so he could perform both duties.

After the Civil War was over Lane sat at the table of the radical Republicans who wanted harsh treatment of the former Confederacy. However, Lane after a while broke ranks with this group. He was harshly criticized back in Kansas for this. The "Grim Chieftain" became despondent and ill health surrounded him, possibly to the point it caused mental illness. He came home to Kansas in 1866 to rest but in a fit of despondence he shot himself in the head, thus ending his life.[40] The restless, vibrant life of James Lane ended.

However, into Tabor another man would come to further the cause of a free Kansas. The man was just as colorful and fiery as Lane. He was the man many said started the Civil War. His name was John Brown.

10

"John Brown's Body Lies A-Mouldering in the Grave"

In 1855 a strange man started coming into Tabor. The man was seen in and out of town many times over the next four years. He was a lanky man for the time, almost six feet tall and weighing less than 150 pounds. He had blue-gray eyes that seemed to pop out when he was speaking vigorously and when he spoke against slavery it was always in an excited manner. He had the manner of an Old Testament prophet. People around Tabor quickly began to know this new visitor was John Brown.

Brown grew up in a hardscrabble life in Connecticut, Pennsylvania and Ohio. When he reached manhood America's promise of prosperity eluded him. He became a tanner like his father, but also dabbled in a variety of occupations such as surveyor, wool merchant, farmer and shepherd. Brown also attempted several business ventures but they all failed.[1]

In 1855 Brown followed his six sons out to the Kansas territory. The sons hoped to make a living farming, while Brown felt his mission was to keep the territory free of slavery. On the way to the territory Brown made his way through Southwest Iowa and Tabor. Brown felt a natural kinship with the people of Tabor. He had lived in the Western Reserve of Ohio. At one time he had even negotiated with Oberlin College for a surveying job and possible land purchase.[2] When Brown set foot in Tabor the town made him feel as if he were back home in Ohio. Brown felt a natural kinship with these fiery Tabor abolitionists.[3]

Out of respect he was often called Captain John Brown while in town.

Tabor was often Brown's base of operations. During the summer of 1856 Brown brought his sick son and his wounded son-in-law, Henry Thompson, to Tabor to recuperate.[4] John Todd and the rest of the town were only too happy to set up hospitals in their houses to help the sick and wounded soldiers of Kansas to recover. While he was in town Brown developed a special relationship with Jonas Jones and George Gaston. Brown usually boarded with the Jones or Gaston families when in town.

The people of Tabor often helped Brown, his family and Brown's fellow travelers. However, Brown and his relatives or fellow travelers took special care to never show the people of Tabor or John Todd their sometimes excessive violent or dishonest nature. During the summer of 1856 Brown's son, Oliver, and William Thompson, younger brother to Henry Thompson, were coming to Tabor via Kansas. When these two got into Nebraska they heard rumors that proslavery men were on their trail. They surprised two unsuspecting horsemen and stole their mounts and headed into Tabor. They never told the people in Tabor how they obtained their horses and they acquired a buggy in town on credit. Thompson and Brown drove the buggy and horses to Iowa City. They sold the buggy in Iowa City and remitted the money for the buggy back to Tabor. Thus they kept John Brown's name and his entourage's reputation intact in this southwestern Iowa town.[5] However, Oliver Brown's and William Thompson's luck finally ran out when they were killed during Brown's raid on Harper's Ferry.

It wasn't unusual for John Brown or his sons Owen, Jason, Oliver or John Brown, Jr., to bring an extra traveler when they came to Tabor. On one occasion they were bringing a mule team of arms and ammunition out of Kansas to be stored in Tabor. The Browns also brought a runaway slave hidden in a one horse wagon filled with hay. Once they were in Iowa and near Tabor, they felt confident enough to let the runaway come out from underneath the hay. The runaway worked for awhile in Tabor before completing his escape on the Underground Railroad.[6]

At another time John Brown had brought two escaping slaves with him to the George Gaston house. The Gastons, John Brown and the slaves were all seated at the dinner table when there was a knock at the door. It was a slave bounty hunter looking for the two runaways. George Gaston went to the door and engaged the slave hunter in conversation.

Meanwhile Mrs. Gaston and John Brown hid the slaves from any unfriendly eyes. George and the slave hunter still were engaging in conversation when finally the slaver asked him if he knew where the escaping slaves were located. Gaston answered him, "If I did I shouldn't tell you."[7] The slaver left empty handed and another successful escape was engineered on the Underground Railroad.

During this time the citizens of Tabor felt threatened enough that they formed a military company of their own. Because it was becoming known that Brown, Lane, escaping slaves and other radicals regularly resided in Tabor, the town often heard rumors of threats by pro-slavery factions about attacking Tabor. At times it was hard to ascertain the veracity of these rumors but the citizens thought it in their best interests to have some sort of military unit in case the town was attacked. George Gaston was elected captain of this unit. A committee was appointed to ask state officials for weapons.[8] However, no attack on the town ever took place.

While coming to and from Tabor, the Reverend Todd wrote, John Brown used his disguise as a surveyor to escape federal authorities. Todd recalled that in one of Brown's trips from Kansas to Tabor he camped several nights with a United States cavalry unit in which the officer in charge had a writ for Brown's arrest. Brown had a light wagon with his surveyor's equipment prominently displayed and a cow tied

John Brown's most controversial trip to Tabor occurred in February of 1859. Brown came into town with a dozen people making their escape to freedom plus several of his own men. They were treated royally, as usual, at first. However, as details of the nature of this escape on the Underground Railroad by Brown came to the attention of the people of Tabor, questions were asked. Brown and his men had killed a plantation owner and had hauled off a lot of property. The people of Tabor censured Brown which deeply hurt him. Brown and his men had often hid their sometimes murderous intentions and their penchant for theft from John Todd and the people of Tabor. Brown then went to Grinnell, where he was treated splendidly. (Kansas State Historical Society.)

on behind it. The cavalry officer was unaware that this supposed kindly old surveyor was the most wanted man in the territory and allowed Brown to travel and camp with his military unit that was attempting to arrest him. Brown, who was also ill at this time, managed to elude this manhunt for him. He reached Tabor safe and sound and the local citizenry made sure he was protected from any arrest.[9]

In June of 1857 John Brown received a letter from William A. Phillips in Lawrence in the Kansas Territory. Brown had wanted Phillips to meet him in Tabor but Phillips could not, as he was taking a census for statewide elections that were to be held in the fall. Phillips had to give Old Brown the bad news that his original land claim had been jumped in Kansas. His prolonged absences in Tabor and his fund raising tours in the rest of America had made it possible for a squatter to take over his claim. To keep enemies off guard Brown often used phony names on his mail correspondence while in Tabor; at this time his was using the name Jas Smith.[10]

Owen and Jason Brown, sons of John Brown, in their later years. Owen and Jason Brown were in and out of Tabor often during the 1850s. They often brought escaping slaves from Kansas when they came to Iowa. They survived the troubles in "Bleeding Kansas," and Owen survived the disaster at Harper's Ferry. The brothers lived to old age, and this picture was taken at their mountain home seven miles north of Pasadena, California. (State Historical Society of Iowa—Des Moines.)

When he wasn't in Kansas or Tabor Brown spent much time back east trying to raise funds and support for his cause. On one of his trips to raise funds Brown met a soldier of fortune by the name of Hugh Forbes in New York City. Forbes had fought with Giuseppe Garibaldi in Italy. While in New York City, Forbes was scraping out a living teaching fencing lessons, being a translator, as he was an expert linguist, editing an Italian language newspaper called *The European* and writing for the New York *Tribune*.[11]

In August of 1857 Brown sent Forbes to Tabor with the intent of training his men in the guerrilla warfare tactics that he was familiar with. Forbes would later reveal that Brown talked to him in Tabor of his plan to attack in Virginia and create an armed slave rebellion in the south.[12] Brown paid Forbes $100 a month and even advanced him $600.[13] Forbes had published a manual on military tactics. While in Tabor he often referred to the manual, which was entitled "The Patriotic Volunteer."

John Todd wrote of Forbes and Brown's time in town when they were training for combat:

> Part of the time they practiced shooting at a target with Sharps rifles.
> In the point of one of the prairie ridges which run north and south and just north of Dragoon hollow they dug a hole of sufficient dimensions to contain a man comfortably. A sheet-like white cloth with a black spot in the center, suspended on two stakes, was placed on the north side of the hole, in which one of their number placed himself with his back to the marksmen, fronting the target, and deep enough in the ground to be safe from any balls that might be fired. There with a long pointer in hand terminated by a black knob about the size of a man's fist to render it more readily distinguishable, sat the indicator awaiting the report of a Sharps rifle half a mile or more away south, whither Colonel Forbes and Captain Brown had repaired to try their skill as marksmen. No sooner was the report of the distant rifle heard than the black knob on the end of the pointer was placed on the hole where the ball perforated the target, which the marksmen, with the aid of a field glass, could readily see and modify their subsequent attempts accordingly.[14]

Todd noted that Forbes' textbook on military training was studied in their classroom and the target practice provided outdoor activity. Thus the summer and fall of 1857 marched by with Brown and Forbes training in Tabor. However, they failed to attract only but a few to their "army." Soon after he arrived in Tabor in August, Brown wrote in a letter to his wife and children enthusiastically about the training Forbes was providing.[15] However, it would not take long before for these two men with strong personalities to begin to clash.

Brown and Forbes argued often while they were in Tabor. They each had plans to start a slave insurrection. They both had their own ideas on how best to start and sustain a rebellion. But both men were hard headed and oblivious to advice. Each thought they only had the true answers. Both thought they were masters of guerrilla warfare that they thought would be needed to maintain a slave upraising. John Brown pored over maps and made a list of federal facilities, forts and arsenals which would have arms to carry on his slave uprising. These two dreamers, John Brown and Hugh Forbes, were in the hamlet of Tabor basically plotting to overthrow the government of the United States in order to destroy slavery. They both mistakenly thought they could do this with only 50 to 100 men trained in the art of guerrilla warfare. Brown had become obsessed with the idea of using pikes in his guerrilla slave uprising or for settlers in Kansas in defending themselves against border ruffians in the territories. He had captured Henry Clay Pate at the battle of Black Jack in Kansas. Pate had with him a number of pikes, a wicked-looking medieval weapon with a double-edged sword attached to the long end of a pole. Brown thought this would be the perfect weapon for use by untrained fighters. While back east Brown, on a fund raising tour, had an order for a large number of pikes made by a blacksmith in Connecticut.[16] He showed the people in Tabor some of these pikes.

However, Old Brown was as usual almost out of money and then he came down with the ague while in Tabor. The people in town nursed him back to health.[17]

Brown felt that pro-slavery elements would interfere with the elections in October of 1857 in Kansas. James Lane, who was in Kansas, was of the mind that it was necessary for anti-slavery men to become guards of the ballot boxes to make sure the elections were not tampered with by the slavery proponents. In a letter to Brown in Tabor dated September 29, Lane urged Brown to send all the guns and ammunition in the Iowa town to Kansas. In an effort to butter up Brown, Lane even addressed the letter to "Genl." Lane also wanted Brown to send the some 200 hundred revolvers that had been sent to Tabor by the Massachusetts Arms Company. Also, Brown was urged by Lane to send all of the military stores in Tabor that he had been acquiring and bring them by wagon to Kansas.[18]

Brown, in a letter dated the next day, begged off and said it "will be next to impossible in my poor state of health to go through on such a short notice." Brown also addressed his letter to "Genl. Jas. H. Lane" and signed it "Very Respectfully Your Friend."[19]

It is not clear if Brown used the ruse that he was too ill to comply with Lane's wishes to avoid handing over this military cache to someone he did not fully trust. Besides, being in control of such a large amount of military goods gave Brown power. At this time both were often at odds with each other. Why should Brown give up control of these military weapons to someone who was somewhat of a rival? Was Brown pretending to be too sick to make the journey to Kansas so that Lane would not come into possession of all of the military stores in Tabor? Brown and Lane were notorious for their in-fighting on who would be the leader in the fight to keep slavery out of Kansas.

Again on October 30 Lane in a letter pleaded with Brown to bring the Tabor military supplies to Kansas. Brown again stated he was not able to do so. In a letter at this time Brown did complain of a serious injury.[20] Yet one wonders why Brown didn't send the arms and supplies with one of his sons.

Lane wrote that he was in Nebraska so the exchange could be made only a short distance from Tabor. Brown still didn't comply. It is interesting to note that at this time it was unusual for there to be so many late model firearms in a small frontier village like Tabor.[21]

In a letter to John Brown in Tabor dated October 2, 1857, friend Samuel L. Adair from Osawatomie in the Kansas Territory advised Brown that he thought in the upcoming elections in October "that the pro slavery men will carry the day." However, Adair didn't think there would be a mass invasion of Kansas by pro-slavery Missourians as there was in 1854 & 1855.[22]

Remarkably, the election

Frederick Douglass, born a slave, was one of the most brilliant speakers and writers in America against the evils of slavery. John Brown had brought Hugh Forbes to Tabor to train his men. After Hugh Forbes left Tabor, Forbes felt he had been abandoned by the abolitionist movement when they didn't support him with money. Forbes went from Tabor to Rochester, New York, to try and get money from Douglass. Douglass found Forbes to be reprehensible. Forbes eventually turned against his mentor John Brown and he became a pariah to the abolitionist cause. (State Historical Society of Iowa—Des Moines.)

on October 7, 1857, in Kansas went off without fraud or terror tactics. In a letter from friend Henry H. Williams in Osawatomie to Brown in Tabor he reported that "as far as this Co. is concerned it went off right." Williams went on to say that one reason things went as planned was the presence of free state men watching the ballot boxes.[23] Both Brown and Lane were in the whole satisfied with how things went and Tabor's weapons were not needed to arm the ballot box watchers. After the election Forbes then left Tabor and embarked on a steamer in Nebraska City and headed back East. The drill instructor was furious with the lack of funds sent to him while he was in Tabor from the abolitionists back East. He would soon try and settle that score. Forbes never returned to Tabor.[24]

Fredrick Douglass met with Forbes in Rochester, New York, right after Forbes had left Tabor and found him reprehensible. Forbes was pleading for money from all the abolitionists, including Douglass, for his proposed ventures with Brown. Douglass introduced Forbes to some of his friends, an act he would later regret. Some were intrigued by an international revolutionary but the romance disappeared when Forbes displayed his penance for endlessly begging for money.[25] Soon Horace Greeley, Samuel Gridley Howe, Fredrick Douglass and other abolitionist leaders in the East against slavery grew tired of Forbes and saw him as a moocher. When he could get no more money from his benefactors he began to tell them if he wasn't given any more cash he would betray Brown.[26]

After leaving Tabor John Brown took the immigrant road and headed into Kansas; much to the dismay of those in Kansas he was without the weapons that were stockpiled in Tabor. He would ride in a wagon driven by one of his sons.

While John Brown was in and out of Tabor he did as James Lane had done. He often changed his demeanor to reflect the piety of John Todd's flock. Brown portrayed the killings he had committed in Kansas as justified self-defense. He never told the residents of Tabor that often the violence he had committed was aggressive in nature and sometimes nothing more than cold-blooded murder.

After Lawrence, Kansas, then the free state stronghold, had been sacked in May of 1856, John Brown went to avenge this deed. He went to a place on Pottawatomie Creek where five families that held slaves were located. Brown and his sons called the men out and brutally executed them. The true facts of incidents like this were kept from the citizens of Tabor and for that matter much of the rest of the country for many years. Many of Brown's apologists helped to muddy the waters on incidents like this.

It is interesting to note that a minister, H. D. King, would visit the Reverend Todd on occasion. The Reverend King had a talk one time with John Brown trying to ascertain his overall religious philosophy. King wrote: "I tried to get at his theology. It was a subject naturally suggested by my daily work. But I never could force him down to dry sober talk on what he thought of the moral features of things in general. He would not express himself on little diversions from common right for the accomplishment of a greater good. For him there was only one wrong, and that was slavery. He was rather skeptical, I think. Not an infidel, but not bound by creeds. He was somewhat cranky on the subject of the Bible, as he was on that of killing people. He believed in God and Humanity, but his attitude seemed to be; 'We don't know anything about some things. We do not know about the humanity matter. If any great obstacle stand in the way, you may properly break all the Decalogue to get rid of it.'"[27]

Throughout 1856 and 1857 many skirmishes and battles occurred in Kansas. Sometimes Brown's men were implicated and sometimes Lane's men were involved. At times Brown's and Lane's men acted in self-defense; at other times they were clearly the aggressors. Very often the wounded or survivors of these firefights would find themselves recovering or restocking their equipment or ammunition in Tabor.

One such skirmish occurred in Kansas in which John Brown, Jr., played a small part. A particularly obnoxious slave owner who dubbed himself Colonel Titus built a fortified cabin and named it Fort Titus. Titus and his men staged raids on free soil settlers, killing and capturing them. A band of free soil partisans surrounded Fort Titus and put the inhabitants under a stream of fire.[28]

A black woman who was at this time the property of Colonel Titus was unfortunately inside the fort when it came under attack. After firing into Titus's fortified position with rifles and pistols the free soil men rolled up a cannon and began to blast the fort. The slave woman was seated on a trunk. A cannonball struck the trunk she was sitting on and it exited on the other side. Even though the Titus fort was burned to the ground by the free state men, this slave woman was able to escape. She later was able to make her way out of Kansas and out of bondage to Tabor. John Todd and the people of Tabor heard her harrowing tale and made sure she was escorted north on the Underground Railroad to freedom.[29] Titus was captured after the battle at his self-proclaimed fort and then later was killed.[30]

There was another account of a black slave woman, known as Ann Clarke, owned by Colonel Titus and George W. Clarke, who was from 40 to 45 years old and some 175 pounds. Ann was a domestic slave. Ann wanted her freedom and escaped from the horrors of that life but was recaptured by slave hunters. However, before Ann's capturers could collect their reward money she managed to escape again. This time she tasted freedom permanently. She made her way on the Underground Railroad to Doc Blanchard's home in Civil Bend. She made her way to Tabor and finally to Chicago.

Ann was able to hide amid the burgeoning black population in the Windy City. She was able to write to her friends in Kansas in subsequent years of her ultimate whereabouts.[31]

John Brown was back in Tabor after returning from Kansas and wanted the military stores there. He had with him some of the men who would later attack Harper's Ferry, Virginia. At Tabor at this time with Brown were his son Owen, A.D. Stephens, Charles Moffit, C.P. Tidd, Richard Richardson, Colonel Richard Realf, L.F. Parsons, William Leaman, and Captain Cook. Cook stated that for the first time John Brown revealed that their ultimate mission was to attack Harper's Ferry with the idea that the arsenal there would be used to support a slave rebellion in the South.[32]

The Sharps rifles that had been hidden in the Todds' basement, the revolvers and other military equipment were taken by wagon from Tabor on December 4, 1857.[33] The caravan proceeded onto West Liberty, Iowa. From this Iowa town they were shipped to John Brown, Jr., in Ashtabula County, Ohio. They were then shipped to Chambersburg, Pennsylvania, and then forwarded to a farm in Maryland only a few miles from Harper's Ferry, Virginia.[34]

John Brown's next appearance in Tabor would be his most spectacular. Some of Brown's men had heard that some slaves in Missouri wanted to escape bondage. In December of 1858 they staged raids on three different Missouri slave plantations. They came from Kansas and invaded Missouri. Brown freed eleven slaves plus teams of horses, oxen, wagons and personal property of the plantation owners. The Brown forces began to loot the plantations on the grounds that some of it had come from Lawrence, Kansas. On the raid of plantation owner David Cruise, while liberating one slave one of Brown's men killed Cruise when he thought Cruise was reaching for a weapon.[35]

On the Underground Railroad, even though there were no published rules, there was a certain protocol that was expected to be followed. One was that if slaves came to your residence or station you were to help them with all diligence. However, it was not acceptable to go onto slave plantations and take slaves from their masters no matter how appealing that might seem. It was also considered deplorable that you would kill someone to help liberate slaves on the Underground Railroad. There was much discussion among the conductors on the Underground Railroad as to the acceptable amount of property a runaway slave could take with him or her. Surely the clothes on his or her back, a blanket, a small amount of food and possibly a horse or firearm would be permissible. After all, hadn't the slave worked his or her whole life? Wouldn't it be fair to expect that after a lifetime of work, if the slave had been paid wages, they would have acquired some property? Weren't these few necessities only a minimal amount of compensation for a lifetime of servitude?

Most Underground Railroad conductors agreed that this minimal amount of property taken was permissible. However, it is evident that Brown and his men went way over the line with their plundering of much of the plantation owner's property. The manner of Brown's capture of these slaves and the killing of Cruise made the whole endeavor, if the facts had been known, an embarrassment to the Underground Railroad.

Brown and his party made their way through Kansas in the harsh winter environment. A baby was born to one of the females on her flight to freedom, now making the runaways a total of 12. Brown and his party made their way into Nebraska City. They eluded a posse of 50 men before reaching Nebraska City.[36]

While in Nebraska City the local paper, the *News*, left little doubt where their sympathies lay when they printed this account of Brown on February 12, 1859: "John Brown, Captain John Brown, Old John Brown of Osawatomie, the 'Old John Brown' Gerritt Smith said had done more for the freedom of Kansas than the whole Republican party, passed through the city Friday evening at the head of a herd of stolen niggers taken from southern Missouri, accompanied by a gang of horse thieves of the most desperate character. They had a large number of stolen horses in their possession—two of which were taken and now held by the deputy sheriff of this county."

Brown then went to Civil Bend and headed for the home of Dr. Ira Blanchard. The U.S. Marshal's posse that had been chasing Brown had reached Blanchard's house before Old Osawatomie got there. The posse thoroughly searched the Doctor's home for Brown. However, rather than staying at Blanchard's place, they left before Brown got there. Brown luckily eluded his pursuers.[37] It is interesting to note that this huge posse didn't follow Brown to Tabor, where by any degree of common sense would tell you he was going next. This attack by Brown on these plantations had hit the newspapers both North and South. President Buchanan had even weighed in and offered a reward of $250 for Brown.[38]

Once in Tabor, Brown and his entourage were treated royally. They were given the local schoolhouse and a cooking stove was placed at their disposal.[39] Brown was happy to be back at Tabor and wrote to his wife and children, "I am once more in Iowa through the great mercy of God. Those with me & other friends are well. I hope soon to be at a point where I can learn of your *welfare* & perhaps send you something besides my good wishes. I suppose you get the common news. May the God of my *fathers* be *your* God."[40]

However, reports had begun to filter back into Tabor as to the methods of Brown's latest rescue on the Underground Railroad. There was starting to be a backlash against him. When Sabbath day came around the whole town went to church as usual. Brown and his group also came and Brown handed the Reverend Todd a note which he wanted Todd to read to the congregation. The note read, "John Brown respectfully requests the church at Tabor to offer public thanksgiving to God on behalf of himself and his rescued captives, in particular for his gracious preservation of their lives and health and his signal deliverance of all out of the hand of the wicked hitherto. Oh, give thanks unto the Lord; for He is good; for His mercy endureth forever."[41]

The rest of that day news swirled around Tabor about Brown's raid in Missouri. A public town hall meeting was called for that Monday to allow Brown to tell his side of the story. Unfortunately the Reverend Todd would be unable to attend the meeting, as he had to preach in Glenwood later that day and then head to Quincy, Iowa, to spend a week with Brother Penfield to conduct a series of meetings.[42]

At the appointed time for the meeting John Brown showed up and began to tell his story. A stranger came into the meeting. He was a pro-slavery advocate, ironically named Dr. Brown, from St. Joseph, Missouri. Dr. Brown was a specialist in town to treat a few cases. The Missouri physician was very familiar with the facts of John Brown's raid.

John Brown, hearing who Dr. Brown was, refused to speak anymore for fear that anything he said might be used by Dr. Brown to further prosecute the case against him. John Brown said if Dr. Brown remained in the hall he would have to leave. The Missouri doctor refused to vacate the meeting hall. So John Brown withdrew from the building. He saw his sons on the streets of Tabor and said that they had better look to their arms, as they were not yet among friends.[43]

Even after John Brown left, very few vacated the Tabor meeting hall. They discussed Brown's raid and slavery in general. Dr. Brown took an active part. The Missouri physician quoted Bible scriptures used by slave holders to justify slavery.[44]

Some of John Brown's men and the citizens of Tabor were quick to respond with counter biblical passages condemning slavery. However, at the end of the meeting the majority of the citizens of Tabor agreed that Brown's latest methods were not the kind of tactics most abolitionists would adhere to in freeing slaves. A resolution was passed condemning Brown and his men. This resolution read, "Resolved, That while we sympathize with the oppressed, & will do all that we conscientiously can to help them in their efforts for freedom, nevertheless, we have no Sympathy with those who go to Slave States, to entice away slaves, & take property or life when necessary to attain that end."[45]

Mrs. George Gaston, in whose house Brown was staying, wrote of his reaction to the meeting and resolution.

Captain Brown was sick at this time also, and not finding the same sympathy as formally, it almost broke his heart. He thought we had sadly lost principle, not realizing that he was in a school with very different teachers from ours. I shall never forget his disappointment and anguish accompanied by many tears, when his men returned from a meeting expressing disapproval of his course. He said he must trust in the Lord alone and not rely on earthly friends. The blow was crushing. He had expected so much, it was hard to be blamed. At other times he was welcomed and had received all he asked for, and he could not understand why we should not take this advanced step with him.[46]

John Brown turned his back on Tabor and with his charges continued on the Underground Railroad through Iowa. Although with the bounty on his head, Brown still went the well known Underground Railroad paths that he had gone on before. In Des Moines, Brown and his lieutenant, John Kagi, looked up *Register* editor John Teasdale. Teasdale paid for the group's ferriage across the Des Moines River. In March of 1859 still trying to justify his actions to the people of Tabor, Brown wrote to Teasdale's paper on why he entered Missouri, "First it has been my deliberate judgment since 1855 that the most ready and effectual way to retrieve Kansas would be to meddle directly with the peculiar institution. Next, we had no means of moving the rescued captives without taking a portion of their lawfully acquired earnings. All we took has been held sacred to that object and will be."[47]

In Grinnell, Iowa, Brown noted a much better reception from Josiah Grinnell and the abolitionists in his town. Brown, still stinging from the rebuke he had received in Tabor, would write to a friend a week later of the great reception he received in Grinnell. Brown wrote of six points in which the Grinnell reaction was more positive than Tabor's resolution of condemnation.[48]

Brown then left Grinnell and went to Springdale and stayed until March 10. Josiah B. Grinnell went to Chicago and arranged for a railcar.

Opposite: **For some reason in 1887, Josiah B. Grinnell accused the people of Tabor of censoring John Brown, not because of the murder and extraordinary theft he had committed, but because they were afraid of retaliation from nearby pro-slavery men. Professor L.F. Parker, head of the Historical Department at the University of Iowa, had an interesting perspective on this matter. He had been in Kansas when it was known as "Bleeding Kansas," he had taught in Grinnell, and had known J.B. Grinnell. Parker had known John Todd and the people of Tabor and he had also known John Brown. Parker pointed out that Grinnell was sadly mistaken on the matter and he had events in the wrong order. Grinnell backpedaled on his charges, and it was obvious he was blinded by his hero worship of John Brown and could not see the man and his shortcomings. (State Historical Society of Iowa—Des Moines.)**

This railcar was sent to West Liberty, Iowa, where it picked up the escaping slaves. They were sent to Chicago where Allan Pinkerton, the famed detective, met them and arranged for a ferry to take them to Canada. John Brown saw his charges ferried to freedom under the flag of the Union Jack.[49]

There has been much discussion about Brown's true motives for going

into Missouri to help slaves to escape. Was he trying to invade the slave state? Was he trying to defend Kansas with the theory that a good offense is a good defense? What was John Brown trying to accomplish?

L.F. Parker wrote to Todd that John Brown had asked him, "What would Oberlin think of his raid?" Parker replied, "Probably as I do, that it was a success as a hint that Missourians live in glass houses and would do well to stop provoking Kansas to throw stones, but as an anti-slavery measure it was a mistake." Brown then stated, "I don't want that. I did it not to defend Kansas but to attack slavery!"[50]

John Brown would claim on this raid he only took one wagon and one team. However, he and his men took much more than one wagon and one team. He took a great deal of livestock and wagons and many portable items of value. Brown tried to justify that all the items taken were held in some kind of a "trust" for the escaping slaves less the expense of transporting them on the Underground Railroad. But there is no evidence to support this notion. Brown and his men were always strapped for cash and it is reasonable to suppose that the escaping slaves saw little recompense for the "liberated" loot that Brown took from Missouri.

Years later this raid by Brown and escape on the Underground Railroad would cause much controversy in the state of Iowa. For some reason Josiah B. Grinnell decided to write an article in the *Iowa State Register* in 1887 detailing Brown's action. The real storm started when Grinnell stated, "Tabor a religious colony in Fremont county, was the nearest station to the slave border, but under threats by incendiaries, and for the general safety, resolved against John Brown and his excursions. This was a grief to the old hero, but the sentiment of that day and the perils to property and persons should be the basis of a charitable opinion of a brave people."[51]

John Todd fired back to Grinnell's baseless charges that the people of Tabor had rejected Brown because they were afraid of retaliation from nearby slave interests. Grinnell wrote another letter to the editor of the *Iowa State Register* backpedaling on this issue. He stated, "In answer to J.T. of Tabor.... Personally I could not have suspicion of the brave and true men of Tabor, whose generous aid to fleeing slaves the world knows. It is my convictions that under all the circumstances, they were deserving of more credit that the citizens of Grinnell, or even the Quakers more remote from the scenes of strife and bloody warfare.... I am the last one to question the action, as I know only the high character of the colony." However, Grinnell went on to say that Brown was somewhat justified in raiding Missouri because the slave faction had produced a plot to kill Brown some two years before this incident.[52]

L. F. Parker was uniquely qualified to discuss this issue with both John Todd and Grinnell. Parker had been an Oberlin College graduate and had gone to Lawrence in the days when that territory was known as "Bleeding Kansas." He later went to Grinnell to teach and became friends with Josiah B. Grinnell. For years he taught history at what was then called Iowa College and later named Grinnell College. After Iowa College, Parker went on to hold the chair of history and comparative philology at the University of Iowa, then the state's largest and most prestigious university.

In a letter to John Todd Parker stated, "J.B.G.'s mistake [was] in saying Tabor was frightened into resolving 'against John Brown.' Parker pointed out Grinnell's misuse of the facts of Brown's actions in Kansas at this time, that Brown had admitted to Parker that he wasn't defending Kansas or himself but attacking slavery when he went into Missouri. Parker went on to say, "which will sustain you as against the forgetfulness of J.B.G. Doubtless Tabor has erred enough to seem human: it is unnecessary to assume that her wise acts were blunders in order to make her humble."[53]

Brown would, however, return to Tabor one more time after the town rebuked him, albeit only for a few hours. He came to this Southwest Iowa town for the last time in September of 1859, less than two months before his raid on Harper's Ferry. Brown stopped by the home of Jonas Jones on a Sabbath day. Jones stepped out onto his porch and Brown told him in a criptive manner, "Good-by, Mr. Jones. I do not say where I am going, but you will hear from me. There has been enough said about 'Bleeding Kansas.' I intend to make a bloody spot at another point, and carry the war into Africa."[54]

On October 16, 1859, John Brown and his 21 men attacked the federal arsenal at Harper's Ferry, Virginia, with the arms that had been stored in the Reverend Todd's basement.

They were successful in seizing the arsenal and other strategic points. Brown's plan was to use the 100,000 weapons stored there to start a guerrilla war in the Blue Ridge Mountains. The weapons would be given to slaves and other sympathizers and Brown felt he could bring the slave states to their knees with this insurrection.

However, his raid proved to be short-lived and in 36 hours most of his men were killed or captured by attacking federal forces led, ironically, by Colonel Robert E. Lee and Lieutenant J.E.B. Stuart. Lee would later lead the Confederate Army in Virginia during the Civil War and Stuart was the most famous of all the Confederate cavalry officers. Old Brown was captured but as defiant as ever. He offered no apologies for the ill-fated raid in Virginia.

Almost immediately the Southern press and members of the Southern caucus in Congress called for the arrest of anyone aiding Brown. The slaveholding interests wanted Brown mainly to incriminate the well known abolitionists and the abolitionist aid societies in Massachusetts and elsewhere.

However, enough people thought of Brown as a madman and the investigations into his raid were not widespread. So the Sharps rifles and other military goods that Brown used were not traced back to Tabor or the Reverend Todd.

The whole country wasn't sure what to make of John Brown. He was condemned even among many abolitionists who counseled the enslaved blacks not to use violence for their liberation. However, the *Liberator*, the voice of William Lloyd Garrison, one of the country's most influential abolitionists and a usual practitioner of the non-violent argument, while critical of Brown for his raid, also warned that as the nation's founding fathers fought for their freedom, the slaves shouldn't be denied the right to fight for their right to freedom.[55]

John Brown was eventually tried for treason and found guilty even though the governor of Virginia was counseled to just put Brown in an insane asylum. The trial became a showcase for the fight against slavery and the protracted argument the nation was experiencing on this subject. Brown was sentenced to death for murder and treason. He was hung and became an instant martyr. He became a hero to many in the abolitionist movement in the North. There has been much discussion as to what role John Brown played in starting the Civil War. Was he the main catalyst to the beginning of this horrible conflict or merely just another player in the march to the inevitable? By the time the Civil War started Brown's image was cemented to the abolitionist community as the radical who saw any means to ending slavery, violent or non-violent, was justified. Brown's martyrdom ensured that his legacy as the premier fighter against the evil of slavery would endure forever.

While many in Tabor saw Brown as a man totally dedicated to the abolition of slavery, as they were, they also saw a deeply flawed human being. Maria Gaston wrote, "He gave his life on the altar of Slavery. He thought his steps were ordered of the Lord ... [such] lives show us much self sacrifice & consecration to the master. To err is human, but I think John Brown a noble specimen of manhood."[56]

Although Brown saw those in Tabor, after his rebuke by the town, as against him, they were only in opposition to some of his tactics, not his message.

11

The War of the Rebellion

John Todd and his fellow abolitionists on the western frontier were excited when Abraham Lincoln, the Republican nominee for the presidency of the United States, won the election of 1860. In a letter from real estate broker E. Fraser from Kansas City, Missouri, to John Todd a few days after the election, Fraser proudly tells Todd that he and 180 other Kansas Citians voted for "Old Abe."[1] These abolitionists naturally hoped that Lincoln would end what John Todd felt was the continued appeasement of the pro-slavery South. Todd also dreamed that Lincoln could somehow end the terrible blight of slavery throughout the southern states and any newly formed territories in the United States.

However, as the election returns came in announcing Lincoln as president, the slave states began to react. The election was held on November 6 of 1860 and by December 14, a call was issued in Georgia for a convention to discuss the formation of a Southern Confederacy. On December 20, the state of South Carolina seceded from the Union. Then Mississippi, Florida, and Alabama seceded from the Union on January 9, 10 and 11 of 1861. Georgia, Louisiana and Texas followed suit. A convention was held in early February of 1861 to form the Confederate States of America. A Confederate Constitution was ratified and passed that had as its cornerstone the preservation of slavery forever.

Jefferson Davis was elected president of the Confederacy and took office before Abraham Lincoln did on March 4, 1861. Virginia, Arkansas and North Carolina seceded from the Union and joined the Confederate States of America. On April 12, 1861, Confederate forces at Ft. Sumter in South Carolina fired upon the Union held fort demanding that the garrison surrender the fort to the Rebels. The War of the Rebellion or as it is

Painting of Abraham Lincoln and Grenville Dodge. E. Fraser excitedly
wrote to John Todd that 180 Kansas Citians voted for Abraham Lincoln

better known, the American Civil War, had begun in earnest. Blood had been shed.

John Todd and the rest of the country were seeing the great union of the United States torn asunder. The newly elected vice president of the Confederacy, Alexander H. Stephens, left little doubt about what the Confederate States of America stood for and what they were all about when he stated in his Cornerstone Address given on March 21, 1861, "Our new government is founded on the opposite idea of equality of the races.... Its corner stone rests upon the great truth that the Negro is not equal to the white man.... [Our] government is the first in the history of the world, based on this great physical and moral truth."

In a sermon given a few days after the Civil War commenced, entitled "Judgment for the Oppressed," John Todd outlined the reasons for the Civil War. In that sermon Todd stated, "The present generation knows nothing of the evils of war, but those evils are upon us. We may have fondly hoped that ... knowledge had banished war forever but the wicked will do wickedly still. The oppressor relaxes his grasp only when compelled to do so ... no more awful scourge can visit than civil war.... It may rightfully be regarded as a judgment for our sins. Slavery ... its moral tendency [is to] corrupt the national conscience. Once it was considered an evil—now it is justified from the bible."[2]

John saw the Civil War as a natural punishment for allowing slavery to exist for so long. Unlike many in America, John also saw as a major national sin the "glorification of the Anglo-Saxon race, as if God had made them lords of earth, & it was their prerogative to trample down others. Might makes right."[3]

John Todd saw the Civil War as God's mighty hand helping the oppressed. In the same sermon he asserted,

> Short sighted, groveling mortals are proof to forget that God has an efficient agency in bringing about passing events. So much accustomed to look at immediate & secondary causes, they fail to discern the hand of the living God.... God interposes in behalf of the weak ... the oppressed against the oppressor.... It is often said that nations are punished in this world, but individuals in the next. Jehovah executes righteousness & judgment for all that are oppressed. He both judges righteously, & inflicts

during the election of 1860. Lincoln's presidency was greeted with excitement by abolitionists like John Todd after the disastrous administrations of Pierce and Buchanan. This painting by C. Everett Johnson depicts a meeting between Lincoln and nearby Council Bluffs, Iowa, resident Grenville Dodge in 1859. Dodge would become a Union general, and Lincoln would tap Dodge to develop the transcontinental railroad. (State Historical Society of Iowa—Des Moines.)

punishment accordingly. If for a time God permits injustice to triumph that men may develop the wickedness of their own hearts, until there seems to be no justice & sense of right in the hearts of men, yet in His own good time He will vindicate His honor & send judgments on the guilty.[4]

John Todd and the rest of Tabor threw themselves into the war effort. Todd spoke out earnestly and eloquently in support of the Union Army and government during the Civil War. Even the early Union losses at Bull Run and elsewhere didn't deter the people of Tabor. They sent their sons, husbands and fathers into the fray. Richard B. Foster, who had founded the Republican Party in Tabor, became an officer for one of the black regiments being raised.[5]

The last few years in the decade of the 1850's and into the decade which began the Civil War much of Iowa had changed its view towards slavery and race. With the election of James W. Grimes first as governor then as United States senator from Iowa and the election of James Harlan as U.S. senator, the state was drifting more to the viewpoint of John Todd and the abolitions, as opposed to the racist mentality as espoused by Augustus Caesar Dodge. The state was being settled more and more by those from free state backgrounds and the support of southern states' slavery laws and views didn't sit well with much of the populace of Iowa. In 1859 when Dodge ran for governor of the Hawkeye state many of his pro-slavery views came back to haunt him in the election and he lost it.

As the war progressed there was some concern in Fremont County that Confederate guerrilla raiders from Missouri might cross the southern border of Iowa and attack somewhere in the county. These bands led by William Quantrill, Bloody Bill Anderson and George Todd (no relation to John Todd) were the scourge of Missouri. For much of the Civil War the regular Confederate Army in the Midwest led by Sterling Price had been driven to the southern part of Missouri, or later completely from the state. Despite forays into the state of Missouri the regular Confederate Army was of little threat to the counties of southern Iowa. In this void Confederate bands sometimes known as irregulars, partisans or guerrilla fighters were formed. Also, the inept occupation of Missouri by the Union Army also drove some Missourians into these bands. Ironically, some of James Lane's Kansas troops in Missouri constantly caused problems for the residents of Missouri for their cruel and sometimes unreasonable conduct towards the citizens of that state.

These Missouri Confederate guerilla bands had as their members many tough customers. Among them were Jesse James, his brother Frank, Cole Younger, Dave Pool, Clell Miller and Archie Clement. These bands stole the best horses in the area and had the latest weapons that they commandeered from various sources. These Confederate raiders were feared all over the Midwest.

In December of 1861, Warren Price and a small group of area Confederate partisans attacked the farmstead of an abolitionist in Southern Fremont County in Iowa, robbing and killing the farmer and molesting his wife. Price's band was broken up with some of his men being killed or wounded.

In 1863 George Todd and his veteran Confederate guerrilla fighters traveled through Fremont County on their way to Nebraska. Since their motives were not known the Fremont County militia trailed them and engaged them in a brief firefight. One of the leaders in the Fremont County militia was killed. However, George Todd and his group left the county without further bloodshed.[6]

William Quantrill rode into Lawrence, Kansas, on August 19, 1863, with 194 men and the intention to kill every man in the town and to burn every house. No females were to be harmed. The one man in Lawrence that Quantrill most wanted to kill was sometime Tabor dweller and now United States senator from Kansas James Lane. Lane had built a new magnificent home in that city. Lane managed to hide from the carnage, but Quantrill's blood bath unfortunately continued. One hundred and eighty-three men and boys lay dead or dying. Quantrill's usual henchmen were with him, Frank James and the Youngers.[7]

Fortunately for its residents, Tabor was not attacked during the Civil War by Confederate partisans or Confederate regulars. The paramilitary units that were raised in Tabor during the troubles of the 1850's would not have to be reactivated. However, death made its way into town, as it always had throughout the ages. Jesse West, the hotelier, restaurateur and blacksmith, was cut down in the prime of life. The man who had provided much aid and comfort to those on the Underground Railroad died November 1, 1861. Todd and the rest of the community were baffled that someone so strong and in the "meridian of life," as John Todd said, could be cut down so quickly by one the many infirmities that were common for the time.[8]

During the war John's brother David became a teacher for the Freedmen's Bureau in Arkansas. The Freedmen's Bureau set up schools to teach newly emancipated slaves to read and write. Under the slave codes it had been illegal to teach slaves to read or write, so a whole generation of freed blacks would be given the gift of literacy. The Rebel Army counterattacked the Union forces in Arkansas and the Rebels were only twenty miles from David Todd's Freedmen's Bureau school. Any white person caught trying to improve the condition of the black race was often executed or imprisoned. All of the teachers except David and another left the school for safety. David managed to hold the school together until the Union Army drove the Confederates from the area.[9]

John Todd and other abolitionists were elated when President Lincoln issued the Emancipation Proclamation on January 1, 1863. Prayer services had been held in Tabor from its inception praying for the end of that vile institution. The Emancipation Proclamation only freed slaves in the Southern states that were not controlled by the Union Army but it still allowed slavery in Southern areas controlled by the Union Army. To all abolitionists, however, it was obvious that slavery as an institution was on its way out of the fabric of the American experience.

The Civil War continued without resolution through the years of 1862, 1863 and 1864. Military blunders by Generals McClelland and other top Union commanders consistently failed to take advantage of the North's superiority in men and materials. John Todd and the others in Tabor followed the news from the war fronts as soon as it was published in the newspapers. Letters from sons and fathers who were on the front lines also provided much information as to the course of the war.

In early January of 1863 the Reverend Todd made a journey to Camp Hamilton in Virginia in the military district of Washington, D.C. Todd was given a military pass through the Union lines. Although the purpose of his trip is unclear, in all probability he was visiting soldiers from Tabor. The military pass he received stated the reason for the pass was for "visiting."[10] The Reverend Todd was always willing to go above and beyond the call of duty to comfort those in his flock.

During the summer of 1864 a call was sent out all over the Union for 100 day volunteers. It was felt the South was on its last legs and if the Union made one big push with a massive build-up in men, then the Confederacy could be brought to the surrender table.

John Todd's eldest son James, age 18, was attending Oberlin College when the call went out for the 100 day volunteers. He joined the 150th Ohio Infantry Company K on May 7 as a private. The company was made up of mostly Oberlin College students. With little training young Todd and his regiment were sent to Ft. Stevens in Washington, D.C.[11]

General Ulysses Grant had been named commander-in-chief of the Union Armies in March of 1864. He began a campaign of constantly engaging the Confederate forces of Robert E. Lee with the ultimate goal being Richmond, Virginia, the capital of the Confederacy. Up until this time Civil War commanders usually would engage in one, two or three day battles and whoever was left on the field of combat was declared the winner. The two sides would then re-supply and gather reinforcements until they were able to fight again. Grant correctly reasoned that the Confederate Armies couldn't sustain the losses in men and material if they were constantly engaged in battle.

Grant's army of blue sliced through Virginia first with the Wilderness

Campaign, then Spotsylvania, then at Cold Harbor, where the Union Army lost 7,000 men in 20 minutes. They then fought at Petersburg and settled into a siege of the town. Robert E. Lee decided to try and take pressure off his position at Petersburg and he sent General Jubal Early and 10,000 of his men on a flanking maneuver to attack Washington, D.C. Early drove up through Maryland to position his men to assault the Union capital. Early's seasoned veterans attacked in the suburbs of Washington, D.C., coming within five miles of the city.[12]

In this grand master strategy of Lee and Grant an eighteen year old private, James E. Todd, found himself. Todd and his fellow raw recruits from Ohio were soon on the front lines of the Civil War. After Early's attack even government clerks deep in the bowels of the bureaucracy of Washington, D.C., armed themselves and joined in defending the capital. Grant diverted troops from the front to help defend the seat of the Union government.

James Todd wrote to his father that starting on July 11, 1864, on a Monday morning at 10 o'clock, the Confederates began attacking Fort Stevens. The fighting lasted until late Tuesday night of the 12th. Early's Rebels were at times within 300 yards of the fort, firing upon the green recruits of Todd's Company K. Fortunately young Todd was not harmed. Company K only sustained one fatality. Todd also reported that President Abraham Lincoln and his aides were in the fort during the Rebel attack.[13]

James E. Todd managed to serve out his term of enlistment with the 150th Ohio Infantry regiment. After Early's attack the regiment mostly did garrison duties at Ft. Stevens. He went back to Oberlin College in the fall of 1864 and continued his schooling and received a bachelor of arts degree in 1867. James then attended Union Theological Seminary in New York for two years. Young Todd then returned to Oberlin and completed his work on a seminary degree. Todd also received a master of arts degree from Oberlin.[14]

On May 9, 1864, a public meeting was called in the Tabor Schoolhouse to make a suitable response to the governor of Iowa's request for 10,000 100 day volunteers. Many in Tabor volunteered to go. Those who didn't go pledged to harvest the crops of those who had left Tabor to join the Union Army.[15]

John Todd was 45 years old when he volunteered to be a chaplain for one of the newly formed 100 day units. Service in the Union Army was a very important ideal for John Todd. Todd's ancestors had a long history of military service to this country. Obviously, because of his age and the fact that he had a congregation in Tabor that needed his full time leadership, service in the Union Army was out of the question. When the concept of the 100 day volunteers came up this seemed to be a perfect solution for John to fulfill his desire to serve the country whose ideas momentarily were more in line with his own concerning freedom and equality. Originally John was to go with the 29th Iowa Infantry but was ultimately assigned to the 46th Iowa Infantry.[16]

The 46th Iowa Infantry was formed in Davenport. John was mustered in on June of 1864.[17] John's mustering in papers stated that he was appointed from civil life by the governor of Iowa.[18] The 46th Iowa Infantry would be shipped out; first the unit went to Cairo, Illinois, and then on to Tennessee.[19] The unit's mission in Tennessee would be to mostly guard railroad tracks and other infrastructure facilities. Confederate regulars and irregulars were constantly attacking trains and tearing up railroad tracks, slowing down the progress of the Union Army in its invasion of the South.

The life of a chaplain in the Union Army at this time was varied and at times trying. While the 46th received very few battle deaths or casualties, death by disease visited the 46th, as it did most of the Union and Confederate armies. It was the primary killer of uniformed men. Once in Tennessee John Todd settled into the grueling life of a field chaplain in the Union Army. A Civil War commentator remarked that sometimes privates, officers and even chaplains changed their attitudes once they were in the field. Oftentimes they would commence to cuss, drink and even carouse around like the other soldiers. A native of Tabor wrote of John Todd, "We know that *his* life in the army was not *the* life in *the* army. It was just as pure in the camp as it was in his own home. His words were just as earnest, just as clean when he talked to the soldiers around the camp fire as when he spoke from the sacred desk here in Tabor. He knew the men."[20]

John received letters on a variety of matters reflecting the often diverse duties of a Civil War chaplain. Chaplain Todd sometimes heard from parents or relatives of the men in his regiment. Many naturally worried about their sons, husbands and fathers. In one case John heard from a father of a soldier who was concerned because his son had never professed his belief in God or Jesus Christ. The father was worried that his son would pass onto the other side without professing to be a Christian.[21] Part of John's duties was to convince parents and relatives that their loved ones were right with God. A parent or wife might write John asking him to check on their loved one who was in the hospital.[22]

John received an unusual letter from a soldier in the officer's hospital in Memphis. John apparently was given a sword that was found by the railroad tracks. The officer who had lost the sword gave a detailed description of it to John in hopes of getting it back.[23]

In a letter from a man named David Worcester, John was asked to give Worcester a recommendation to become a chaplain in the Union Army, possibly a chaplain to a black unit. Worcester, who was stationed on Island 63 below Helena, Arkansas, tells of the fine crop of cotton being raised on the island by freed blacks. Worcester also related to Todd that the island was being guarded by two companies of black troops.

Letters from home were always appreciated and John's wife, Martha, and his daughters wrote often. They told of family news and of the news of the people of Tabor and of his church. Letters from home were always morale boosters. In one letter John's daughter Maggie tells of the president of the Tabor Literary Institute, William Brooks, going down to St. Louis to visit a freedmen's school located at the Benton Barracks in that city.

During the summer and fall of 1864 Northern Missouri had been wracked with violence by Confederate guerrilla fighters who attacked trains and stages and took any other disruptive measures they could. Most of these actions were undertaken by the men of Bloody Bill Anderson. Anderson's men would include Jesse James, Frank James, Arch Clements, Cole Younger and many others who would later ride with the James-Younger gang. Maggie wrote that Brooks made it to St. Louis without being attacked by the guerrillas but Brooks did say he had seen one "copperhead" from Sidney.[24] A copperhead was a northerner who was not in favor of the Union war effort against the Confederate States.

John's abilities as a chaplain were never in doubt. One man in his regiment felt that John treated everyone the same whether they were private or officer, black or white. This man reported, "Father Todd not only preached every Sunday, but we had a prayer meeting on Wednesday evening, too. There was one of those little earthworks where we used to go and hold prayer meeting. Father Todd was there always.... One of the most earnest prayers I ever heard from mortal lips I heard from him. It was beside the cot of a ... colored man, who had just been taken from slavery, and the musket put in his hands, and who was mortally wounded. He was one chaplain who was earnest, constant in season and out of season, doing his duty no matter where it was."[25]

Although the 46th Iowa Infantry saw no action in any major battles, they were involved in skirmishes and other military action. This action usually was the result of Rebels trying to disrupt railroad travel or ambushing small groups of federal soldiers. On one occasion two members of the 6th Illinois Cavalry had been captured by the Confederates. About a dozen and a half men were sent out to try and get them back from the Rebels. This group of the 46th Iowa Infantry was then ambushed by a much larger party of Rebels and was forced back into camp. The unit took several casualties and four men were taken prisoners.[26]

John Todd served out his term of enlistment. After being mustered out of service with the rest of the 46th Iowa Infantry, he headed back to Tabor, Iowa. There he was reunited with his family and friends and resumed his position as pastor of the Tabor Congregational Church. The 100 day recruitment program by the Union Army had given many veterans needed rest and at places like Ft. Stevens they had played an important role in blunting Confederate advances. However, the program didn't bring the Confederates to the surrender table as it was hoped.

Grant would continue his siege of Petersburg, Virginia, in what would become World War I type trench warfare. The siege would last for 10 months. General William T. Sherman would begin his "march to the sea" in November to December of 1864. Union General George Thomas completely destroyed the Rebel forces of General John Bell Hood at the battles of Nashville and Franklin. The Confederate Armies were being ground down, taking casualties and expending material that could not be replaced.

John Todd read the accounts of the Union victories but the Confederate States would not give in. Suffering terrible hardships, the soldiers and civilians of the Rebel states wouldn't unconditionally surrender—the only terms that Grant would accept. As 1865 rolled around the Union war machine was in full bloom. Grant, Sherman and Thomas commanded huge armies. In Tabor the summer of 1864 had been very hot and wet, providing a good corn crop.[27] The farms around Tabor were supplying the war economy with as much as they could. The Union was taking all the excess crops Fremont County could produce.

As January of 1865 rolled around John Todd received a letter addressed to "My Dear Chaplain" from an Army comrade. In the letter the writer expresses, "A triumphant thrill [passes] through my heart when I converse with Coy [a freed slave] and look at the decaying carcass of slavery."[28] The end was coming. Slavery was in its death throes. This horrible institution was finally ending in the country that proclaimed in its Declaration of Independence, "We hold these truths to be self-evident, that all men are created equal, that they are endowed by their Creator with certain unalienable Rights, that among these are Life, Liberty and the pursuit of Happiness." On April 2, 1865, Grant took Petersburg and then Richmond; the Confederate capital fell. Lee and his men retreated to Appomattox. Finally on April 9, 1865, at the Appomattox Courthouse, Lee surrendered to Grant. Tabor celebrated as did the rest of the nation over the end of the great national struggle.

However, jubilation was short lived, as the assassination of President Abraham Lincoln on April 14 brought the joyful mood of the country to a standstill. The abolitionists of Tabor were stunned when their hero, "Old Abe," had been murdered. Lincoln had not only freed the slaves, he was also advocating giving them the vote and seeing that they were assimilated into the society as a whole. This was the point of view that the people of Oberlin and Tabor had long advocated.

As the sons, fathers and husbands of Tabor came back from Civil War service it was decided that the citizens would hold a celebration for the "boys in blue." Tabor had managed to escape the carnage of death and casualties that many communities in the North and South had experienced, although, most notably, George Gaston's son Alonzo had died during his service to the Union cause in 1863. On August 2, 1865, at a public meeting the citizens of Tabor formed a committee to formally welcome back the Union Army veterans.[29]

John Todd knew that even though slavery had ended there was still much work to be done to help the newly freed humans. John and especially his wife Martha helped to financially support a student at a freedman's school in Tougaloo, Mississippi.[30]

During the 1850's John Todd had concentrated his energies on the Underground Railroad and the Jim Lane Trail. In the early 1860's the Civil War had consumed Todd's energy. Now he could channel his vision, heart and mind in creating a college like Oberlin, one that would be an institution that promoted equality among the races and genders. The idea of equality and a college that promoted this ideal had been John Todd's dream.

12

A Dream Fulfilled

After the bloody conflict of the American Civil War was over John Todd and the citizens of Tabor were elated that the institution of slavery was defeated. They were trying to put their lives back into some kind of perspective and normalcy. Their first priority, of course, would be to build a school that would resemble Oberlin College and its ideals.

However, four years of the Civil War plus the previous years of sacrifice had left the town in less than prosperous conditions. The years of the Underground Railroad, John Brown, the James Lane Trail and the Kansas immigration through Tabor had left many in the town devoid of much extra cash needed to finance a college. Tabor's generosity to the cause of freedom had left many in the position of just keeping their heads above water.

However, the subject of the college was always on everyone's mind. Shortly after Tabor was founded a group of 38 pioneers came from Oberlin to settle in Tabor. They brought with them a bell to hang from the college's chapel.[1]

In 1857 Origen Cummings went to Oberlin to find a principal for the Tabor Literary Institute. Since the town didn't have the funds to support a college it was decided to open an academy and high school. This institution was named the Tabor Literary Institute. While in Oberlin James H. Fairchild recommended an up and coming student who had just graduated from Oberlin College named William Brooks for the principal position in Tabor. Brooks had been teaching in rural areas during his vacation and Fairchild thought he would do a splendid job in Tabor. Brooks was highly recommended by various professors at Oberlin.[2] He hoped to use the funds he earned at the Tabor Literary Institute to continue his theology studies at Oberlin Seminary.

Brooks made the tiresome journey from Oberlin to Iowa via train and stagecoach and at one point he even rode in a lumber wagon to get to his destination. After he reached the Southwest Iowa town in late October, the directors of the school agreed to pay Brooks $500, all his travel expenses above $50 and two dollars a week for room, board and laundry.[3]

Brooks wasted no time in getting the school started and commenced classes on November 3, 1857. Seventeen scholars attended this first session. Brooks did a marvelous job teaching all phases of English, algebra, geometry, physiology, Latin and Greek.

After the end of his first year Brooks decided to stick with his original plan and use the money he had earned at Tabor to continue his religious studies at Oberlin Seminary. Many in the Tabor community tried to change Brooks' mind but he was earnest in his convictions to obtain a seminary degree and he left Tabor for Oberlin.

George B. Bushnell was then hired to teach and run the school the second year. However, Bushnell, in the words of John Todd, was "radically defective."[4] George Gaston's opinion of Bushnell was hardly any better; Gaston called him a "miserable failure."[5] The school had to be closed after only 10 weeks with many of the students saying they would not go back if Bushnell was the teacher. Others in Tabor, such as Jonas Jones and Edwin Hill, wrote to Brooks telling him of the dire predicament the school found itself in with the ineffective Bushnell.[6]

Many Taborites felt that without the return of Brooks the whole college project was in jeopardy. John Todd wrote to Brooks offering $500 per annum plus whatever more Brooks could realize from tuition bills. Todd pleaded with Brooks to come to "our aid."[7] George Gaston also wrote to Brooks wanting him to return to Tabor. Gaston pointed out that Brooks' skill as a teacher was a "calling" just as was the ministry. Gaston also wrote to Brooks of a brick building 40 by 60 feet and three stories high that Tabor was planning to build for the school.[8]

On March 31, 1859, a despondent group met to discuss the future of the Tabor Literary Institute. A union school or grade school was discussed, as the idea of a college or academy seemed out of the question. Without the proper leadership the Tabor Literary Institute could not be turned into Tabor College. The Tabor colony's dream for an Oberlin type of institution seemed out of reach. It was decided to go with a grade school or union school. However, two weeks later on April 14, 1859, a letter was read at the town meeting that electrified the group. William Brooks had agreed to come back and be principal and teacher of the academy. The dream of an Oberlin type college was still a possibility. Brooks would receive his $500 a year salary and he was allowed to collect an additional $100 per year in tuition payments from those who attended from another school district or who were over twenty-one years of age.[9]

Fortunately, the discouraged scholars of the year before decided to give the academy another chance. However, another danger raised its head that had the potential to derail the college and town of Tabor. This danger was "gold fever." Just as the California gold rush of 1849 about ruined the Todd-Gaston plans for immigrating to Tabor, the Pikes Peak "gold rush" of 1859 caused some panic in town. Some of the citizens wanted to abandon their plans for a western Oberlin for the "riches" of the Colorado gold fields.

Wagons began rolling into Iowa marked "Pikes Peak or Bust." Gold had been found in Colorado and many were talking of heading West, even those in Fremont County and Tabor. The only paper in Fremont County at that time, the *Fremont Herald*, reported, "The tides of immigration continues to pour through our streets, and today there are a dozen or 15 immigrant wagons and about a hundred head of oxen lined up waiting to load supplies for the trip to the gold fields." The *Fremont Herald* went on, "We learn 700 or 800 head of cattle have been brought into the vicinity of McKissick's Grove. The idea seems to be to have them handy to Sidney for the emigrants who will outfit here for the goldfields."[10]

John Todd was worried that even some of the faithful in Tabor might succumb to the promise of gold riches. If the fledgling town lost much of its population it could possibly scuttle the college project. In a letter to William Brooks the Reverend wrote, "There is however just now an increase disposition among the people in this region to go to the gold mines in the spring. Even some of our staid people think of going. Pike's Peak & Cherry Creek are becoming the absorbing topics of conversation. People are already abroad buying cattle as a preparatory step. Money has been very scarce, but this stir is likely to improve the money market or rather the market for produce of all kinds. We begin to feel its influence already & expect it to increase for months to come. We have such information respecting the mines, from a reliable source, that thousands will doubtless be found rushing westward with the opening spring. Many exaggerated statements are found in newspapers yet it is not all humbug—its influence will, I fear, be disastrous to the religious interest of the country for 'how hardly shall they that have riches enter into the kin. [Kingdom] of God! Oh! how bewitching is the love of gain!' Yet 'if any man love the world the love of the Father is not in him.'"[11]

John Todd was able to keep most of Tabor focused on the important work they had to do in Iowa, such as the Underground Railroad and the college. The exodus that the gold rush seemed to predict auspiciously never materialized in the Reverend Todd's flock. However, one who left for the gold fields of Colorado had a tragic ending. Henry Carpenter had left Tabor for the supposed riches of the glittering gold fields. He did not find the treasures he had hoped for. On his way back to Tabor he was murdered near Salt

Creek, Nebraska, in the middle of March in 1859. The Reverend Todd held belated services for Carpenter in Tabor on May 22, 1859. The town remained intact and concentrated on their Underground Railroad duties and their work to keep Kansas free from slavery. The college project was never far from everyone's mind.

When the Civil War broke out of course plans to build the college were put on the back burner. However, John Todd was true to his promise to let William Brooks explore other avenues of income. While Brooks was principal of the Tabor Literary Institute he also added to his income the position as the superintendent for the Fremont County Schools during the Civil War. In 1864 Brooks' salary as the superintendent of the Fremont County Schools was $200 per year.[12]

After the Civil War ended John Todd and the citizens of Tabor met several times to consider starting a college. Financing the college was, of course, a major consideration. George Gaston came forward with an incredible offer. Gaston stated at a town meeting, "I have felt ever since coming into the West, and especially when in a most spiritual frame of mind, that I was making property for this one object—to put into an institution, where the young people who should be educated, should go out into the world as Christians, and I will now give from my capital all that can be spared from my business and carry that forward successfully. I am willing to leave it to others to say how much that shall be, I will devote my income to the college; and, if necessary to its success, I will put in every dollar I have, and begin anew." Gaston gave some $2,000 in cash plus notes for $2,000. His property was assessed on the tax books for $4,000 with a real value of $9,000.[13]

John Todd, on a yearly salary of $800, pledged $1,000 and over the next few years another $1,000 was given. Todd taught at the college three years and never took a dime in salary. He acted for many years as librarian, again at no salary. At various times he served as secretary, treasurer and auditor for the college with no compensation. Three of the Reverend Todd's children graduated from Tabor College but he never availed himself of the free tuition given to children of ministers in active service, but preferred to pay the tuition in full for the sake of the college.[14]

William Brooks noted that the first nineteen donors in Tabor gave 60 percent of the assessed value of their property. He noted that more than one half of the adult population of Tabor had donated to the college.[15]

When $25,000 had been raised by the citizen of Tabor, the Tabor Literary Institute became Tabor College. The dream of an Oberlin-like college was becoming a reality. Mrs. Todd's uncle, Josiah Atkins, donated his private library and that became the nucleus of the beginning of the Tabor College library.[16]

Gaston Hall of Tabor College. After the Civil War had ended the residents of Tabor felt they could put their energies into building an institution of higher learning like Oberlin College. They named it Tabor College. Gaston Hall was named for George Gaston and had its cornerstone placed in June of 1886. It was dedicated in April of 1887. Gaston Hall served the college for many years. The building was demolished in 1951. (Todd House Museum Archives.)

However, building a college on the prairie was no easy matter. Within twelve miles of Tabor seven institutions of higher learning had been attempted with no success. In Louden, a town eight miles from Tabor, an institution with the prestigious name of Columbia University was attempted. An impressive three story building was built at a cost of $16,000, a large sum for the time. A tornado whipped through the town and blew the building down, thus Columbia University of Louden, Iowa, ended before even one student had entered the university.[17]

The college started and with minor exception went off without a hitch. Men and women and persons of color were admitted. However, trying to create an endowment and financing for the college proved to be a never ending project.

In a letter to the Reverend Theron Baldwin of the Society to Aid Western Colleges and Seminaries, John Todd solicited funds for Tabor College.

John also wrote that he was upset by the news that the friends of the Congregational college in Grinnell, Iowa, had been telling funding sources in the northeastern part of the United States that they should only support one congregational college in Iowa. That college of course was the one in Grinnell and not the one in Tabor. John went on to write that Grinnell was 200 miles from Tabor and they were not in competition with each other for students.[18]

The Reverend Jonathan Cable was hired to go east to some of the Congregational strongholds and try to raise money in the larger cities such as New York and Philadelphia. However, this proved not to be successful. He did raise some small amounts of money but not in the sums needed to create financial freedom for the college. In one case Cable received a donation of a sewing machine that he thought they could sell and turn into cash.[19] The Reverend Cable managed to get donations of books for the college but only slight amounts of cash donations.[20]

The people of Tabor were resourceful to keep costs to a minimum. When a new building was constructed for a dormitory and dining area in 1868–69, Tabor College purchased the window and door frames from the defunct Columbia University.

Tabor College provided course work in the scientific, classical and literary disciplines. Two degrees were conferred by the college, a bachelor of arts or a bachelor of science degree. Men and women attended classes on equal footing. A two year teaching course was also offered, as was a three year ladies' diploma, if a four year degree was not needed.[21]

After the Civil War was over John Todd turned his natural crusading nature from the abolition of slavery to that of the growing temperance movement to discourage the drinking of alcohol. Liquor had always been part of the American frontier. Heavy drinking had been accepted among many of the veterans of the Civil War. However, many felt the human misery that was caused by alcoholism, how it contributed to poverty and illness, and the toll on family life were not worth it. The per capita consumption of hard liquor was twice as much before and after the Civil War as it is now.

John Todd and many other reformers saw the abolition of drinking as a solution to this problem of drunkenness and all the social woes that came along with it. For the most part they sought to have people sign pledges to stop drinking and to petition the state legislature in Iowa to abolish the consumption of alcohol, as Kansas did in 1880 by constitutional measures. It was a quixotic project. But John Todd attacked it with the fervor he had used with all his other crusades.

However, one of Tabor's crusades to keep its citizens on the honorable high ground might have been a little bit of moral overkill. A circus was making its rounds in Southwest Iowa and was performing in Glenwood. John

Todd and others got wind of this and decided it would be best if the people of Tabor not be subjected to the circus. A petition was passed and signed
by many of the leading citizens of Tabor. People were told not to grant the
circus permission to let them use their land for a performance. John Todd
and Dr. John F. Sanborn were assigned the task to contact the managers of
the circus to tell them to bypass Tabor. Their mission was not successful and
the circus did perform in the Tabor area.[22]

The incident of the circus was a good indication that while Todd and
Gaston and other leaders in Tabor were highly respected, their word was
not the final say. They allowed those in Tabor to express their free will. And
they never exerted undue pressure on the people of the town to conform to
their wishes.

On May 1, 1873, one of the lions of Tabor died when George Gaston
passed away at age 50. John Todd said of Gaston's passing, "For days our
village wore a subdued aspect. All seemed to feel that they had lost a friend.
He is missed at home. He is missed on the streets, missed at the Town Council, missed at the prayer-meeting, missed at the church meeting, missed in

**Adams Hall of Tabor College. Named for Deacon Samuel Adams, this
structure served the college for many years. The building still stands and
was converted to apartments a few years ago and still is being used.
(Todd House Museum Archives.)**

the choir, missed in the Sabbath school, missed by many who looked up to him as in a spiritual father."[23]

Even in his death George Gaston continued giving to the town of Tabor and the college. He left in his will a piece of real estate for the college. As the town of Tabor grew it became apparent that the Congregational Church would need its own building. The Reverend Todd was building the flock at a rate that it was becoming one of the larger Congregational churches in Iowa even though Tabor didn't have a big population base. What became known as the chapel building for the college had served the town as a church, a school and as a meeting house. A separate building would be needed to house Todd's church.

The Congregational Church in Tabor was designed by the Reverend J. K. Nutting, then the pastor at the Congregational Church in Glenwood. Nutting had been the pastor at the famed "Little Brown Church in the Vale" near Nashua, Iowa, when it was built. So it was not surprising that the Tabor Congregational Church was patterned after it. Finally in June of 1875 the building was completed.[24]

Tabor College of course welcomed all minorities and although great numbers of minorities did not attend the college its fame as a hospitable place for blacks became well known. In 1880 two young black men, William Bankston and Edward Blacksheler, came north out of Louisiana to study at Tabor College. They had been born in slavery. It was believed that Bankston was from a small town some 90 miles north of New Orleans. It was believed that Blacksheler graduated from the college but it was thought that Bankston was not a graduate. Bankston remained in Tabor for the rest of his life. He raised potatoes, onions and other small vegetables on a large scale. He had a large potato planting and digging machines and a large potato cave to keep the produce fresh as long as possible.

Bankston was always generous to Tabor College and the church with his gifts. He lived frugally and acquired a 40 acre farm and another 18½ acre plot. Bankston also owned some stocks. He died in Tabor on June 21, 1935, and was greatly missed by those in the town.[25]

The star of the faculty at Tabor College was James E. Todd, eldest son of John Todd. James was born in Ohio.[26] He grew up in the Underground Railroad days of Tabor and under his mother's tutelage he learned Greek before age eight.[27] He became a young man during the Civil War. James entered Oberlin College as a freshman in 1863.

By 1864 the pull of this struggle between slavery and freedom became too great and James, as mentioned before, joined the 150th Ohio Infantry as a 100 day recruit. He saw action at Ft. Stevens in Washington, D.C. After his term of duty was up young Todd went back to Oberlin, where he continued his academic career and graduated from that institution in 1867.

James then went to Union Seminary in New York for two years but returned to Oberlin. During his senior year he filled the pulpits at Amherst and South Amherst, Ohio. It was never young Todd's intention to become a minister but rather to understand the complex questions that concerned the religious and scientific communities at that time.[28] The biblical accounts were being brought into question by new scientific information and methods, such as the discovery of dinosaur bones and the theory of evolution. James wanted to understand both sides in such a way as not to compromise either his beliefs or his intelligence.

He graduated from Oberlin Seminary in 1870 and also received a master of arts degree from that institution.[29] Young Todd then for a year continued his advanced scientific studies at the Scheffield Scientific School at Yale.[30]

James Todd then went to Tabor College, where he spent the next ten years directing its department of natural science. After this stint at Tabor College James then spent two years as a professor at Beloit College in Wisconsin. He returned to Tabor College for another nine years. In 1893 Todd accepted a position as professor of geology and mineralogy at the University of South Dakota. James stayed at this university for ten years. For two years at that institution he acted as president. While in South Dakota Todd also took the position as state geologist. From 1881 to 1907 James Todd was an assistant geologist for the United States Geological Survey.

In 1907 James Todd crowned his distinguished academic career by becoming a professor of geology and mineralogy at the University of Kansas. He held this position until his death 15 years later. He was well respected at all of his posts. Professor Todd wrote for many of the leading scientific and scholarly magazines of his day and also produced a book. In preparing one of his articles for the magazine *The American Naturalist*, he corresponded with Charles Darwin, the famed theorist and scientist.[31]

James was unusual in that he was a scientist who also was trained in a seminary. Professor Todd had the intellectual honesty not to ignore scientific truths to bend to the shifting sands of current popular religious dogma. New discoveries in the scientific community only strengthened James' faith; they did not make him run from common sense or the betterment of mankind.

While heading the science department at Tabor College Professor Todd turned it into one of the best in the nation for a school of its size. While James was in charge the natural science department boasted of having over 10,000 specimens. Some of them were on loan from the Smithsonian Institute.[32]

One of the factors that deeply impacted Tabor and its college was the lack of a railroad. It was ironic that the town that was so deeply involved in the Underground Railroad was bypassed by the overland railroad. During this time in the history of the United States to be bypassed by the railroad was almost a death knell for a town or any kind of enterprise.

In 1889 plans were developed to create a railroad from Tabor to Malvern, Iowa, the nearest railhead. The distance was only ten miles. The college would own the railroad and its equipment. A person from the college would be president of the small railroad line. This enterprise was called the Tabor-Northern Railroad. It lasted for almost ten years until the college decided to get out of the railroad business.

The Reverend John Todd never stopped trying to evangelize for the church, from the early days before the Civil War when he rode a circuit and tried to start churches in communities that had no places of worship to the later years when his duties in Tabor took up most of his time. His influence in this area of Iowa was tremendous and he was revered almost to the point of adulation. He was known then and is still revered today as "Father Todd."

John Todd and the college were very influential in the surrounding area of Tabor. They helped established churches in the area and promoted Southwest Iowa. One such church was in Shenandoah, Iowa. John had very prophetically written about this area even before the town was in existence. In a letter to his father-in-law, Q.F. Atkins, in 1857, John Todd mentioned the sale of vacant lands "on the boundless prairie 10 or 18 miles E. of Sidney."[33]

However, it took almost 14 years before the area was settled and the town of Shenandoah was formed. A Dartmouth College graduate and headmaster for a successful New England Academy, A. S. Lake, followed his brother David to this town when it was little more than prairie. Lake, a strong Congregationalist, after a few years in Shenandoah wanted to begin a church. John Todd sat on the board to help counsel Lake and his fledgling worshipers. Before a church building was erected services were held and John's son, James E. Todd, conducted the first of these religious services. After Lake and his fellow residents of Shenandoah had built their church William Brooks conducted the first worship meeting. The Shenandoah church was able to hire William Plested of New York City as their first full-time pastor.

It is interesting to note that the members of this church turned this Southwest Iowa town into one of the leading seed and nursery capitals in the nation, with at one time several thousand acres of growing trees and shrubs in the surrounding area. The town was also headquarters to dozens of lawn and garden centers. The Lake, Henry Fields, Earl May, Rankin and Welsh families all called this Shenandoah church their home. Earl May and Henry Fields were pioneers of radio broadcasting in the Midwest with the May family amassing a large broadcasting empire.[34]

Dr. P. Adelstein Johnson, who later became President of the Congregational Conference in Iowa, said this about Father Todd, "When he led in the pastoral prayer ... the worshiper felt the Lord had been fully advised with reference to our human needs ... his venerable appearance with his patriarchal white beard seemed to warm the whole atmosphere of the church.[35]

In 1883 at age 65 John Todd decided to retire from his pastorate at the Tabor Congregational Church. John had held only two pastorates. One was in Clarksfield, Ohio, and the other one in Tabor. Although John retired from the ministry, he didn't retire from life. He kept active in the college and other causes he felt were important for the betterment of mankind. John did, however, speak from the pulpit in Tabor on various occasions after his retirement. The parishioners always enjoyed those times.

John Todd and his wife enjoyed a large circle of friends and relatives with whom they had regular correspondence: John's sister in Pennsylvania, his brother and cousins in California, friends and relatives in Ohio and Michigan, friends in Mississippi, her sister in New York, and relatives in Louisiana and other states.

In an interesting letter Martha's sister Mary begged the Todds to come to Louisiana as missionaries as the South was reconstructing after the Civil War. She coyly stated, "We [Mary and her husband] never go to church & I seldom go out of our yard, Don't you think yours would be a missionary life, should you come?"[36]

On July 20, 1888, tragedy shook John Todd's life to its foundation. His beloved helpmate and companion Martha died. Martha Todd had grown up in a nice middle class family and could have taken an easy path in life, but instead she chose the extremely hard existence of a frontier minister's wife.[37]

Mrs. Todd had a beautiful singing voice and was an important part of the Oberlin College music contingent. While living in Tabor Mrs. Todd was the first schoolteacher in Ross Township. During the early years of Tabor College Martha taught vocal music. During John Todd's regular church services Martha would sing. Many parishioners looked forward to her musical offerings.[38]

Martha Todd had suffered from epilepsy for some twenty years before her death. As she neared her end she also suffered severe pain and other infirmities. In a letter Pastor G.G. Rice of Council Bluffs tried to comfort John Todd and tell him his dear wife was free from these challenges.[39]

John missed his wife deeply. Without his mate he seemed lost. During the winter of that year he traveled to California to visit friends in the Golden Bear state. When summer came around he helped his daughter Minnie secure a homestead claim in Drakola, Kingsbury County, South Dakota.[40]

John came back to Tabor a very lonely man. But fate intervened and John met a refined lady named Mrs. Anna K. Drake. On March 26, 1891, they quietly married. One of the most touching letters in the Todd House collection occurred at this time when John had remarried. Martha Todd's sister, Bertha Judson, who had carried on a regular correspondence with her and John throughout the years, wrote an extremely poignant letter to John after her sister had passed away and John had remarried.

The sometimes awkward mores of the Victoria era often prescribed that true feelings be submerged in favor of a rigorous adherence to conformity to society's wishes for "proper appearances." Bertha stated that she still considered John her brother even though his wife, her sister, had died. Bertha was happy to hear that John still thought of her as a sister. She closed her letter with "with love to yourself & wife ... ever your sister."[41]

John spent his remaining years with his new wife and carried on correspondence with friends and relatives who were too far away for personal visits. The newlyweds seemed happy. They did some traveling and visited the World's Columbia Exposition in Chicago during September of 1893. When in Tabor John carried on with his usual reform efforts.

On January 31, 1894, John and Deacon J. M. Hill had divided the town into two parts to get signatures to sign a temperance petition. The state of Iowa was going to pass laws to ease certain restrictions on alcohol consumption. John and the temperance movement were against this modification and hoped to petition the state legislature. Hill would get signatures in half the town and John would get signatures in the other half. They had to work fast, as they needed to get the petition in the mail that day. They only stayed a few minutes at each stop.

John seemed to be in good health and even teased with one signer when she said, "Yes, I can sign anything you present to me." John joked, "Don't be too sure of that!"[42]

John Todd proceeded to the farm of Reuben Reeves that was about a half a mile outside of town. There was a considerable hill to climb to get to the Reeves farmhouse and the cold January air made his lungs ache.

After Todd had arrived at the Reeves home the farmer, seeing something wasn't quite right, offered John a chair to rest and warm himself. John sat down and in only a minute after he was seated he threw up his hands and let out a gasp. The grand old man of the Underground Railroad was dead.[43]

John Todd died as he would have wanted—engaged in doing God's work to make mankind's lot in life better. His funeral and memorial services would be major events in Southwest Iowa. Pastor Cowan, who took over John's pastorate at the Congregational Church in Tabor, The Reverend G.G. Rice from Council Bluffs and J.K. Nutting of Glenwood and others spoke at his funeral.

After John was gone the college that had been his dream struggled. Even though Midwest business mogul N.P. Dodge was on its board of directors for a number of years, the college needed constant financial transfusions.[44]

The college received another serious setback a year and a half after John Todd's death when William Brooks resigned, as he was of retirement age. The board of trustees talked him into staying another year. Brooks an asthmatic would retire to California to help his medical condition.[45]

Tabor College had a good succession of faculty and presidents but its nagging problem of not having a significant endowment plagued the institution. For the first two decades in the 20th century the college became the lifeblood of the town. Its graduates became teachers, ministers, missionaries and business people. It is interesting to note that in 1903 Tabor College held a debate. It was like many debates held at the college but the topic was of interest to the local history. The topic was, "Resolved that the south is justified in disfranchising the Negro." The judges decided the side that offered the resolution that the south was justified in disfranchising the blacks was the winner. The newspaper in Glenwood asked if the people in Tabor and the college had gone back on their founding principals of the Underground Railroad. One of those in attendance to the debate was Deacon Samuel Adams. In a newspaper article in the June 26, 1903, edition of the *Tabor Beacon* Adams assured the Glenwood paper that Tabor had not gone back on her founding principals but that in fact the one side had bested the other in the debate. Everyone seemed satisfied with Adams' answer. Adams, the last of the lions of the Underground Railroad, passed away on February 26, 1910.[46] Everyone once connected with the Underground Railroad in Tabor or Civil Bend had either moved or passed away. Now only the faint, far away footsteps of those heading for freedom could be heard in the town.

The college struggled even more after the end of World War I. Commodity prices in the Midwest dipped and money dried up in the area. Finally, in the commencement of 1927 the president of the college, Dr. Frederick Clayton, announced the college would not be able to reopen in the fall. Dr. Clayton, in particular, had worked very hard even putting some of his own money to keep the college open but to no avail. The institution had managed to stay open some 23 years after John Todd's death.[47]

Several attempts to reopen the college occurred over the next decade and a half, but to no avail. Its work was done.

Now only the echoes of John Todd, John Brown, James Lane, George Gaston and the college are heard over this quiet town. Its nice streets and arching trees belie the sound of the wagons with escaping slaves aboard or the report of a Sharps rifle being fired by John Brown. Maybe the saying "they entertained every stranger so they wouldn't miss entertaining an angel" should be the epitaph of their era.

Appendix:
Letters and Documents

The following appendix contains letters and documents pertaining to the Todd family, the Underground Railroad and other abolitionist activities including the Kansas Free State Movement. All spellings, punctuations and grammar have been kept intact as they were written. Most of these letters and documents were handwritten and an attempt has been made to keep all spacing, marks, indentation and other peculiarities as they were written. Unless otherwise noted all these letters and documents have been reproduced courtesy of the Todd House Museum.

⚜ 1 ⚜

This first letter represents the finest example of the Reverend John Todd's anti-slavery beliefs. It is written to his cousin, Mrs. Margaret G. Strohm in Dayton, Ohio, while John was still a student at Oberlin College. Although Mrs. Strohm is from Ohio she believes as did many in the Northern states, that while slavery was a bad institution it was probably best not to get rid of it, and most of all don't agitate against it. Mrs. Strohm's point of view might be best summed up by saying she was for the status quo and she was apparently very alarmed at the goings on at Oberlin College. The letter is stamped Oberlin O Feb. 23. On the return address is John Todd Feb. 21st 1842. The original of this letter resides in Oberlin College Achives and is reprinted here courtesy of the Oberlin College Archives, Oberlin, Ohio.

Oberlin February 21, 1842

Dear Cousin

The expectation you cherished as expressed in your postscripts must long ere this have died in disappointment. But you doubtless know the reason, and I shall therefore add no apology. I returned on Saturday and found your letter in the P.O.—there perhaps since November. I commenced my school in Ill. the same day you wrote to me. You shall have the first letter I write, and, that you may understand the phenomenon of the kinds of ink on this page, let me say that in commencing to write I found my ink had been frozen and was unfit for use.—My health is good and has been so during the winter, and I left our folks in Ill. in full enjoyment of the same blessing—a precious boon indeed, which we are slow to appreciate! My visit to the west has been very pleasant, and I hail with joy the privilege of again engaging in study. The treasury of knowledge are vast & deep, & patient, laborious & candid investigation alone can lead to their possession.

I had entirely forgotten the subject matter of the letter I last addressed to you, but by your remarks I am reminded of a considerable portion of it. You seem to express not a little surprise at some of our "doings" here, especially at our Antislavery efforts. I had forgotten that you were not a thoroughgoing Abolitionist. I do not however regret that the enemies of our cause are thereby informed of our proceedings; for I am willing that the universe should know the ground we take in this matter; & our reasons too for pursuing the course we have insured, & which we still intend to pursue. You style the subject of Slavery a "vexed question." The discipline of it may be, & truly is a vexing question to tyrants & slaveholders, but to the ardent lovers of liberty—to those who holds that "all men are created equal"—to those who possess the spirit of the gospels nothing can be more pleasing than the elucidation of those principles, upon which our present prosperity is based—the "Magna Charta" of our heaven-born freedom. You say you are not one of those Anti-abolitionists who will not read on the subject & promise to read my address should it be published. So far good.—You shall have a copy, if it should be published, & perhaps it will. But you add that you don't know enough about the subject to have an obstinate opinion of your own. Can it be that this has become a "vexed question" to you, before you know enough about it to form an enlightened opinion on the subject & This seems too much like condemning before the case has a hearing. At no time since the commencement of the Anti-Slavery movement, has the prospect of its success been so flattering as at present. The fundamental principles of this reform are eternal truth & cannot be shaken. Many of the most learned openly know them. The most devoted Christians are the strongest advocates. Some of our most eminent statesmen boldly proclaim them in the national Capitol. Slaveholders tremble at the thought of public discussion on the subject But discussed it must be & discussed it will be. The nation is becoming alive to the encroachments of Slavery & will not long endure its despotic way. Liberty & Slavery cannot long exist in the same governments—They are themselves antagonist principles & cannot long coexist in juxtaposition. And who, that possesses a spark of true patriotism, can consent to sacrifice at the shrine of Slavery!—To speak plainly, Margaret, I came very near lecturing on the subject this winter, and <u>probably</u> shall do so next winter. What do you say to that? Heh? Will you call me a fanatic? But you know that we are commanded to "remember them that are in bonds as bound with them." How can we obey this command & be deaf to the cry of the suffering slave?

But you more than insinuate that we are in league with the British. So did Henry Wise of Va. Charge J.Q. Adams, in Congress, of being partial to the English. But who believed it? Not I certainly. If to clothe the naked, feed the hungry, to do others as ye would that they should do to you = & deliver the poor from the hands of the oppressor, be "Conspiracy," I glory in such Conspiracy. If the philanthropists of England, imbued with the spirit of the gospels, are set upon freeing the world from oppression, shall we not write with them in so glorious a cause? And when the poor exiles have reached a land of freedom, what beast can be so destitute of the feelings of humanity as to deny them the privileges of a "Manual labor institution" or any other means to forward their elevation & improvement?—Are we multiplying the enemies of our country? Certainly not. If they are enemies when freed from the lash of taskmasters, & in a land of freedom, would they not much more be enemies when smarting under the driver's whip!! You say that "<u>few</u> in <u>your</u> neighborhoods would justify a clandestine egress of slaves to a British province I might say that there are <u>few</u> in <u>this neighborhood</u> that would <u>not</u> justify such a course; & which community is the more intelligent on this subject? Who have thought most, & judged most, & read most? But public opinion in itself is no guide to duty. If it were, Paul would never have lifted his voice in idolatrous Athens, nor the sound of the gospel have reached the ends of the world. Had not Luther lifted his voice against the Church of Rome, the dark ages might still have enshrouded the world in gloom, & you & I bowing to Catholic images.— But I go farther, the slaves would be justifiable in rising & asserting & maintaining their liberty by force. (Although I should advise them to wait in hope of obtaining a peaceable deliverance) I don't believe any man in the world can justify the war of the American Revolution & at the same time condemn the slaves for rising to obtain their liberties. "All men are created equal." Is that a rhetorical flourish? Or is it sober truth? If so, then the <u>African</u> has right to pursue <u>his</u> happiness, that the <u>American</u> or <u>European</u> has to seek <u>his</u>.—But you will be ready to say this is a "<u>vexed letter</u>." I will therefore stop, although the subject opens to the minds a <u>vast field</u>?

You are I trust enjoying a high degree of hymeneal bliss. May that love, peace, harmony, & prosperity, which secures the highest conjugal felicity, attends you through all your future life. My best respects to that new male cousin, whom you by your charms have known. Remember me to uncle, aunt, & Eloisa.

David has not returned yet, but I am expecting him daily.

There is a very great interest here at present in the subject of religion, & powerful revivals have attended. Pres. Mahan's & Prof. Finney's preaching at the east—Remember me also to Cousin Samuel & family, & all inquiring friends. And now, Margaret, I only ask you to ans. since this in due time either personally or by proxy & you will oblige your cousin <u>John Todd</u>

2

The following is a copy of a handwritten document of a speech John Todd gave at the commencement exercises at Oberlin College in 1841. It caused something of a sensation. John Todd had a basic understanding of the forces of economics. He comes to a thoughtful conclusion that if the benefits of slavery are so economically advantageous to all why hadn't the Southern slave states seen tremendous prosperity. John Todd felt that slavery could be successfully attacked by logic and not necessarily only on an emotional level. This was the kind of logical argument he would likely use against slavery, often devoid of an emotional element. In this talk a young John Todd oversimplifies many of the issues of the day but he does hit home on several, including the boondoggle in Florida by slave interests. This speech is a little more flowery, as was the custom of the times, than the ones a more mature John Todd would give. This document is reproduced in a transcribed version courtesy of the Kansas Collection Spencer Research Library, University of Kansas Libraries.

Political Economy of Slavery

Another anniversary of our nation's birth has passed away. That independence declared to be our boon by the patriots of "Seventy six" has been secured to our country to this day. The lapse of 65 years has transformed an embryo people just merging into existence, into a full grown & mighty nation. The tide of emigration, which had then but touched our shores, has risen higher & spread itself farther & evidence scaled the Allegiances & poured its flood into the great western valley. Where then the dense & towering forest stood unbroken & undisturbed where thousands of Indians pursued in noble independence & manly dignity of Spartan chase; now the tall spires of populous cities meet the skies, or the whistling plough boy traces his long furrows. The winding footpath & bark canoe have been exchanged for railroads & [mighty?] steamboats. Distance is well nigh annihilated, & distant points brought into juxtaposition. But while our country, as a whole is moving onward with rapid stride, <u>some positions</u> once fair & flourishing are now falling into decay, & exhibit all the symptoms of decrepitude. While the states on the one hand are increasing in wealth, strength, security, & happiness. [Those on the other] are waving & sinking in that political horizon, where they once shone as stars of the first magnitude.—Paradoxical as it may seem our nation protests at the same time the most perfect freedom & the most object Slavery. Grace the boundaries of these & you trace the line which separates intelligence & enterprises from ignorance & degradation.—It is a fundamental principle in political economy that caeteris paribus, the increase of wealth is as if industry, excited, but industry will be exerted in proportions as every man is permitted to enjoy, in the most unlimited manner, the advantages of his labor. Hence, since the slave receives no advantage of his labor, there is no incentive to industry, &, no industry there will be no increase of wealth. So that from the nature of the case, slavery tends only to poverty, & carries in itself the seeds of its own destruction. Facts prove the same.

Forty years ago, the present slaveholding region had in population a majority of more than 3,000, & now has a minority of more than 2 million. In confining our view to a smaller portion, & comparison states that have longer tested the merits of freedom & slavery, we find a still more striking exhibition of the baneful effects of the latter. In 1790 Virginia had more than twice the population of N.Y. Now N.Y. has twice that of Virginia. While the population of Va. increased less than half a million, from double the population of N. York, that of N.Y. increased more than two millions from half the population of Virginia. N.Y., with an extent of territory less by 18,000 sq. miles than Va, has a value of property greater than that of Va. by $442,069.492.

Here are the facts. What is the cause of this wide difference? Does Virginia labor under greater natural disadvantages than N.Y.? Is this climate less favorable? Is her soil less fertile? Are her resources less extensive? Or were her sons originally less enterprising? Nay verily—occupying the most central position on the American seaboard, with the Ocean before her waiting to do her bidding & behind her the Ohio, as it rolls majestically onward, inviting to inland trade & certain wealth; what more could she ask at the hand of heaven? Nor have the sons of the "Old Dominion" been lacking in learning & intelligence. She has given birth to spirits, who have been an ornament to our nation. They saw the corroding cancer preying upon their country's vitals, & deeply deplored without being able to remedy the evil. Tis Slavery makes the startling odds. These two positions of our country began their political career together. The one has already been far outrun, & no prophet here is needed to predict the ultimate triumph of freedom. But Slavery instead of laying aside its besetting weights has striven by throwing obstacles in the way, to impede its swiftfooted competitor. Instead of changing herself to freedom, she has sought to change Freedom to Slavery. This is manifest both from her public influence & private conduct. Slavery & Freedom being directly opposed, their interests also are directly opposed.—The omnipotent energy of freedom needs but permission to prosecute unmolested any given course in order to secure complete success. Open to her the treasures of the deep—Let the allurements of commerce be spread before her, & soon will there be no climb that her sons have not traversed—no wave under heaven that her heels have not parted—Nor a breeze that blows, to which her banner has not been unfurled—Again close the gates of commerce, & she grows sick from her own resources. She lays the soils under tribute—makes the mountain cataract her manufacturer—Yokes the steam to her cars—drives asunder the flirty ribs of her rocky mountains, & draws forth their hidden stores. In shores free industry can adapt itself to any course, but a change must inevitably be attended with vast expenses & loss. Aware of this, her jealous rival has improved every opportunity to change the national policy, & this necessitates a change in the directly of free industry. In 1807, the North, by an Embargo was driven from the ocean, & in a few years when she had fully invested her capital in manufactures, its repeal again invited to foreign trade. A declaration of war, another southern measure, soon followed, & the ocean must be again forsake. After the sacrifice of thousands of lives & millions of money, peace is restored & with its free trade. Old Ocean is soon burdened with American ships & whitened with American canvas. But soon, the South made the discovery that home manufactures must be protected. A tariff must be passed Northern merchants needed no tariff—they asked none—nay they protested loudly against it. The south had no manufactures to protect. But the slave power predominated—S. Carolina originated the tariff—the whole south invited in demanding it, & the dough-faced North complied.—The immense & lucrative trade to the E. Indies was annihilated in a day. Goods, contracted by northern merchants could never be sold—

Commerce languished & multitudes were involved in bankruptcy. Thus has our national policy ever veered to suit the southern interest. More recently we are involved in a Florida war, or more technically a National slave hunt. Forty millions of the public funds have been expended to capture fugitive slaves, under the pretext of taking possession of the ceded territory of Florida. Shameful pretext, when the whole value of the disputed territory would not be sufficient to purchase the medicines expended upon the sick soldiers. What a mockery! What a truckling to southern aristocracy!

Freedom tends to wealth—Slavery to poverty. Hence when their interests are invited, the one must be maintained at the expense of the other. Let facts speak—Boston in 1824 was merged in general bankruptcy. She had withstood the shock of Embargoes & non-intercourse acts, of war & tariff, but now she was attacked in a new form & prostrated. The South had become her debtors, & refused to pay.—They pay nothing for raising their cotton & why should they for manufacturing it?

In 1826 N.Y. was prostrated by a tornado of bankruptcies which in its course greatly injured Boston. This is the fact. The cause is found in the cotton speculation which commenced at the South—Southern credit revived sufficiently to contract debts at the North, & then become insolvent.—We all remember the pressure of 1837. It too had its origin at the south. Southerners were then indebted to N.Y. city alone 100 millions of dollars, 10 per ct. of which could not be recovered. Little Newark N.J. lost 5 millions, & other cities at the north proportionally. Another cotton speculation commenced in 1836, which caused a rise in the value of slaves. Mississippi, to improve the harvest thus afforded, purchased slaves of Va. Md. Valley to the amount of $90 millions.—Then, taking advantage of an old law which prohibited the importation of slaves, refused to pay. Thus she rendered her creditors insolvent, who again had contracted debts at the North. Hence the North must bear the loss—During 1834, 5 & 6 the South drained the U. S. bank of 30 millions never to be repaid, & as a consequence specie payment is suspended to this day.

But what shall I say more? Time would fail me less of Embargoes & now intercourse acts, of wars & tariffs, of banks & bankruptcies of Nullification & gags & slave hunts, of lynching also & dwelling & card playing & cathauling & horseracing & a thousand evils—the legitimate offspring of slavery which infects the morals & paralyzes the energies of our nation. I set out to show the Political Economy of Slavery—but where is the Economy? Economy is wealth. But where is southern wealth? The question returns: where? The defrauded freemen of the North cry; where? The hungry creditors of England & Holland ask: where? The empty coffers echo back, "It is not." Three hundred millions of money have been lost in the Pontine marshes of the south; & still she cries; give! give! Injured as we have been in the matter of dollars & cents, it is by no means the only point attacked. Despairing of ever being able effectually to cope with freedom, while wealth & power attend her as certainly as light—attends the sun, Slavery has arrived at reducing the free laborers of the North to same degradation with her own vassals. She has enslaved those whose skins are white as our own—She has threatened to preach insurrection to the white slaves of the North—she has violently seized, free citizens & sold them into hopeless bondage.—She has apprehended & publicly punished freemen, when honestly engaged in benevolent effort.—she has dared to dictate to the legislative of a free & sovereign state.—She has appointed southern aristocrats to preside over the free territories of the North.—She has, in violation of the Constitution, denied to freemen the right of petition.—She has demanded of a sovereign state the surrender of her citizens to be punished for crimes not known by her laws. When we have attempted a defense of our rights, she has taken advantage of our patriotism, & threatened a dissolution of the union. We have petitioned—we have demonstrated, but our remonstrance have been unheeded, & our petitions trampled upon. (But a brighter day is about to dawn. After a close engagement in the halls of Congress, which was renewed for 8 successive days. Slavery's great champion fell at his post, & was carried from the field of battle—They have acknowledged themselves vanquished—Freedom has triumphed—The right of petition is restored. Now let the petitions flow in until their tables groan beneath the load—let free principles rally around the ballot box.—Let our faces be set as a flint against oppression, & let us prove ourselves worthy sons of the worthy sires of seventy six.)

All this, & yet the North has nothing to do with slavery! Is it nothing to have our pockets rifled—the hard earning of free industry stolen & appropriated to the support of a lordly aristocracy? Is it nothing that we are made to toil without wages? Is it nothing that we are denied a hearing when we would state our grievances? Is it nothing that the press should be fettered, & freemen slain when standing in defense of their property? Will not the heat, which sets southern combustibles on fire, bring Northern doughfaces to a crust?—Dissolve the union! Why the sooner than better. Amputate the dead & decaying member. Why should the loathsome member be left to waste the energies of life? But, in the hope that soundness may yet be restored, let the last—the only remedy be faithfully applied—Let truth be disseminated—Let free principles rally around the ballot box.—Let our faces be set as a flint against oppression—& let us prove the worthy sons of the worthy sires of "Seventy Six."

John Todd

⟨≈ **3** ⟨≈

Martha Todd's younger brother, Arthur, went to Oberlin's prep school but never entered the college. He always seemed to get into trouble and was very irresponsible and had problems with alcohol. In this letter Arthur apparently went on a forbidden raccoon hunt. Rather than sending any money to Arthur, Martha Todd's father, Q. F. Atkins, would send the money he had earmarked for Arthur's school expenses to John Todd for him to disperse on Arthur's behalf. Mr. Atkins knew this way the money would go where it was supposed to. John made an accounting of the money. Arthur was the youngest and only boy in the large family and frankly had been spoiled by his sisters. Young John Todd looked to his future father-in-law as a mentor type. John always wanted to please his father-in-law to be and gave a full accounting of the money. John always informed Mr. Atkins of his activities as if to impress the older man of his worthiness to his daughter's hand. John would always be sure to mention any anti-slavery or abolitionist or temperance meetings he or Martha would attend while they were students at Oberlin College. In the letter Todd makes a comment to Mr. Atkins that "Can it be that a <u>slaveholder</u> shall again fill the highest office in the gift of a <u>free people</u>?" This is a reference to the fact that William Henry Harrison, who had owned slaves and had died early in office while president, was being succeeded by John Tyler, also a slaveholder. Mr. Atkins was a prominent attorney originally from Northern Ohio. John always enjoyed discussing the news of the day with Mr. Atkins and of course the topic of the anti-slavery movement. Mr. Atkins was deeply involved in the Underground Railroad and abolitionist movement. The liberty meeting John refers too was an anti-slavery meeting. It is interesting to note that Mr. Atkins always promptly replied to his correspondence, while most everyone else writing to him apologized for their tardiness in replying. Mr. Atkins would write on the outside of the envelope when he received his mail and when he wrote his reply to that particular piece of correspondence. John Todd later adopted this practice.

Oberlin Sep. 20th. 1842.
Mr. Atkins,

Respected Sir, Your last was duly received, with the five dollars enclosed to be appropriated for Arthur's benefit. All his dues had been paid, so that there was no pressing urgency for further funds. You are desirous to know what amt. of money more will be needed to carry him through the present term. This query I will answer—by giving you an account of his entire expenditures.

Q. F. Atkins in acct. with J. Todd.

Cr.		Dr.	
May 24th. By Cash – – – – $13.00		To board from May 24th. to Nov. 2nd. 23 Wks. at $1.00 – – – – – – $23.00	
July 5th. By " – – – – 4.00			
Aug. – – By " – – – – 5.00		To Tuition from May 25th. to August 24th – – – 6.00	
Aug. 16th By " – – – – 3.00		" " " Aug. 24th to Nov. 2nd – – – – 4.25	
Sep. 12th. By " – – – – 5.00		To Books – – – – – – 3.50	
By 2½ Wks Absence from board – – – – – – 2.50		To Axe & helve – – – 1.00	
	32.50	To sundry small items 1.87½	
		$39.62½	
		32.50	
		7.12½	

The above is I believe a true statement of the money received by me &
also of all the money already expended together with the amt. necessary
for board & tuition until the close of the term. There will probably be
some additional expense necessary for articles needed from time to time,
e.g. he carried his shoes to be mended to day & was told that they were
not worth mending. Of course, he must have shoes of some kind. I
thought perhaps he had better get a pair of coarse boots.

    I can only say of Arthur that he does tolerable well, & scarcely that.
He went off one night on a "cooning" expedition without informing either
Prof. Allen or myself & that too when on a former occasion he was strictly
forbidden to go. The consequence is that he has been required to give the
Faculty a written acknowledgement of his guilt & if deemed advisable by
them, it will be read before all the members of the institution. Arthur has
made the acknowledgement, but it has not been publicly read yet. Our
health is as well as usual. Martha purposes going to the Washingtonian
Convention at Medina tomorrow. Many are going from here.

    Yesterday we had a most interesting Liberty Convention at Elyria.
Judge King & _____ Lewis each gave us a fine speech. The court house
was crowded to overflowing, & we doubt not many went away fully satisfied not only that our actions were not prompted by fanaticism, but by
the best reasons & the soundest judgment. We rejoice in the hope that
the pure patriotism of '76 is about to be revived in the breasts of Northern Freemen, & the principles of the Declaration of Independence again
to become dominant. Can it be that a slaveholder shall again fill the
highest office in the gift of a free people? I have inquired a good deal

about a house & lot for you, but every nook & corner seems to be occupied. There is at present a large house nearly opposite Mrs. Cole's which is unfinished. The owner has been disappointed in procuring funds to complete it, but promise to complete in six weeks, if $75.00 in cash, can be furnished him. Mr. Fairfield thinks of occupying 5 or 6 rooms & there will be 4 or 5 large rooms left besides the kitchen & back part, which is now occupied by Mr. Spencer himself but will be vacated during the winter. There is ½ an acre of land connected with this house. For rent Mr. Spencer asks $16.00 per annum for each of the rooms, which are about x14 ft. square & one of them larger. I cannot tell whether such a house would meet your wishes, & there are so many conditional circumstances that I cannot speak with much certainty respecting it. But if 25 or 30 dols. could be furnished now, I think you might have 4 or 5 good rooms, in 6 or 7 weeks, for the above mentioned rent. If this would <u>at all</u> meet your wishes, you would, I think, do well to come & see. Mr. Spencer wishes to know as soon as possible, that he may make his arrangements.

Mr. Fitch finished his course on the Millennium, last evening, & I know not that he has made a single convert. We regard him as a man of <u>lovely spirit</u>, but a very superficial interpreter of scripture. To night Prof. Cowles answers him, but he will not stay to hear.

Love to you all. Yours in haste

Q. F. Atkins Esqr.   John Todd
Cleveland, Ohio

Let us hear from you <u>as soon as possible</u>

4

John Todd's younger brother David attended Oberlin College at the same time as did John. During the winter months and summer months students at Oberlin would fan out into the adjoining states to teach or preach at some rural communities, many of them too poor or new to be able to afford a full-time teacher or pastor. While David was in slave state Kentucky he was charged with trying to incite a slave revolt. At this time in a slave state any contact by an unknown white person and a black person was viewed with deep suspicion, particularly if that white person was from Ohio or especially Oberlin, Ohio. David apparently was not convicted of this alleged "crime." As you can tell from the summation the evidence is flimsy at best. The fact that David Todd would have been charged with such a crime would have been a "badge of honor" at Oberlin College. The following is what appears to be a prosecuting attorney's summation to a jury charging David Todd for attempting to incite a slave revolt in Kentucky.

May it please the court & Gentlemen of the Jury.

Called together today under circumstances peculiarly important.
You have heard the indictment. The crime alleged is a flagrant one.
Its influence as extensive as the interests of our beloved country. Your
responsibilities are truly very great—your labor arduous & painful—if you
acquit yourselves like men: & if other wise; What? With these remarks
you will be prepared to examine the testimony in the case before us.

Lift the affidavits These showing that here was an insurrection of
slaves discovered.

For this then must have been a cause not the operation of the natural elements but what? Are adequate to produce the effect: How great was
the effect? To several plantations in counties—is great cause, What was
the cause? The prisoner or some one else? Nothing to do at present with
others than prisoners. Was he the mover? Evidence that he was. <u>Was
Seen</u> , etc. Several cases combine. Was absolutely at such places at such
times. What for? For something. The insurrection shows that there was
some cause more than common operating.

No other cause, known, to produce this uncommon event there—
must it not be that the presence of the prisoner was the cause? But this
insurrection was discovered in the very places where he was. Then how
manifest that he was the cause. If he had no ill designs why did he take
such a course as to act privately? Can you (?) No, impossible. Such a
course is inexplicable with the supposition of a good intention. The last
that he seen with slaves would excite suspicion of some evil. The following events would leave no doubt on any mind. But what was he seen
doing? See the affidavits Just what he would do if aiming to excite an
insurrection. In how many places was he seen & what doing? From these
circumstances you will abuse your own reason & judgment to suppose he
was not guilty of the crime alleged to him. Not only is the supposition of
his innocence absurd but the supposition of his guilt makes everything
plain. If anymore evidence is wanted let me tell you where he came from.
Ohio What are in Ohio? Abolitionists a set of disorganizers. In all kinds
of business. He's probably of that sect or influenced by them. This last
only circumstantial evidence, But etc.

[There are 4 lines crossed out at this point]

Gentlemen of the Jury Does the evidence of the prisoners guilt
satisfy you? If so remember that and be on your guard how the prisoner's
learned counsel seduce your minds from their steadfastness. Remember
that the prisoner was seen doing so & so, here & there. No alibi—if so
the oaths are false. Remember too that you have to do with how the law
of the land, & see that they do not beguile you with any new fangled

philosophy. Beware too of appeals to your sympathies. Your reason & judgment here have to rule. Justice is our sovereign here & you must obey stern & rigid though it be. If you are referred to the prisoner's mother, brothers & sisters—their sorrow—think of yours if you let loose such a malefactor among us. Your families will be periled & can you have it so through your fault? If he is guilty irrespective of such thing? You <u>ought</u> to condemn him.

I have charged you thus carefully & perhaps excessively on account of the <u>deep interest</u> I take in this case. Such an important case my professional duties heretofore have never called me to please. (The looks of the prisoner, his eyes full of enmity

Now in ____ let me urge you to be calm & let your reason & judgment prevail & I doubt not you will be able to do justice & equity in this case.

State of Kentucky Harlan Co. against Wm. S. Westervelt
David Todd   September 26th 1842.

 **5**

John Todd's first pastoral assignment was in Clarksfield, Ohio. John and his young wife are disappointed by the lack of emotional and intellectual interest in religion and the anti-slavery movement. The letter gives a good example of what Martha Todd's life was as minister's wife in the 1840's. The Todds are disappointed at the deficient progress on their parsonage. One of the interesting things mentioned in the letter was Mrs. Todd's use of bad ink. All married couples have those little items that one of them does that drives the other spouse to distraction. In the case of the Todds it was Martha's use of bad or frozen ink. This drove her husband crazy. However, as other letters attest to, Mrs. Todd never changed her ways. They many times wrote joint letters to family and friends. John's ink was always strong and readable. Martha's was at times weak and unreadable. This letter was addressed to Mrs. Sally Atkins Care of E. Wade Esqr. Cleveland Ohio. Sally Atkins was Martha Todd's mother. She was in ill health and was often in the care of her sister, Mrs. Edward Wade. Edward Wade would be a United States congressman from Ohio from 1853 to 1860. His brother was Benjamin Franklin Wade, longtime Ohio United States senator. Edward Wade was actively involved in the Underground Railroad. It is clear that Martha and John have great concerns about her wayward brother, Arthur. The "Pa" mentioned in the letter is Martha Todd's grandfather; John and Martha always addressed her father as "Father."

Clarksfield, Dec. 29, 1846

My dear Mother,

When we received Pa's letter, which was one week less Thursday, we thought we would write to have you & Arthur both come on here, but then again we hardly knew where to find a place for you know our house is very small, and we hardly knew what A would employ himself about, if he were able to do anything, yet I do wish you could come. I think we could stow you away (if I may so speak) somewhere... We were truly glad to hear of Arthur's good resolutions, and may he constantly realize whence all his strength must come, if there is any permanent goodness in him. Can you not both come and make us a visit, if you do not stay. You could remain three or four weeks at least we would endeavor to meet you as before, but perhaps you would come by the way of Auygles, if you go to Tallmadge. We have not been there yet. I have been hoping it would be sleighing so we could make them a visit. I think I could find enough for you to do so you need not be troubled, on that account. My knitting has all been deferred "till snow then comes" until I am without stockings, and I have had to sew up some for James. Why have you not written us? I hoped to get a letter last week from C. and indeed almost every week for sometime past. We have had not particulars respecting A's last sickness, nor did we know anything of your coming ____ until Pa wrote us a week or two since. How glad I should be to have you decide to come. I am not afraid but that we should live. We have more than we had last winter, and had we not enough then? How will Pa be employed this winter? We must write him soon. How long a time will you probably spend in Tallmadge? We long to hear from you.

My fall business such as making soap, dipping candles, taking care of the pork, etc are all done with I believe, and I am calculating upon considerable leisure for reading etc but I may be disappointed. We have had very little company this fall past, so I have passed along with less hard labor than I expected, yet my sewing is somewhat behind. They are doing little or nothing at the parsonage as yet—but if we remain next year, we hope to be among our people another winter. There is no particular religious interest here, still we have some hope that a discussion upon Universalism, which Mr. Todd is expecting to be drawn into, will arouse the community in some measure, so that they will be led to inquire after truths and may result in much good. Surely it is our most earnest prayer that the Spirit of God will attend the truth.

Perhaps Mr. T. will find time to write a little in this, and there remains but little for me to say. How does L and family prosper? I wonder she does not write. It is altogether uncertain when we shall obtain those peaches, for we have not opportunity of sending. We might possibly obtain them soon if you could get them to O. but I have not stood in need of them as yet for we have an abundance of green apples. Little James does not walk yet but he pulls up by things, and we are hoping he will soon be getting about. He has been very well, with the exception of an attack of the croup. I was able to arrest the disease by bathing, so he has taken nothing internally, as yet. I must close, Do write soon. Cannot A. write me a long letter. We wish he would. Love to.

Your daughter Martha..

Dec. 30. Dear Mother, Martha has attempted to write you on the preceding pages of this sheet, but in consequence of using bad ink I fear you will hardly be able to decipher it. If you should be unable to read it, I trust you will be able to read what I now write. We were very glad to hear from you, but would be quite as well pleased to have the news directly from Cleveland as round by way of Geneva. We shall be very glad when you can come & stay with us. I should be pleased to have Arthur here too, but as Martha says I do not know what he could be profitably engaged in, & surely he could not be satisfied without some employment. Yet if he could not stay a great while, he might while recovering his strength, spend a few weeks with us. I hope Arthur will keep the new leaf he has turned over unsullied. Should he prove himself to be a new creature in Christ Jesus, it must prove an inexpressible joy to his parents as well as the entire connect (partially blurred). Mother come if you can. We did expect to see you here a month ago. At least let us hear from you & relieve us from all suspense in relation to your coming.

Yours Affectionately,

John Todd

6

The following letter was written when the Todd family was on its way to Iowa, then a frontier area. The letter gives the reader somewhat of an idea of how travel was accomplished in those days. The Todds left Clarksfield, Ohio, and went to Granville, Illinois, where they rested and wrote this letter, and stayed with John's parents and brothers. They then left Granville and went to Southwest Iowa. John Todd remarked one time that the ruggedness of travel at this time prepared a person for the harshness of frontier living. The letter was written to Mrs. Todd's father, Q.F. Atkins.

Granville Ill. Monday June 10.1850.

Dear Father,

I now sit down to redeem Martha's promise made to some of you there, that we would report ourselves from this place. We left Cleveland about 7 o'clock on Tuesday eve, &were soon out far from land on the calm bosom of Lake Erie. The fishing boats &sail vessels, the wake of our boat, &many other novelties deeply interested the children. The evening was calm &beautiful, &we fixed a lingering gaze upon the city of our home, &intently watched its departure from our view, until the dimness of twilight began to gather around us. We soon retired to rest, &, on awaking, next morning found ourselves in the Detroit river &near the city. At 7 o'clock we took the oars, after taking breakfast at the Temperance house, for New Buffalo, where we arrived in the evening of Wednesday after a ride of a little more than 12 hours. There we took passage to Chicago, &reached that city about midnight, but were permitted to remain on board undisturbed until morning. We took breakfast at the Lake St. Temperance house—found that Arthur had left Chicago on Monday, &would not be back for 2 or 3 days. Horatio had gone to Green Bay, so that we failed entirely to see either of them. At eight we set off on the canal mail packet for Peru or Leadalle, which we reached by six o'clock on next (Friday) morning. We then hired a wagon to carry us over to Granville (6 miles) which we reached by noon, in the midst of a shower of rain. We are all pretty well. The children have had no ague &took the journey better than we had feared they would. Our friends here were well—had just received the letter I wrote the week before we started—&came home from the P.O. to go to Peru after us, but found us already here. We shall probably leave here on Thursday for St Louis. The country here is not now suffering for rain, though the upper part of the Illinois river is low &only the lightest class of boats can navigate the river. Michigan seemed to be suffering with drought, but there was a slight shower on Wednesday as we passed along, &perhaps ere this both Michigan &northern Ohio have received a refreshing. The corn appears more forward here than any that we have seen anywhere... Perhaps what I have written above will suffice to gratify your present desire to know how we have been prospered thus far, &when we shall have reached our destination, if we are in the Providence of God permitted to do so, we shall again write you. Please remember us to all the dear people of yours & Mr. Wade's families, Uncle Josiah etc. I hope mother will not be entirely alone, as the contrast between the noise of our children, &perfect quiet must be painful.

Affectionately Yours

John Todd

꧁꧂   **7**   ꧁꧂

The following was a letter written to Q.F. Atkins from Jonas Jones. They had become friends when Atkins, Martha Todd's father, came to visit in Tabor. John Brown often stayed at Jones's house when he resided or visited in Tabor. The letter is unusual in that it directly mentions activities on the Underground Railroad. So often the residents of Tabor were reluctant to outwardly mention any of these illegal activities; however, they did mention them on occasion. The letter, as did most of the letters of this time, mentions who is ill and who has passed away. These were unfortunate realities on the frontier. Then Jones goes onto mention the farming activates and commodity prices, very important items to the survival of the small town of Tabor. When Jones mentions that a better man will be returned to the U.S. Senate, he is referring to incumbent Senator Augustus Caesar Dodge, the anti–Underground Railroad Senator from Iowa. This letter is an edited version.

This letter is addressed to Hon. Q.F. Atkins, Respected Friend, Tabor, Fremont County Sept. 5th, 1854.

Yours of the 24th Ult. From Cleveland was rec. this morning and I hasten to reply. I will here acknowledge your very kind letter from Chicago. I intended to have answered it long before this but before its reception, I had commenced preparations for making the unburnt Brick and from that time to the present it has required and demanded my constant attention and labor. This P.M. we are having a fine rain and indeed a great rain ... the measles and whopping cough were prevailing when you left ... and some of the children were pretty sick for a few days. Our youngest daughter Anna had a severe illness ... she is now convalescing ... No physician has been called to the place. There has been a good deal of sickness South of us and on the River. The crops here are generally good. Wheat(both fall and spring) are very good, also oats ... In Missouri the crops have been cut off in part or by whole by the severe drought. Good wheat has been selling for 85 cents to a dollar ... quite amount of hay already cut and put up ... As to the settlement and prospects of Tabor there has been no great change since you left although there has been progress ... The schoolhouse is (used as a) chapel ... and for other meetings ... to build such a house or dwelling of the brick I have been making I have been making bricks ... the brick have (been) done in the states of Ohio and Michigan and should do well here and if they should do well made of this soil it will be of great value to this country ... (these bricks) will have to be tested by trial ... We will be most joyful to see you back this fall as we all shall be ... We are expecting friends from Ohio here soon to look for themselves and decide what they will do.

I have not found time to read but little of the political news of late,
I believe our state election has been a gain on the score of human rights,
and we expect a better man to be returned to the U.S. Senate than the
present incumbent. You have doubtless been informed by Br. Todd of the
escape of five "human chattels" from their master on the 4th of July. We
expect they are safe now. I would love to fill my sheet now. I have much
to say but time will not allow it now ...

My family joins in kind regards and wishes for your happiness—

Very Truly Yours
Jonas Jones

8

The following letter brings up many interesting points about the Todds'
move into Tabor. Q.F. Atkins wants to buy land in the area but John points
out the lack of timber, a material so important to a growing town. John very
astutely points out that if the Nebraska territory is settled that will drive
down land prices in Tabor and the surrounding area. In this letter John
queries his father-in-law about Ira Blanchard and his past. They compare
the differences between Ohio and Iowa and of the unforgiving travel conditions should Mr. Atkins want to come out to Iowa. In the last part of the
letter Mrs. Todd condemns the pitiful conditions of the frontier mail services. Tabor still doesn't have its own post office and the people of the town
must travel several miles south of town to Dawsonburg to get their mail.

Dawsonburg P.O. Fremont Co. Iowa Jan 3, 1854.

Dear Father,

I have just returned from the P.O. where I found another letter
from your familiar pen, & I hasten to atone for past neglect—no I cannot
atone for it, & must confess myself sadly remiss in not sooner answering
letters before received. Perhaps a full account of the matter might contain
some apology. The fact is my mind was not charged with the pressing
nature of the case. Martha more generally commences your letters I
believe, but this she regarded as mine to answer, because you had inquired
about land etc. In one of your letters you mentioned the middle of May
as a time when you might reach us, and thus I was led to suppose there
was no particular haste called for.—Furthermore I hardly knew whether
to direct to Cleveland or Chicago, but I suppose there could not be more
than 24 or 36 hours between them. Such have been the thoughts which
induced the delay in writing. Take them for what they are worth, still I do
not deem my neglect excusable, nor will I harp upon want of time, for I

despair of ever again being much at leisure, & yet it seems like laboriously doing nothing.

We have entered, as you see, upon a new year, all in continued good health & spirits. Our house seems very comfortable although not entirely finished. We have had a mild winter thus far—frost on the 27th of August then mild & pleasant without frost until the 20th Oct.—then cold—6 inches snow on the first of November—mild again & pleasant from the middle of Nov. till the middle of Dec. & for the last two weeks variable from below zero up to & above 32—most of the time fine working weather & roads dry & smooth—We have none of the Western Reserve mild here ever, nor anything like it.

In relation to the matter of land let me say that there is plenty of prairie land, as good as can be found, to be had yet at government price, but all the timber is either claimed or entered & will therefore cost more. A scarcity of timber is the chief difficulty with which this country has to contend, & it is a serious difficulty, but will be overcome, because of the other superior advantages. Some of our community have deemed it desirable to enter as much land as possible in our immediate vicinity, in order to prevent foes from speculating to our cost, & consequently the land is about all entered within a mile & half or two miles from here. The nearest rail road route surveyed passes 8 or 10 miles N. of us, and I think perhaps most of the land is taken in the vicinity of it, but of this I cannot speak with certainty, as we can only learn what lands are entered by going to the land office. Though the timber is all claimed there are 5 or 6 persons within a few miles of here who have timber that they wish to sell, & if Nebraska should be opened for settlement soon, many more will want to sell. I think you would do well to come & see, before purchasing. Some think our country too uneven. Some don't like it at all, & others are charmed with it. One thing is certain lumber is high & fencing materials scarce. An enterprising Kentuckian has commenced a farm about 7 miles N. of us—out on the open prairie, 3 or 4 miles from timber. He proposes to build houses of brick & fences of sods, to serve until the Machura can grow sufficiently to form a protection to crops. The soil does not heave by frost—cellars do well without any wall, & walls are seldom if ever used in wells except a little above the water. It is generally supposed that unburnt bricks will do well for building purposes in this country. I am not sufficiently acquainted with agricultural chemistry to give you an analysis of our soil. For several feet from the surface the soil is of a dark brown color, gradually growing lighter as you descend, & soon appears like clay though of a different quality from that of the W. Reserve. On our hill, & generally through the country on the high ground wells are dug from 45 to 60 or 70 ft deep without finding a single stone even, &

we have a young Englishman among us who sunk one of our wells over 30 feet in one day. But no statement of particulars will serve the purpose so well as to become an eyewitness of our country. We like it on the whole, & shall be glad to greet you with a hearty welcome next spring, should Providence permit. If we had Jack out here, I think we could cure him of the heaves, as no horses have that disease here, & some that were far gone before coming here, have entirely recovered. We have had a good supply of venison this fall. Deer are plenty but not easily caught on these prairies. Our nearest neighbor shot a buck a few weeks ago that weighed 135 pounds when dressed. Dr. I. D. Blanchard of Civil Bend has a fleet horse, with which he caught three deer last winter in one day by running them down on a fair race in the open prairie. By the way, do you remember the circumstances respecting his crime committed, I think in Ashtabula, in his earlier years. He purloined money from a merchant there I believe. Can you tell how much it was that was taken, & the circumstances connected with it. A more full acquaintance with him increases my curiosity to know, nor is it an idle curiosity.

We have a good school in operation here now, & James & Louisa attend. Curtius is growing to be a large boy, & Maggie is a real little prattler, speaking most everything quite distinctly.

You have not hinted anywhere in your letters how you design to reach us, whether by land or water, by private or public conveyance. Should you come by private conveyance, you had better not attempt it, I think, in the winter. You <u>might</u> indeed find pleasant winter weather, but you would be liable to have a very tedious time of it, & much of the way across our state, no comfortable accommodations. We have usually a good deal of wind in the spring, but not much rain until the middle of April or first of May. But if you come, more definite information respecting the way can be given, if desired, at a future time.

From your last we learn that your health is not good, & your trip to Chicago postponed on that account. We hope you may soon recover, & that we may hear of Bertha's recovery too. Martha says she would like to write a few lines, & I will yield to her the privilege of filling the remainder of the sheet.

Affectionately Yours, <u>John Todd</u>
<u>Q.F. Atkin.</u>

Dear Father, I have felt quite unpleasantly about your letters being so long unanswered, but we have been in such confusion much of the time that we have not been aware how time was passing or that so many weeks had gone away. I hope it will not always be thus yet it seems as if there would be no end to very pressing calls of labor on Mr. T's time so that he can study no more. He alludes to our having venison but some how or other I cannot make very savory dishes out of it. The meat is so exceedingly dry that it seems impossible to obtain moisture sufficient to cook it well. We shall hope to see you here ere many months, but I fear things will be so different from Ohio that it will not be pleasant to remain still the journey may do you good. James says he has a good many things to write but there is no room this time. He will have to _____ a letter himself, so we hope it will not be long before another is started. Martha

Our County paper states there are now post-masters between Kanesville(Council Bluffs, Iowa) & Ft. Des Moines that cannot read, and if the stage driver cannot attend to the distribution of the mails, it has to be thrown aside till some one comes along who can read. If such be the fact (as I doubt not) we can well account for it taking four weeks & more for letters & papers to come to me from O. I presume it is not much better though Missouri.

9

The following letter was addressed to Q.F. Atkins, Racine, Wisconsin, from Tabor, Dec. 25, 1856. It was written by Martha Todd and James E. Todd, son of John and Martha. It was received in Racine on Jan. 9, 1857. At this time James E. Todd was 10 years old. James as an adult became an educator and he taught at Tabor College. Later he became acting president of the University of South Dakota and became a government geologist. He ended his prominent career in education as the professor of geology at the University of Kansas. The Todds go into some detail on Underground Railroad escapes and the harshness of frontier life.

Tabor, Dec. 25, 1856

My Dear Grandpa,

I wish you a merry Christmas. Louisa and Curtius are going to school. I go to one of our neighbors to draw once or twice a week. Flora has had the earache lately and her nose does not smell so bad as it did. Saturday before last one of our neighbors, named Lealyn was frozen to death. He went out in the afternoon about three miles after a load of wood, and as he was coming home he lost his way, and as he did not come home his wife thought likely he would stop at a neighbors so she did not feel much concerned until morning then she sent to that neighbor and he started out to hunt him up, they traced him nearly to his home and then he turned and went away from it, they found him about two miles from home dead.

G B Gast Thursday three Missourians came to Mr. Gastons after a
couple of Negroes that had been here. Louisa has been so afraid they
would come again that she did not want to stay at home alone Sunday to
take care of Flora. Last night Father married two couple, one was Sherman Pearce to Sarah Gardner and the other was Leemuel Webb to Eliza-
beth Heill. From your

Affectionate grandson

James E Todd

Dear Father.

    James thinks he has written all he can, and I feel quite loth to have it
leave without adding a line or two tho' there be no new of importance to
communicate. Our children have recovered, still Flora is a great deal of
trouble, especially nights. I think she can hardly feel well any of the time.
Our little place has been visited again by a slave catcher from Jackson Co.
Missouri, and he expresses great fears for our town. We supposed warrants
would be obtained to search all our houses, but they have not appeared a
second time as yet. The alleged slaves, who had escaped from Lexington
and Kansas City through Kansas, but lost their way in Nebraska, fell into
the slavery hands, were taken and lodged in Linden jail. By setting fire to
the jail they escaped and finally came here, tho' they had been warned of
this place, as a place "where the people got rich by selling slaves to New
Orleans." We hope they are now safely on their way to a land of freedom,
tho' some may be base enough to betray them in this state. We feared not
their warrants because of finding them but because of some arms & placed
here by authority designed for K[Kansas]. They were assured that we were
well provided with means of defense and have perhaps given up hope of
accomplishing anything, but I more think they were deterred from coming
by a severe wind & snow storm that occurred the following day. We have
had three very severe snow storms this month. I can but think they are
fighting the battles of Kansas, for Who can stand before this Cold?. still
there must be great suffering among the new settlers. We have heard of a
number of deaths by freezing during those storms. We supposed from
Ophelia's letter that you would spend the winter with her, so directed a
letter to you there, which you will probably obtain. Our steam mill was
disabled during the first storm occurring the 2nd ins. and they can do
nothing until it becomes warmer. Many have been depending upon it both
for lumber and food. Unless it should moderate so that they can raise the
chimney (which was blown down) we may suffer for food, still we hope for
the best. The people here are generally nice tho' Mrs. Matthews is failing
gradually with the dropsy. Write soon & often, tho' I can seldom write.

Good bye, Martha

10

Mrs. Todd's whole family was involved in the Underground Railroad. The following is a very interesting letter that Martha Todd's sister Bertha wrote to their father, Q.F. Atkins. The language is very unique and is probably referencing some activities on the Underground Railroad. The phase "Old Jack enjoys his liberty," "we lost three men over the falls" and "after Mr. Wade's horses leave which will be tomorrow or the next day" is very indicative of some kind of code to hide Underground Railroad activities. Also, Bertha's description of traveling in Canada is very revealing. The Mr. Wade mentioned is probably Edward Wade, a known Underground Railroad conductor. This letter was addressed to the Hon. Q.F. Atkins, Wolcott, New Haven Co., Conn., Post marked Cleveland O. Also, written on the outside of the envelope: Bertha A. Judson July 26th 1853 ... Recd at Wolcott, Connecticut July 29th 1853 and answered July 30th/53. Mrs. Judson resided around Niagara Falls, New York, at one time; however, it is addressed from Brooklyn; the state was not given. In all of the hundreds of letters and documents in the Todd House Museum Archives concerning Q.F. Atkins, many of them dealing with his business transactions, he seems to have no business affairs in Canada. Wilbur Siebert lists Atkins and Edward Wade as active participants on the Underground Railroad. The most logical assumption that can be drawn from his apparent trips to Canada are to take escaping slaves to that country.

Brooklyn Tuesday Evng July 26

My Dear Father

Your last letter penciled in Mass—Mr. Judson for'd—home this evening—your other written at Toronto came last Friday—it seems to me it takes a good while for letters to come from Canada—at least longer than it wo'd to go the same distance in our own country. Oscar & Frankie had a letter from their Father written at Toronto. We were very glad to hear that you all enjoyed your journey so well—at least you and Mr Wade— from Mary we hear nothing—save as your speak of her I tho't you wo'd enjoy that route down the St. Lawrence—it seems to me from what I have heard of its beauties that it must be delightful—and I am glad you co'd visit it with such congenial companions. You have probably heard ere this, of this painfuly exciting scene that occurred at the Falls a few days after you left—the loss of the three men over the Falls. We have had warm and very dry weather—no rain since you left until yesterday and then normal nearly all May—and some to day—we found on measuring it this morning that there was over two inches—we needed rain very much the grass in the door yard looked crisped and the corn leaves curled—the cisterns failed—and great quantities of dust to annoy us—but to night it is beautiful. Old Jack seems to enjoy his liberty very much. We have had him harnessed only once—but may oftener after Mr. Wade's horses leave which will be tomorrow or next day. Cousin Frank drives to Andover with the children where they (the horses) are to remain until Mr. Wade goes for them. The hens are contributing their share to our comfort and sure to be doing well—I can hardly speak for things at home as I have been there but a few times—Cato visits us every day and seems glad to get a pleasant word. Our family are all in usual health—talk about the absent one's considerable—When may we expect you at home? We shall all be glad to see you—Ophelia goes in the morning to Oberlin—back in the P.M. to see about a house or houses which Cousin Wm has written about. I think she intend to remove there about the 1st of Sept. Oscar sits by me—and says give my love to Grandpa—Cousin Frank. ditto—he adds— that he expects you can tell some long stories about the hard times the early settlers had in Ohio—There has a joint—letter to you & I arrived from Martha which I will keep unless you wish it forwarded. Your papers are laid by safely for future perusal. Mr. Judson wishes to be remembered to you and is glad to hear from you. I hope we shall hear often from you— and that you will come back to us improved in health etc–

    Your affectionately Bertha

✎ 11 ✎

Even Mrs. Todd's wayward brother, Arthur, cheered on the escape of a runaway in Chicago, Illinois. In a rare letter to his family Arthur lets them know his whereabouts. He was a seaman who would often take off, probably in some form of inebriation, for long ocean voyages. Here he seems at this time to be sailing around the Great Lakes region.

Chicago June 3/51

Dear Mother

    I am at the _____ to sail & shall do so most probably in the course of an hour or so I take this opportunity of keeping you informed of the State of my health & prospects

    I do not expect to sail the Crumen all season But may I have not seen my owners since last spring so do not know whether I suit them or not—I am ready & anxious to quit & the first word of grumbling I get from them I mean so to do

    I mean to come home about the 4th if possible & spend a week with you & see the friends by Summerlight

Sailing this season has been a hard trip up But—Ive been so far one
of the fortunate ones Hornito is by Green Bay & will not be back before
the 1st July when he means to go to some place out South & get a better
half Do not say anything about it to any one as he wishes me to keep still
so that he could astonish the C friends I believe it is Annie Morrison
that he marries There is a good deal of excitement here on act. of a Fugitive Slave being claimed by its masters & the Chicago folks sure to feel
inclined to turn out enmasse to the rescue I do not think they will get
away with him but they may

Write as soon & oft as convenient & be sure I shall be glad to get
the news from that quarter Do you hold your office ___ etc etc

I remain as ever

Your Son Arthur Atkins

Love to all tell B she is indebted to me a letter

✦ 12 ✦

The following is a tract from the American Reform Tract and Book Society. The propaganda war between the abolitionists and the slavery interests
was intense. Tracts like this were sent out to Sunday schools and churches
in the North to be read by children to win their hearts and minds over to
the abolitionists' anti-slavery cause. The tract paints a very positive picture
of the Underground Railroad. At the top of the tract was a woodcut picture
(on page 117) of a slave auction of a family in Washington, D.C., or as it was
referred to in the pamphlet, Washington city. This type of propaganda was
a powerful tool in moving the Northern States like Iowa to an abolitionist
stance. It is interesting to note that the tract not only mentions black slavery but the slavery of people of Asian origin and white slavery.

A Tract for the Sabbath Schools

Slaves are people held as property. They are bought and sold, as if
they were cows or horses. Some of them are black, some yellow, and some
white. In Washington city, where the President of the United States
resides, where Congress meets, and the great men of the nation resort,
there has been in times past one of the greatest slave markets in the
world. One specimen of the sales of families in that city will now be
given. It was a young man, his wife and babe. They were placed on an
elevated platform, that the bidders might see if they were healthy and
sound. This family expected to be all sold to one man; and did not, at
first, manifest so much feeling as might be expected.

The auctioneer began with the husband, and he was sold. He next

began to cry off the wife; several men bid for her, but the purchaser of her
husband was not one of them. Intense anguish was exhibited in the coun-
tenance of the hapless pair. She was sold to a second person, and forever
separated from her husband. The big tears rolled down their sable cheeks,
and fell in great drops at their feet. Sadness and despair was evidently
flowing from the deepest recesses of their souls. Last of all the babe was
sold, and to a third person. The cold-hearted wretch came forward to seize
his prey. The babe threw its little arms around its mother's neck, and
closely clung to her; the mother held it with the grasp of despair and
death; her agonizing shrieks pierced the skies, as the clinging child was
torn from her bosom. The little boys of Washington city had become so
hardened at such scenes of cruelty, that they made sport of this bereaved
and shrieking mother. Now, children, how would you feel, if your father
and mother were thus sold from each other, and you sold from them?
"You should remember them that are in bonds as bound with them."

The poor black children feel just as you would do, if you were sold
from your parents to see them no more. Black fathers and mothers love
their children, just as your white fathers and mothers love you. Black
husbands and wives love each other just as white husbands and wives
do; therefore it is just as wicked to make black people slaves, as it would
be to make slaves of white people.

Now I will tell you what a black mother did. She was a very black
woman and a slave. She first sent her husband to Canada, a place to
which a great many slaves run for freedom. After the husband has
escaped to the land of liberty, this black mother took her babe in her
arms, in the dark of night, and in a skiff crossed the great river Ohio into
a free state. She came to the house of a gentleman, and knocked at his
door in the night. He arose from his bed, opened the door, and saw the
poor slave mother with her babe in her arms. He was moved with com-
passion for her. "Don't be afraid," said he, "I am an abolitionist, but I
have never come out, yet; I'll help you." This poor black mother had to
travel in the night three hundred miles, and carry her babe in her arms.
This she had to do to escape the slave-catchers, a horrible class of men,
who catch fugitive slaves for money, and return them to their enraged
masters to be cruelly whipped, sold, and driven to the South to labor
under the lash of brutal overseers to the end of life. Many kind people in
Ohio helped this poor mother, and she got safely to Canada, and there
met her husband, and their meeting in a land of freedom after so much
toil and danger was most joyful. They labored together and procured a
good farm, on which to live. This mother had left six children in slavery.
After four years she traveled more than three hundred miles back to
get her children. She went into Kentucky, and lay concealed in her old

master's garden a whole day in order to see her children. At night she took away four of them and a grand-child. Two of them she could not get, because they slept in the room in which the master and mistress had their bed. Daylight came on before she could get over the river. Now she was obliged to hide with her four children and an infant grand-child in a field of green corn, and had nothing to eat but the ears of green corn. The field was near a town in which many bad people lived, and having an infant child that might cry aloud, she was in great danger of being discovered and taken. The Lord preserved her in this time of distress. The next night she got over to the house of a good man who lived on the bank of the river, who took her in and concealed her and the children during the day. At night she started upon her long and dark journey to Canada. Many good people in Ohio helped her on her way, and by their instrumentality the Lord preserved her from the slave-catchers, and she arrived safely again in Canada. Two of her younger children are still in slavery. A young man followed her into Canada, hoping to get her children. The colored people assembled to kill him, but she dissuaded them from their purpose. She treated him kindly, and sent him away in peace. She returned him good for evil, as her Saviour taught her to do. Now this mother had a black skin, but she had a white heart and a noble soul. And the Lord will bless those good people in Ohio, who helped her to escape with her children from the cruel slave-catchers. This, children, is a true narrative of what this mother really did, and it shows that the black mother loves her children, just as much as the white mother does. It shows how cruel slavery is, and how much black people will do to be free and to have their children free.

Children you should believe in the Saviour, and love him. He loves and pities all the poor, both black and white, and does them good. You should be like him, and do as he does.

13

The following letter is written to Mrs. Todd's mother, Sally Atkins. She had been in ill health for some time and the Todds want her to come live with them. She never does. Probably the poor travel conditions make it impossible for such an ill person to travel from Ohio to Iowa. The jarring of a stage ride would be detrimental to a healthy person, let alone one who was not feeling well. John talks of all the free-state immigrants who are holed up in Tabor. There are reports of a large number of pro-slavery men on the Kansas-Nebraska border waiting to intercept these men and their supplies and arms. Todd talks of the poor condition of the immigrant as far as sup-

plies as they come through Tabor. John also voices his concerns as he reads
newspapers from Chicago and the East of all the money and men that are
being raised to send to Kansas. He asks, where are the men and where has
the money gone?

Tabor, Fremont Co. Iowa Sep 12, 1856

Dear Mother,
      Yours of the 2nd inst. was received yesterday. We were glad, as usual,
to hear from you, but sorry to hear of Arther's disappointment & loss.—
hope he may yet be able to recover himself. It seems to me that if you can
in any way get here, you would do well to come & live with us. Some of
our people have gone to Ohio, & others are intending to cross the state
____ fall soon & if you could think it expedient or possible to get your
effects to Burlington or Davenport, provided I could devise means to
bring them across the state, & so you come yourself across by stage, I
wish you would inform us. I submit the proposal to you & if you enter-
tain such an idea, please write immediately, & state the probably amount
of baggage, etc. to be brought, & when you could probably have it forwarded to Davenport or Burlington. If the movement is impracticable to
you, I will not enter into any arrangements, but if it strikes you as practicable & desirable, let me know immediately, & I will try what I can do.
You shall not be left in want, while I can prevent it.
      We are all very busy. Kansas matters are now perilously exciting.
Emigrants have been here now for nearly 3 weeks waiting for the collection of a sufficient force to enter the territory, as it is blockaded by a force
of Missourians, which numbers according to rumor from 900 to 1500
men. The free State men are hemmed in, in the vicinity of Lawrence by
3 or 4 thousand "Ruffians," beside those that are guarding the northern
line against the entrance of Free Statesmen, so that the fate of Kansas
is well nigh sealed. There are not more than 1800 free statesmen in the
territory. 300 of these were at Topeka, according to our latest intelligence,
& were expecting an attack, with the certainty that they could not hold
out, if strongly attacked. The rest were fortifying themselves at & around
Lawrence, embracing a scope equal to about 5 miles square. They had
gathered in their cattle, horses, & provisions, & were standing in their
defense. They had neither home nor meal & were completely hemmed
in by their foes, living on potatoes, green corn, beef & pork, which must
result in dysentery & death to many. We have provisions, but cannot
raise men enough to carry it safely to them. Oh! It is too bad! I cannot
feel reconciled to the conduct of the people of the North. It seems as
if they never would do anything. They bluster & talk, but do nothing.
Chicago, in the time of excitement, agreed to raise 500 men & 15000

dollars, but where is it & what has it amounted to? Not more than 6 or 7 hundred men <u>in all</u> have come this way to Kansas, & they come in a destitute condition—poorly armed & without money or provisions almost. Lane & others have gone forward with the expectation of being backed up, but now they seem to be doomed to destruction-few if any emigrants are on the way, & we cannot raise a sufficient force to carry provisions or open the road. Alas! Alas!! Shall Kansas & those brave men be deserted in this their extremity? I fear that its fate will indeed be decided before deliverance can come. My heart is pained at the prospect. Some are preparing to go from here to aid if possible in opening the way into the territory & myself among the rest. Yet all told—emigrants & all— we cannot muster over 200 & perhaps not so many & what are these against such fearful odds. There are 20,000 dols. worth of provisions, ammunition ect. to be escorted in, & I fear it will fall into the hands of the Missourians.

Affectionately John Todd

🙢 14 🙠

The following letter is addressed to Mrs. Todd's father, Q.F. Atkins. John had sent 20 gold pieces for the sale of some land that his father-in-law owned in Iowa. However, someone, Mr. Ladd or the bank, has changed that into the less valuable paper money, causing much consternation. Buying land from afar or sending money during this time was often a huge problem. Todd goes on to write of more land matters, a much discussed topic in the new lands of the West, then a short dialogue of Kansas matters. Abolitionists in the summer of 1857 were very concerned about the outcome of the elections in the fall of 1857 and whether pro-slavery men or abolitionists would be elected. It was obvious John had friends writing to him about Underground Railroad matters in Ohio. Mechanicsburg, Ohio, was an important Underground Railroad center, with many of the citizens shielding runaways in the town. It was one of the best know stations in central and southern Ohio. The Poindexter case probably refers to a black barber in Jackson, Ohio, named Poindexter who aided in many Underground Railroad escapes by conveying escapees across the Ohio River at Portsmouth. In the last line of the letter Todd sees only doom over the question of slavery in the United States.

Tabor, Fremont Co. Iowa June 18, 1857

Dear Father,
  Yours of the 28th & 29th ult. were received to day–All satisfactory.

The money I sent you was ten twenty dollar gold pieces. I sewed them up in a belt, for Mr. Ladd's accommodation in carrying them, with my own fingers, & if anybody has palmed off upon you poor paper instead of gold, it was not owing to any design or act of mine. I presume it was an act on the part of the Bank to secure to itself the benefit of so much specie. Well I hope the matter will be so arranged that you will lose nothing by it.

The taxes on your land for the two yrs. past amount to $6'60, which I paid at the proper time, & did it most cheerfully, "hoping for nothing again." Your patents are probably at the Land Office in Kanesville & can be obtained by presenting your duplicate. The patents are made out on good substantial parchment, & are all recorded in the Land Office at Washington as indicated in the patent itself.

I have supposed that it was unnecessary to have recorded here, but perhaps I am mistaken, & will get it recorded if you desire it. I shall probably have an opportunity to send for the patent soon.

I don't wonder that you are surprised that all the land has already been picked up, but such was the rush in the spring of 1856 that every odd 40 was entered, even without being seen by the buyer, & often the competition was so great that the land was sold much above the minimum price. For more than a year none of us here knew of an acre metered anywhere in the region, except swamp lands. But within a few days it has been ascertained that a township or more (reports says) of vacant lands have been formed out on the boundless prairie 10 or 18 miles E. of Sidney. These are now subject to preemption, & preemption only, for the land office has been closed against all others since the passage of the bill granting lands to R. Roads. That vacant land is being picked up now very rapidly by preemptors. The lands too in Nebraska are now subject to preemption & are being entered rapidly.

We have had a cold backward spring. For a few days past we have had frequent showering from the N.W. Corn is small for the season. All eatables have been very high since last fall, & wages too are high.

We are glad to hear thro' you of the health & prosperity of the friends generally. You have probably ere this learned of the death of the only child of Stella Riordan, Clara Emily, on the 13th ult. One week ago last Monday a Mr. Clinton of Vienna on the W. Reserve was interred in our graveyard. He came West & purchased a farm in Nebraska with the intention of removing there as soon as practicable—had completed his business, & was about to start for Ohio, when he was taken ill-deranged from the first—lingered a few days & died, without leaving to surviving friends any good ground of his having made his peace with God. What soul-harrowing tidings to be home to his (pious?) parents, who were hopefully & anxiously waiting his return! It comes to us as a solemn warning against seeking the treasures of earth to the neglect of the one thing needful.

We are all in usual health, & the community generally are well. We have had some valuable additions to our community this spring & more are coming.

What are your hopes for Kansas? Will the party in power succeed in making it a Slave state in spite of the majority of its inhabitants? What about that Dept. U.S. Marshall who was imprisoned at Springfield Ohio, for arresting 4 men at Mechanicsburg in Champaign County for aiding the escape of 2 fugitives? I really hope that Ohio will show backbone enough to sustain the rights of her citizens against all the power of the general government, if need be.—That was a capital decision in the Poindexter case.

It seems to me that our general government is fast hastening toward despotism concentrated. May the good Lord in weary avert the threatened doom. Love to all the friends.

Q. F. Atkins.

Yours Affectionately
John Todd

✑ 15 ✑

John Brown's last trip on the Underground Railroad proved to be very controversial. When he got to Tabor he was censored by the town for the murder and the taking of large amounts of the slave owners' property. Brown felt very humiliated by this from the town that had protected him on so many occasions. When Brown proceeded to Grinnell, Iowa, he was treated as a hero. Many years later J.B. Grinnell brought this matter up and tried to portray himself in a positive light and the people of Tabor as afraid to help Brown because they were afraid of retaliation from nearby pro-slavery men in Nebraska and Missouri. As Parker points out, Grinnell's points didn't make sense. Professor Parker, the writer of this letter, was in a unique position to comment on this matter. He had been in Kansas in the 1850's when she had her troubles, he knew John Brown, and he knew John Todd and the people of Tabor. Parker also knew J.B. Grinnell and the people of that town.

The letter is on State University of Iowa stationary which states: CHAIR OF HISTORY AND COMPARATIVE PHILOLOGY. Leonard F. Parker, Professor. The letter is addressed to Rev John Todd. The J.B.G. is a reference Josiah Bushnell Grinnell.

Iowa City, 2/19/1887

Dear Brother "J.T";

"J.B.G's" mistake in saying Tabor was frightened into resolving "against John Brown" and his request for "a charitable opinion of a brave people" surprised me, yet I am still more surprised by his present expression of disapproval of "a murderous raid into a state with which we were at peace" coupled with his declaration that "in saying this I do not condemn John Brown." He intimates that the killing which Tabor disapproved was done by Brown in resisting a plot to kill himself, i.e. "by his striking the first blow."

Clearly Tabor was, and is, right in this matter, and "J.B.G." and John Brown wrong, for the Doyles whom he slew by "striking first" were killed in May 1856, while the killing Tabor disapproved was done in December 1858, two years and a half later, viz. in his invasion of Missouri solely to liberate slaves.

Sanborn in 'Life and Letters of John Brown' (which you may have) gives all these facts very clearly, as also the Tabor action in this matter. If "J.B.G." is right now in expressing his disapproval of "a murderous raid," etc. Tabor was right when she did the same thing in 1859.

If that ruggedly honest and resolutely truthful old man were alive today he would repudiate the idea that he made that raid into MO in Dec. 1858 in self-defense. He never made such a claim and never would. He always acknowledged and asserted the truth in the matter. I remember well his asking me what Oberlin would think of his raid, and I remember his reply, too, when I said, "Probably as I do, that it was a success as a hint that Missourians live in glass-houses, and would do well to stop provoking Kansas to throw stones, but as an anti-slavery measure it was a mistake." He answered, "I don't want that. I did it not to defend Kansas but to attack slavery."

Sanborn quotes Brown's own "indication of the invasion" which is as follows:

"1. It was in accordance with my settled policy.
2. It was intended as a discriminating blow at slavery.
3. It was calculated to lessen the value of slaves.
4. It was right."

Not a word from him about self-defense in all this as there was nothing of it in fact. It was nothing more or less than the prelude to the tragedy at Harper's Ferry.

Among (the next word all is crossed out) the good words of John Brown which his head and heart would honestly accept would be these: "He periled life" for the slave alone in Mo. as he did in Va."—words which will not justify his act or his judgment, but which will sustain you as against the forgetfulness of 'J.B.G..'

Doubtless Tabor has erred enough to seem human: it is unnecessary to assume that her wise acts were blunders in order to make her humble.

Yours truly,
L. F. Parker.

Chapter Notes

Chapter 1

1. Letter to Q.F. Atkins, Racine, Wisconsin, father to Mrs. John Todd, from Mrs. John Todd and her son James, Tabor, Iowa, dated December 25, 1856. Hereafter cited as Letter, Mrs. Todd, Dec. 25, 1856. All letters are located in the Todd House Archives unless otherwise noted. A complete transcribed version of this letter is in the Appendix.

2. Letter, Mrs. Todd, Dec. 25, 1856.

3. John Todd, *Early Settlement and Growth of Western Iowa or Reminiscences* (Des Moines: The Historical Department of Iowa, 1906), 65–66. The page numbers used are from the version reproduced by the Tabor Historical Society. This version is more accessible. Hereafter cited as Todd book.

4. Wilbur H. Siebert, *The Underground Railroad From Slavery To Freedom* (New York: The Macmillan Company, 1898), 419. Hereafter cited as Siebert.

5. Letter, Mrs. Todd, December 25, 1856.

6. Iowa Freedom Trail Program Proposal Publication. Department of Cultural Affairs, State Historical Society of Iowa, Community Programs Bureau, December 1999, 4. A chart that shows some Fremont County townships where over 30 percent of the residents formerly resided in slave states.

7. Records of Public Meetings in Tabor, Fremont County, Iowa. Taken from the section on Reminiscences of Samuel H. Adams, 102–103. Located in Todd House Archives. Hereafter cited as Tabor Public Meetings.

8. Oswald Garrison Villand, *John Brown: A Biography Fifty Years After* (Boston, New York:

Houghton Mifflin; Cambridge: The Riverside Press, 1911), 270, 274. Hereafter cited as Villand. Richard J. Hinton, *John Brown and His Men* (Funk and Wagnalls, 1894), 60. Hereafter cited as Hinton. Delight Ansley, *The Sword and the Spirit: A Life of John Brown* (New York: Thomas Y. Crowell Co., 1955), 113. Jules Abels, *Man on Fire: John Brown and the Cause of Liberty* (New York: Macmillan Co., 1971), 114, 147. Hereafter cited as Abels. Todd book, 69.

9. Letter to Mrs. Margaret G. Strohm, Dayton, Ohio, from John Todd, Oberlin, Ohio, February 21, 1842. Letter resides in Oberlin College Archives. Hereafter cited as Strohm letter. A transcribed version of this letter is in the Appendix.

10. Letter to Q. F. Atkins location not given from Jonas Jones, Tabor, Iowa, September 5, 1854. Hereafter cited as Letter Jonas Jones. Edited version of letter in Appendix. Todd book, 59.

11. Tabor Public Meetings, Reminiscences of Samuel H. Adams, 103.

12. *Ibid.*

13. Todd book, 59.

14. Adams, Deacon, "Tabor and Northern Excursion: Deacon Adams' Own Story." *The Annals of Iowa*, 3rd Series, Vol. 23 (October 1955), 130. Hereafter cited as Deacon Adams.

15. Tabor Public Meetings, Reminiscences of Samuel H. Adams, 103.

16. Todd book, 60.

17. Deacon Adams, 131.

18. Tabor Public Meetings, Reminiscences of Samuel H. Adams, 103.

19. Robert Gaston, Family papers, from un-

dated newspaper article from 1903, *Tabor Bea-con.* Hereafter cited as Robert Gaston.

20. Todd book, 60.

21. Gaston Manuscript, 17. This document is located at the Todd House Achieves. This material was gathered by W.E. Gaston, son of James Gaston. This manuscript contained information on the early history of Tabor. There were also recollections of the Gaston, Cummings and Townsend family pioneers and their children on events in early Tabor. Hereafter cited as Gaston Ms.

22. Gaston Ms., Addenda, 12.

23. *Ibid.*

24. Gaston Ms., Addenda, 6.

25. *Ibid.*

26. Todd book, 63.

27. Gaston Ms., Addenda, 9.

28. *Ibid.*

29. *Ibid.*, 10.

30. Villand, 267–268.

31. Letter Mrs. Todd, Dec. 25, 1856.

32. Gaston Ms., Addenda, 11.

33. *Ibid.*, 13.

34. Tabor Public Meetings, Maria Gaston, Reminiscences, 102.

Chapter 2

1. John Todd's Alumni File located in the Oberlin College Archives. Hereafter cited as John Todd's Alumni File.

2. J. H. Fairchild, *Oberlin: Its Origin, Progress and Results* (Oberlin: Shankland and Harmon, 1860). 9. This address was made by J. H. Fairchild, longtime president of Oberlin College, to an assembly of alumni at Oberlin on August 22, 1860. His address was put into book form. Hereafter cited as Fairchild.

3. Albert Temple Swing, *James Harris Fairchild or Sixty-Eight Years with a Christian College* (New York, Chicago, Toronto, London and Edinburgh: Fleming H. Revell, 1907), 65. Hereafter cited as Swing.

4. Fairchild, 5.

5. *Ibid.*, 4–5.

6. Todd book, 7.

7. David Todd's Alumni File located at Oberlin College Archives. Hereafter cited as David Todd's Alumni File.

8. Muster roll of the 2nd Regiment, 1st Brigade, Pennsylvania Militia, dated September 14, 1814. Document resides in the Pennsylvania State Archives, Harrisburg, Pa. Hereafter cited as Pennsylvania Muster Roll.

9. Todds of Hanover Genealogy Chart. This genealogy chart resides at the Todd House Museum in Tabor, Iowa. Much of the information on the chart was compiled by John Todd's brother, David Todd. Mrs. Gretchen French

Chamberlain of Mount Vernon, New York, provided some information, and the present day chart that is in Tabor was prepared by R.C. Todd of Middletown, Ohio, in 1937. Much of the information on the chart appeared in the book edited by William Henry Egle, *Notes and Queries: Historical, Biographical, and Genealogical Relating Chiefly to Interior Pennsylvania* (Harrisburg, Pa., 1896). The Todds of Hanover genealogy chart will hereafter be cited as Todd genealogy.

10. John Brannan, ed. *Official Letters of the Military and Naval Officers of the United States During the War with Great Britain in the Years 1812, 13, 14, and 15 With Some Additional Letters and Documents Elucidating the History of That Period* (Washington, 1823), 441.

11. Walter Lord, *The Dawn's Early Light* (New York: W.W. Norton & Company, 1972), 274. Hereafter cited as Lord. Ivan Molotsky, *The Flag, The Poet and The Song* (New York: Dutton, 2001), 79.

12. Letter from Major General Nathan Watson of the Pennsylvania Militia to Pennsylvania Governor Snyder written from Baltimore on September 20, 1814, stating that the first units of the 2nd Regiment, 1st Brigade were scheduled to arrive in Baltimore that morning. This letter is located in the Pennsylvania State Archives, Series 6, Volume 7, page 833. This letter was found by Louis Waddell, associate historian, at the Pennsylvania State Archives.

13. Todd genealogy.

14. Lord, 296.

15. Pennsylvania Muster Roll.

16. Todd genealogy.

17. *Ibid.*

18. *Ibid.*

19. Robert Samuel Fletcher, *A History of Oberlin College From Its Foundation Through the Civil War Vol. II* (Oberlin: Oberlin College, 1943), 615. Hereafter cited as Fletcher Vol. II.

20. Strohm letter.

21. Fairchild, 35.

22. Robert Samuel Fletcher, *A History of Oberlin College from its Foundation Through the Civil War* (Oberlin: Oberlin College, 1943) Vol. I, 380. Hereafter cited as Fletcher Vol. I. Fairchild, 36.

23. Fletcher Vol. I, 381.

24. Fletcher Vol. I, 178. James H. Fairchild, *Oberlin the Colony and the College, 1833–1883* (Oberlin: E.J. Goodrich, 1883), 64. Hereafter cited as Oberlin Fairchild. William E. Bigglestone, *Oberlin from War to Jubilee 1866–1883* (Oberlin: Grady Publishing, 1983), xi–xii. Swing, 76–77.

25. Fairchild, 29. Oberlin Fairchild, 74.

26. Fairchild, 26.

27. Oberlin Fairchild, 116.

28. *Ibid.*, 13.

29. Strohm letter.
30. Fletcher Vol. I, 395.
31. *Ibid.*, 396.
32. Fairchild, 27.
33. A prosecuting attorney's handwritten summation before a jury in Harlan County, Kentucky, charging David Todd and Wm. S. Westervelt of trying to incite a slave revolt. The date on this document is September 26, 1842. A complete transcribed version of this letter is in the Appendix.
34. Fletcher Vol. I, 251.
35. Handwritten copy of John Todd's commencement address in 1841 at Oberlin College entitled "Political Economy of Slavery," located in the Kenneth Spencer Research Library, University of Kansas. A complete transcribed version of his text is in the Appendix.
36. John Todd, "Christ's Last Passover," *Oberlin Review*, August 1846, 44–52.
37. Martha Atkins Todd's Alumni File located in the Oberlin College Archives. Hereafter cited as Martha Todd's Alumni File.
38. Letter to Q.F. Atkins, Cleveland, Ohio, from John Todd, Oberlin, Ohio, dated September 20, 1842. A complete transcribed version of this letter is in the Appendix.
39. Letter to Mrs. S. Atkins (Martha Todd's mother), Toledo, Ohio, from Q. F. Atkins, postmarked Cleveland, Ohio, dated May 4, 1849.
40. Martha Todd's Alumni File. Todd book, 8.
41. John Todd's Alumni File. Todd book, 20.
42. Martha and John Todd's Alumni Files. Todd book, 8, 20.
43. Copies of these ordination papers are on file at the Todd House Archives.

Chapter 3

1. Letter to Mrs. Sally Atkins, Cleveland, Ohio, from Martha Todd, Clarksfield, Ohio, dated December 29, 1846.
2. Letter to Q.F. Atkins, Geneva, Ashtabula, Ohio, from Martha and John Todd, Clarksfield, Ohio, dated June 15, 1847.
3. *Ibid.*
4. Todd genealogy.
5. Todd book, 14–15.
6. Letter to Q.F. Atkins, Cleveland, Ohio, from Martha and John Todd, Clarksfield, Ohio, dated May 11, 1849.
7. Letter to Q.F. Atkins in Geneva, Ashtabula, Ohio, from A.R. Hanna, Mercer, Pa., on March 19, 1846 asking Atkins to lecture in Mercer. Letter to Q.F. Atkins identifying him as being on the Central Committee of the Men of Liberty for Cuyahoga County. Letter is from Detroit, Michigan, dated September 14, 1844. Writer of the letter only identifies himself as "your fellow citizen."

8. Letter to Q. F. Atkins, Wolcott, New Haven Co., Conn., from Martha Todd's sister, Bertha Judson, letter postmarked Cleveland, Ohio. However, Bertha indicates letter was written from Brooklyn (no state given). A transcription of this letter is in the Appendix.
9. Siebert, 419.
10. Letter to Sally Atkins, mother of Martha Todd, no address given, from her son, Arthur Atkins, Chicago, Illinois, dated June 3, 1851. A transcription is in the Appendix.
11. "A Pioneer Daughter," *The Oberlin Alumni Magazine*, December 1, 1931, Volume 28, No. 3.
12. *Ibid.*
13. Letter to Q.F. Atkins, no address given, from his daughter, Mary Atkins, Benicia, California, dated Sept. 28, 1856.
14. *Ibid.*
15. Over 900 sermons located in the Todd House Archives attest to this methodology.
16. Todd book, 12.

Chapter 4

1. *Lorain County News*, Oberlin Ohio, June 12, 1873. Obituary of George Gaston written by John Todd. Hereafter cited as Gaston Obituary. Maria Cummings Gaston unpublished autobiography found in Tabor Library. Hereafter cited as Maria Gaston autobiography.
2. Tabor Public Records, Reminiscences of Elvira Platt, 94. Gaston Ms., 8.
3. Maria Cummings Gaston Alumni File located in the Oberlin College Archives. Gaston Obituary.
4. Gaston Ms., Addenda, 8. Maria Gaston autobiography.
5. Robert Gaston, Loren Hume Story #2, 6.
6. William M. Brooks, *The Story of Tabor College*, Tabor, Fremont Co., Iowa (Rochester, N.Y.: E.R. Andrews Printers, 1885), 3. Hereafter cited as Brooks. Todd book, 8.
7. Gaston Ms., 1, taken from a letter written by Cora (Gaston) Rice, granddaughter of George Gaston.
8. W. Wedel, ed. *The Dunbar-Allis Letters on the Pawnee* (New York & London: Garland Publishing, Inc. 1985), 642. Hereafter cited as Dunbar-Allis.
9. Mrs. Elvira Gaston Platt, "A Teacher Among The Pawnee," *Collections of the Kansas State Historical Society 1915-1918*, Vol. 14, 789. Hereafter cited as Platt-KSHS.
10. Dunbar-Allis, xii.
11. *Ibid.*, xv.
12. *Ibid.*, 654.
13. *Ibid.*, 645, 654.
14. *Ibid.*, 599–600.
15. *Ibid.*, 689.
16. *Ibid.*, 672–674.

17. *Ibid.*, 660.
18. *Ibid.*, 645.
19. http://www.oberlin.edu/~archive/ WWW?files/platt. Last visited 1/19/2001.
20. Dunbar-Allis, 656–659.
21. Mrs. Elvira Gaston Platt, "Reminiscences of a Teacher Among the Nebraska Indians, 1843–1885," *Transactions and Reports of the Nebraska State Historical Society Vol. III*, Hammond Bros., Printers, Fremont, Neb., 1892, 125–127. Hereafter cited as Platt-NSHS. Platt-KSHS, 784–785.
22. Jackson and Spence, eds., *The Expeditions of John Charles Frémont, Vol. 1, Travels from 1838 to 1844* (Urbana, Chicago, and London: University of Illinois Press, 1970), 283. Platt-NSHS, 132.
23. Platt-NSHS, 133. Platt-KSHS, 785.
24. Platt-KSHS, 786.
25. *Ibid.*, 785, Dunbar-Allis, 735.
26. Platt-KSHS, 788.
27. Platt-NSHS, 131.
28. *Ibid.*, 136.
29. Platt-KSHS, 786.
30. Platt-NSHS, 138.
31. Platt-KSHS, 787. Platt-NSHS, 138.
32. Platt-KSHS, 787. Platt-NSHS, 139.
33. Gaston Ms., 1, taken from a letter of Cora (Gaston) Rice, a granddaughter of George Gaston.
34. Oberlin College Archives, Platt Family Papers, 1848–1960, Biographical Sketches. Stephen K. Hutchinson, *Frontier Nebraska: Boone County Stories of Hardship and Triumph in the 1870s* (Lincoln, Neb.: Foundation Books, 1998), 213–214.

Chapter 5

1. Gaston Obituary. Brooks, 4.
2. Brooks, 5.
3. *Tabor Beacon*, March 3, 1910. Samuel H. Adams' obituary.
4. *Tabor Beacon*, June 28, 1907, Samuel H. Adams, "Why I Went to Oberlin."
5. Todd book, 24–25.
6. Todd book, 25.
7. Tabor Public Meetings, Quarter-Centennial Church History by John Todd, 85.
8. Tabor Public Meetings, Reminiscences of John Todd, 110–111.
9. Todd book, 28, 34. Tabor Public Meetings, Reminiscences of John Todd, 111.
10. Todd book, 28, 34.
11. *History of Fremont County, Iowa*, Iowa Historical Society, Iowa Historical Company, 1881, 711. Hereafter cited as Fremont.
12. Letter to Q.F. Atkins, Cleveland, Ohio, from John and Martha Todd, Clarksfield, Ohio, dated January 29, 1849.
13. Letter to Q.F. Atkins, Cleveland, Ohio,

from John Todd, Clarksfield, Ohio, dated May 11, 1849.
14. R.E. Cunningham, ed., *Southwest Iowa's Heritage: A History of Page and Fremont Counties*, Shenandoah, Iowa: World Publishing, 1973, 122-A. Hereafter cited as Southwest Iowa Heritage.
15. Robert Gaston, "A flood of fish," 2.
16. Catharine Grace Barbour Farquhar, "Tabor and Tabor College," *The Iowa Journal of History and Politics*, October 1943, 341. The writer was the granddaughter of Rachel Tucker, and this quotation was from Rachel Tucker's diary that was in the possession of Catharine Farquhar. Hereafter cited as Farquhar.
17. Letter to Q.F. Atkins, Cleveland, Ohio, from John Todd, Granville, Illinois, dated Monday, June 10, 1850. A complete transcribed version of this letter is in the Appendix. Todd book, 36–37.
18. *Tabor Beacon*, June 28, 1907. Reminiscences of James E. Todd.
19. *Tabor Beacon*, June 28, 1907, Mrs. Darius Matthews, "From Oberlin to Tabor."
20. Farquhar, 340.
21. Lowell Blikre, "Phase 1 Intensive Survey of Seven Potential Historic Archeological Properties in The Civil Bend Vicinity, Benton Township, Fremont County, Iowa," prepared for State Historical Society of Iowa, 8. Hereafter cited as Phase 1.
22. Brooks, 6. Tabor Public Records, Reminiscences of Elvira Platt, 97.
23. Todd book, 40. Brooks, 6.
24. Todd book, 42.
25. *Ibid.*, 42–43.
26. Julia Ann Cummings Matthews, Historical Reminiscences, from the family papers of Dale Matthews.
27. Tabor Public Meetings, 1.
28. *Ibid.*, 7–10.
29. Robert Gaston, Loren Hume reminiscences, 3.
30. Robert Gaston, History of Fremont County, 3.
31. Tabor Public Meetings, Reminiscences of John Todd, 113.
32. Tabor Public Meetings, Reminiscences of Mrs. M.C. Gaston, 100.
33. Tabor Public Meetings, Reminiscences of John Todd, 113.
34. Todd book, 13, 39–40.
35. P. Adelstein Johnson, *The First Century of Congregationalism in Iowa 1840–1940* (Cedar Rapids, Iowa: Torch Press, Congregational Christian Conference of Iowa, 1945), 125. Hereafter cited as Johnson. Todd book, 12–13.
36. Letter to John Todd, Gaston, Fremont County, Iowa, from George Whipple, No. 48, Beckman St., New York, N.Y., dated Sept. 9, 1851.
37. Robert Gaston, Loren Hume story #5, 4.
38. Robert Gaston, Loren Hume story #4, 2.

Chapter 6

1. Lord Richard Acton and Patricia Nassif Acton, Chapter Four, *Outside In: African-American History in Iowa 1838-2000* (Des Moines: State Historical Society of Iowa, 2001), 61.

2. Todd book, 40.

3. Sermon by John Todd in Tabor, Iowa, titled "Oppression," May 10, 1857.

4. Sermon by John Todd in Tabor, Iowa, titled "Western Book and Tract Society," June 23, 1867.

5. Charles E. Payne, *Josiah Bushnell Grinnell* (Iowa City: State Historical Society of Iowa, 1938), 114–115. Hereafter sited as Grinnell.

6. Brooks, 6.

7. Louis Pelzer, *Augustus Caesar Dodge* (Iowa City: State Historical Society of Iowa, 1908), 143–144. Hereafter cited as Dodge.

8. *Ibid.*, 146.

9. G. Galin Berrier, Chapter Three, *Outside In: African-American History in Iowa, 1838-2000* (Des Moines: State Historical Society of Iowa, 2000), 50–51.

10. Dodge, 148.

11. *Ibid.*, 150–151.

12. *Ibid.*, 190.

13. Articles of Incorporation for Tabor Literary Institute. These were the exact articles used for the formation of Tabor College in 1866.

14. Robert Dykstra, *Bright Radical Star: Black Freedom and White Supremacy of the Hawkeye Frontier* (Cambridge, Mass.: Harvard University Press, 1993), 110–112.

15. Gaston Manuscript addendum, 11.

16. Todd book, 79.

17. *Ibid.*

18. Fugitive Slave Act (1850): Sections 5, 6, 7.

19. Levine, Bruce, *Half Slave and Half Free: The Roots of Civil War* (New York: Hill and Wang, 1992), 187.

20. Sermon by John Todd in Tabor, Iowa, titled, "Judgment for the Oppressed," April 28, 1861.

21. http://www.sos.mo.gov/archives/local recs/conservation/dredscott/intro.asp. Last visited 4/25/2004. *Frank Leslie's Illustrated Newspaper*, June 27, 1857.

22. Lloyd Lewis, "The Man Historians Forgot," *Kansas Historical Quarterly*, February 1939 (Vol. 8, No. 1), 87. Hereafter cited as Lewis.

23. Larry Gara, *The Presidency of Franklin Pierce* (The University of Kansas Press, 1991), 32, 48–49.

24. Siebert, 410.

25. Tabor Public Meetings, 11–13.

26. Letter written by Q.F. Atkins from Tabor, May 25, 1854. This letter was written for the *Cleveland Morning Leader* for publication.

27. Letter to Q.F. Atkins, no address, from John Todd, Dawsonburg, Fremont County,

Iowa, dated Jan. 3, 1854. A complete transcribed version of this letter is in the Appendix.

28. Todd genealogy.

29. Letter to John Todd, Dawsonburg, Iowa, from David Todd and James Todd, Granville, Ill., brothers of John Todd, dated June 16 and June 21, 1852.

30. Letters to John Todd, Dawsonburg, Iowa, from David Todd, Granville, Ill., dated June 16 and June 26, 1852. Letters to John Todd, Dawsonburg, from James Todd, Granville, Ill., dated July 8 and July 13, 1853.

31. *Ibid.*

32. Letter to Q.F. Atkins, Racine, Wisconsin, from John Todd, Tabor, Iowa, dated Jan. 19, 1857.

33. Letters to Q.F. Atkins, Geneva, Ohio, from John Todd, Tabor, Iowa, dated May 18 and June 18, 1857.

34. Letter to John Todd, Dawsonburg, Iowa, from George Whipple of the American Missionary Society, New York City, dated May 22, 1853.

35. Letter to John Todd, Dawsonburg, Iowa, from S.L. Jocelyn and George Whipple of the American Missionary Society, New York City, March 9, 1854.

36. Letter to John Todd, Tabor, Iowa, from George Whipple of the American Missionary Society, New York City, June 3, 1856.

37. Letter Jonas Jones.

Chapter 7

1. Todd book, 60.

2. Letter, Mrs. Margaret Strohm, February 21, 1842.

3. *Tabor Beacon*, Centennial Issue, July 23, 1952. Unfortunately, a wildly inaccurate article in the *Council Bluffs Nonpareil* newspaper on August 26, 1926, perpetuates this misinformation of underground tunnels.

4. Todd papers in the Todd Museum archives and Gaston Manuscript or other documents from that era are devoid of any mention of tunnels.

5. Larry Gura, "An Epic in United States History," *Underground Railroad*, produced by the Division of Publications, National Park Service, Washington, D.C., 12.

6. Richard B. Sheridan, editor and complier, *Freedom's Crucible: The Underground Railroad in Lawrence and Douglas County, Kansas, 1854-1865: A Reader* (Lawrence: The University of Kansas, 1998). Hereafter cited as Sheridan.

7. Todd book, 61. It is known that Williamson was a major player in the assistance of the Nuckolls slaves' escape from Nebraska City.

8. Charles L. Blockson, *The Underground Railroad: First-Person Narratives of Escapees to Free-*

dom in the North (New York: Prentice Hall Press, 1987). Hereafter cited as Blockson.

9. Todd book, 75.

10. *Des Moines Capitol*, May 7, 1924.

11. A.A. Minnick, "The Underground Railroad in Nebraska," Nebraska State Historical Society, Publication, 2nd Series, Vol. 2, 73–74.

12. Harriet C. Frazier, *Runaway and Freed Missouri Slaves and Those Who Helped Them* (Jefferson, N.C. and London: McFarland and Co. 2004), 152, 154, 158–59. Hereafter cited as Frazier. *Missouri, A Guide to the 'Show Me' State*, Complied by the Workers of the Writers' Program of the Work Projects Administration (New York: Duell, Sloan and Pearce, 1941), 287.

13. Glenn Noble, *John Brown and the Jim Lane Trail* (Broken Bow, Neb.: Purcells, 1977), 107; hereafter cited as Noble.

14. These anti-slavery articles are located in the Todd House Museum Archives. They are often pasted in pages of a journal or an old expense book.

15. These tracts are located in the Todd House Museum Archives.

16. Photocopy of a handwritten notice for an anti-slavery meeting in the county seat of Fremont County, Sidney, Iowa, on September 1, 1855, located in the archives of the Todd House Museum. The original copy of this note resides in the Iowa Historical Society's Archives.

17. *Des Moines Capitol*, May 7, 1924.

18. Letter to Q.F. Atkins, Racine, Wisconsin, from John Todd, Tabor, Iowa, dated January 19, 1857. Letter to Q.F. Atkins, address unknown, from John and Martha Todd, April 29, 1857. Letter, Mrs. Todd, December 25, 1856.

19. Frazier, 100.

20. *Ibid.*, 101.

21. *Iowa State Register Morning Edition* newspaper clipping. Partial date of 6, 1887. No month available. Resides in Todd House Archives. *The Iowa State Register* was the forerunner to the *Des Moines Register*. Hereafter cited as *Iowa State Register*.

22. Letter to Q.F. Atkins, Geneva, Ashtabula, Ohio, from John Todd, Tabor, Iowa, dated May 3, 1858.

23. Jacob Van Ek, "Underground Railroad in Iowa," *Palimpsest*, May 1921, 135.

24. Hitchcock House, www.hitchcockhouse.org/conductor.htm. Last visited January 17, 2004.

25. Author's notes while at the Hitchcock House in Lewis, Iowa.

26. Charles Edward Smith, unpublished thesis at Northeast Missouri State College in August of 1971, 59.

27. G. Gailin Barrier, *Outside In: African-American History in Iowa 1838-2000*, Chapter 3, 49.

28. Curtis Harnack, "The Underground Railroad." *The Iowan Magazine*, June-July 1956. Harnack made a drawing of sites on the Underground Railroad in Iowa. Some of these cites have been verified; others have not.

29. *Iowa—A Guide To The Hawkeye State*, compiled and written by the Federal Writers' Project of the Works Progress Administration for the State of Iowa (New York: Viking Press, 1936), 101, 343.

30. *Appanoose County History*, Western Historical Co. (Chicago: 1878), 373. Hereafter cited as Appanoose.

31. Appanoose, 372.

32. Johnson, 74.

33. Blockson, 189.

34. Letter to John Todd, Tabor, Iowa, from K. Day, Denmark, Iowa, dated Feb. 6, 1862.

Chapter 8

1. *Tabor Beacon*, Centennial Issue, July 23, 1952.

2. Tabor Historical Pageant, Episode IV, 6. June 9–12, 1917.

3. S.F. Nuckolls' name has been spelled different ways, Nuckolls, Nuckols, and Nuchols, in newspapers and other publications. Nuckolls seems the most credible.

4. *Nebraska City News*, August 13, 1859.

5. *Nebraska City News Press*, November, 24, 1860.

6. File on S.F. Nuckolls located at the Morton-James Library in Nebraska City, Nebraska, 1926–1927. Hereafter cited as Nuckolls.

7. Todd book, 61.

8. Todd book, 61–62.

9. Robert Gaston, Loren Hume story #1, Phase 1, 11.

10. Phase 1, 12.

11. Fremont County Clerk's Office, Court Case No. 30, *Henry Garner vs. S.F. Nuchols* [sic], etc. March Term District Court 1859. Bob and Gertrude Handy, *Some Day: A Tale of Civil Bend by the River* (Interstate Publishers and Printers, 1973). 43. Hereafter cited as Handy.

12. Nuckolls, 1928.

13. Todd book, 61.

14. Fremont, 571.

15. Todd book, 62.

16. *Nebraska City News*, undated article.

17. Fremont County Clerk's Office, Court Case No. 30, *Henry Garner vs. S.F. Nuchols* [sic], etc. March Term District Court, 1859.

18. Fremont, 393, 394, 519.

19. Nuckolls, 1928.

20. Todd book, 62.

21. Federal Census, 1860, Otoe Co. mss, Family #20, including Census of Slaves.

22. File on Alexander Majors located at the

Morton-James Library in Nebraska City, Nebraska, 1691.

23. Alice A. Minick, *Underground Railroad in Nebraska.* Proceeding and Collection of the Nebraska State Historical Society Second Series, Vol. 2 (Lincoln, Neb.: State Journal Company Printers, 1898).

24. Hinton, 458.

25. W.E. Connelley, "The Lane Trail," *Collections of the Kansas State Historical Society*, Vol. 13 (1913–1914), 269–270. Handy, 36.

26. Noble, 93.

27. Handy, 39.

28. Letter to Q.F. Atkins, address unknown, from John Todd, Dawsonburg P.O., Fremont County, Iowa, dated January 3, 1854.

29. Fremont, 576.

30. Kevin Abing, "A Holy Battleground: Methodist, Baptist, and Quaker Missionaries Among Shawnee Indians, 1830–1844." *Kansas History* (Summer 1998): 132.

31. Tabor Public Meetings, Quarter Centennial of Tabor Congregational Church by John Todd, 86.

32. *Ibid.*

33. Fremont, 542.

34. Register of marriages performed by John Todd located in the Tabor Library.

35. *Ibid.*

36. Robert Gaston, Hume reminiscences, 2.

37. *Taylor County Tribune*, October 4, 1860.

38. Todd book, 66. Undated transcribed newspaper article from *The St. Louis Democrat* found in Todd House Archives. Hereafter cited as *St. Louis Democrat*. This same article was published in the *Page County Herald*, November 9, 1860. Hereafter cited as *Page County Herald*.

39. *St. Louis Democrat, Page County Herald.*

40. *Ibid.*

41. *Ibid.*

42. *Ibid.*

43. *Ibid.*

44. Farquhar, 362.

Chapter 9

1. Letter to Q.F. Atkins, address unknown, from John Todd, Tabor, Iowa, dated March 26, 1856.

2. Todd book, 51.

3. Noble, 30.

4. Laura Richards, editor, notes by F. B. Sanborn, *The Letters and Journals of Samuel Gridley Howe*, Vol. 2 (Boston: Dana Estes & Co., 1909), 423–424. Hereafter cited as Howe.

5. John Speer, *Life of Gen. Jas. H. Lane, The Liberator of Kansas* (Garden City, Kan.: 1896), 12. Hereafter cited as Speer.

6. Lewis, 91.

7. Hinton, 55–56.

8. Noble, 36–37.

9. Jay Monaghan, *Civil War on the Western Border 1854-1865* (New York: Bonanza Books, 1955), 70. Hereafter cited as Monaghan.

10. Thomas Henry Tibbles, *Buckskins and Blanket Days: Memoirs of a Friend of the Indians* (Chicago: Lakeside Press, reprint 1985), 19–20. Hereafter cited as Tibbles.

11. *Ibid.*, xxix.

12. W.H. Stephenson, "The Political Career of General James H. Lane," *Publication of the Kansas State Historical Society* (Topeka, 1930) Vol. 3, 74.

13. Monaghan, 69–70.

14. *Ibid.*, 70.

15. Todd book, 58.

16. Tibbles, 20–21.

17. *Ibid.*, 21.

18. Noble, 93. Letter to Thaddeus Hyatt, address unknown, from A.D. Searl in Tabor, Iowa, on August 21, 1856. Hereafter cited as Searl Letter. Letter resides in the Kansas State Historical Society.

19. Howe, 425, 427.

20. Monaghan, 73.

21. *Ibid.*, 74–75.

22. Todd book, 53.

23. Joseph G. Rosa, *They Called Him Wild Bill: The Life and Adventures of James Butler Hickok,* (Norman, Okla.: University of Oklahoma Press, 1964), 18, 22.

24. Speer, 128.

25. Shaler W. Eldridge, "Recollections of Early Days in Kansas," *Publications of the Kansas State Historical Society* (1920), Vol. 2, 110.

26. Lawrence L. Knutson, newspaper article carried by Associated Press, "From Milwaukee newspaper to key role in 1868 impeachment vote," *Milwaukee Journal Sentinel*, January 31, 1999. Hereafter cited as Milwaukee.

27. Noble, 36, 39.

28. Milwaukee.

29. Hinton, 120.

30. Noble, 51.

31. Searl letter.

32. Letter to Sally Atkins, mother-in-law, address unknown, from John Todd, Tabor, Iowa, dated Sept. 12, 1856. Hereafter, cited as Letter, Sally Atkins, September 12, 1856. A transcribed version of this letter is in the Appendix.

33. Tabor Public Meetings, Maria Gaston Reminiscences, 100–101. Todd book, 53–54.

34. Letter to Sally Atkins, September 12, 1856.

35. *Ibid.*, Todd, 54.

36. Todd book, 54.

37. *Ibid.*

38. Letter, Sally Atkins, Sept. 12, 1856.

39. Southwest Iowa Heritage, 148.

40. Lewis, 15.

Chapter 10

1. Merrill D. Peterson, *The Legend Revisited: John Brown* (Charlottesville: University of Virginia Press, 2002), 3–4. Hereafter cited as Peterson.

2. Villard, 31–33.

3. *Ibid.*, 273.

4. Todd, 53. Tabor Public Meetings, 101.

5. Noble, 25.

6. Villard, 262.

7. Tabor Historical Pageant, Episode IV, June 9–12, 1917, 6.

8. Tabor Public Meetings, 25–26. Todd book, 52.

9. Todd book, 57.

10. Letter to John Brown, Tabor, Iowa, from William A. Phillips, Lawrence, K.T., dated June 24, 1857. Letter resides in the Kansas State Historical Archives.

11. Abels, 146.

12. Villard, 313–314.

13. F.B. Sanborn, ed., *The Life and Letters of John Brown, Liberator of Kansas and Martyr of Virginia* (Boston: Roberts Brothers, 1891), 388–389. Hereafter cited as Sanborn. Peterson, 7.

14. Todd book, 68.

15. Letter to Mary Brown, address unknown, from (Nelson Hawkins) John Brown, Tabor, Iowa, dated August 17, 1857. Letter located at the Kansas State Historical Society.

16. John Anthony Scott and Robert Alan Scott, *John Brown of Harper's Ferry* (New York, Oxford and England: Facts on File Publishers, 1988), 127.

17. Stephen B. Oates, *To Purge This Land With Blood* (New York, Evanston and London: Harper and Row, 1970), 211–215.

18. Letter to Genl. John Brown, Tabor, Iowa, from James Lane, Falls City, Nebraska, dated Sept. 29, 1857. Letter resides in the Kansas State Historical Society, Sanborn, 402.

19. Letter to Genl. Jas. H. Lane, probably Falls City, Nebraska, from John Brown, Tabor, Iowa, dated September 30, 1857. Letter resides in the Kansas State Historical Society.

20. Sanborn, 400, 405.

21. Noble, 75.

22. Letter to John Brown in Tabor, Iowa, from S. (Samuel) L. Adair, Osawatomie, K.T., dated Oct. 2, 1857. Letter resides in the Kansas State Historical Society.

23. Letter to John Brown in Tabor, Iowa, from Henry H. Williams, Osawatomie, K.T., dated October 12, 1857. Letter resides in the Kansas State Historical Society.

24. Todd book, 68.

25. William S. McFeely, *Frederick Douglass* (New York and London: W.W. Norton & Co., 1991), 193.

26. Sanborn, 425–427, 431–432.

27. Villard, 298–299.

28. *Ibid.*, 311–312.

29. Todd book, 55.

30. Sanborn, 287, 312.

31. Sheridan, 142–143.

32. Villard, 308.

33. *Ibid.*, 311.

34. Sanborn, 423–424.

35. Villard, 368–369.

36. Villard, 383.

37. Hinton, 225.

38. James Redpath, *The Public Life of Captain John Brown* (Boston: 1860), 221.

39. Professor J.E. Todd, "John Brown's Last Visit To Tabor," *Annals of Iowa*, April–July, 1898, 458. Hereafter cited as J.E. Todd. Todd book, 70.

40. Villard, 384.

41. The original of this note is located in the Iowa State Historical Archives in Des Moines, Iowa. A photocopy of this note resides in the Todd House Museum Archives.

42. Todd book, 70.

43. J.E. Todd, 459. Todd book, 70.

44. J.E. Todd, 459.

45. Villard, 385. Sanborn, 488.

46. Tabor Public Meetings, Maria Gaston's Reminiscences, 101–102.

47. Villard, 386.

48. Sanborn, 488–489. Grinnell, 108–112.

49. Grinnell, 110–111.

50. Letter to John Todd, Tabor, Iowa, from L.F. Parker, Iowa City, Iowa, dated February 19, 1887. Hereafter cited as Parker letter. A complete transcribed version of this letter is in the Appendix.

51. *Iowa State Register*, 1887, undated newspaper article.

52. *Iowa State Register* newspaper article, dated Feb. 16, 1887.

53. Parker letter.

54. Todd book, 71. J.E. Todd, 460–461.

55. *Liberator*, October 21, 1859.

56. Tabor Public Meetings, Maria Gaston's Reminiscences, 102.

Chapter 11

1. Letter to John Todd, Tabor, Iowa, from E. Fraser of Boarman and Fraser Real Estate Brokers and General Agents in Kansas City, Missouri, dated November 15, 1860.

2. Sermon, "Judgment for the Oppressed" by John Todd given at the Tabor Congregational Church on April 28, 1861.

3. *Ibid.*

4. *Ibid.*

5. Todd book, 51.

6. Fremont, 570–71.

7. Monaghan, 281–286.

8. Funeral sermon for Jesse West on Nov. 3, 1861, given by the Reverend John Todd.

9. Letter to John Todd, Tabor, Iowa, from his brother, David Todd, Pine Bluff, Arkansas, dated June 6, 1864. Letter to John Todd, while chaplain of the 46th Iowa Infantry stationed in Colliersville, Tenn., from his sister, Mary Sloan, Harrisburg, Pa., dated August 11, 1864.

10. Photocopies of military documents from the Headquarters Military District of Washington dated Jan. 8, 1863, giving John Todd a pass within the lines of the United States Forces. Also, a document from the Office of the Provost Marshal, Camp Hamilton, Va., notifying guards to pass Mr. Todd. These photocopies were found in the Tabor Library.

11. Letter to John Todd while John was chaplain of the 46th Iowa Infantry in Memphis, Tenn., from son James Todd, Ft. Stevens, Washington, D.C., dated July 19, 1864. Hereafter cited as Letter, James E. Todd, July 19, 1864. Fremont, 711.

12. Geoffrey C. Ward, Ric Burns and Ken Burns, *The Civil War* (New York: Alfred A. Knopf, 1991), 310–311.

13. Letter, James E. Todd, July 19, 1864.

14. James E. Todd Alumni File, Oberlin College Archives. Undated newspaper obituary from the *Tabor Beacon* of James E. Todd.

15. Tabor Public Meetings, 63.

16. Todd book, 12.

17. John Todd's mustering-in papers from the Union Army located at the Todd House Archives state he was mustered in on June 29, 1864. However, a certificate issued by the state of Iowa signed by the Adjutant of the 46th Iowa Infantry, stated Todd's date of mustering-in was June 14, 1864.

18. John Todd's mustering-in papers from the Union Army located at the Todd House Archives.

19. Letter to John Todd, while chaplain of 46th Iowa Infantry, addressed to Cairo, Ill., from Mrs. John Todd, Tabor, Iowa, dated June 30, 1864.

20. Todd book, 12.

21. Letter to John Todd while chaplain of the 46th Iowa Infantry, Memphis, Tenn., from James R. Pinnio, Tipton, Iowa, dated July 14, 1864.

22. Letter to John Todd while chaplain of the 46th Iowa Infantry, Colliersville, Tenn., from L. Williams, Glenwood, Iowa, dated August 30, 1864.

23. Letter to John Todd while chaplain of the 46th Iowa Infantry, Colliersville, Tenn., from Lt. Alexander Rliedang, Memphis Officer Hospital, August, 10, 1864.

24. Letter to John Todd while chaplain of the 46th Iowa Infantry, Memphis, Tennessee, from Mrs. John Todd and daughters Maggie and Flora, Tabor, Iowa, July 27, 1864.

25. Todd book, 12.

26. *Roster and Records of Iowa Soldiers in the War of the Rebellion Together With Historical Sketches of Volunteer Organizations, 1861-1865*, Vol. 5, p. 1374 (Des Moines, Iowa: E.H. English, 1908). Letter to John Todd while he was chaplain of the 46th Iowa Infantry in Memphis, Tenn., from Mrs. John Todd and daughter Flora, Tabor, Iowa, dated August 5, 1864. The letter contained an undated newspaper article describing the skirmish.

27. Letter to John Todd while he was chaplain of the 46th Iowa Infantry, Colliersville, Tenn., from the Reverend Origen Cummings, Tabor, Iowa, dated July 7, 1864.

28. Letter to John Todd, Glenwood, Iowa, from Dr. B. Henderson on stationery from the Headquarters Board of Enrollment for the Third Congressional District State of Iowa, Dubuque, Iowa, dated January 30, 1865.

29. Tabor Public Meetings, 69.

30. Letters to Mrs. John Todd, Tabor, Iowa, from Wade Thomas, Tougaloo, Mississippi, dated January 26, March 23 and June 5, 1880. Letter to Mrs. John Todd, Tabor, Iowa, from L. J. Hines, Tougaloo, Mississippi, dated Feb. 16, 1880.

Chapter 12

1. Brooks book, 7.

2. Letters of recommendation for William Brooks were written from these Oberlin College professors: James Monroe, dated June 10, 1857; Charles Penfield, dated June 19, 1857; and John Morgan, dated June 11, 1857. These documents reside in the Todd House Museum Archives.

3. Farquhar, 364.

4. Letter to William Brooks, Oberlin, Ohio, from John Todd, Tabor, Iowa, dated January 14, 1859.

5. Letter to William Brooks, Oberlin, Ohio, from George Gaston, Tabor, Iowa, dated January 27, 1859.

6. Letters to William Brooks, Oberlin, Ohio, from Edwin Hill, Tabor, Iowa, dated November 28, 1858 and January 10, 1859. Letter to William Brooks, Oberlin, Ohio, from Jonas Jones, Tabor, Iowa, dated January 27, 1859.

7. Letter to William Brooks, Oberlin, Ohio, from John Todd, Tabor, Iowa, dated January 14, 1859.

8. Letter to William Brooks, Oberlin, Ohio, from George Gaston, Tabor, Iowa, dated January 27, 1859.

9. Tabor Public Meetings, 41–42.

10. Southwest Iowa Heritage, 148.

11. Letter to William Brooks, Oberlin, Ohio,

from John Todd, Tabor, Iowa, dated January 14, 1859.

12. Southwest Iowa Heritage, 148.

13. William Brooks, "History of Tabor College," presentation given at the Quarter Centennial Anniversary of the Tabor Congregational Church, October 11, 1877. Brooks, 11.

14. Todd book, 14.

15. Brooks, 12–13.

16. Tabor College newspaper article from the *The Cardinal* dated Dec. 8, 1925.

17. Farquhar, 369.

18. Letter to the Reverend Theron Baldwin D.D., address unknown, from John Todd, Tabor, Iowa, dated July 11, 1868.

19. Letter to John Todd, Tabor, Iowa, from Jonathan Cable, New York, dated May 28, 1868.

20. Letters to John Todd, Tabor, Iowa, from Jonathan Cable, Danville, Iowa, dated March 26, 1868; from Philadelphia, Pa., dated April 13, 1868; from Philadelphia, Pa., dated May 9, 1868; from New York, New York, dated May 18, 1868; from New York, New York, dated May 28, 1868; from Providence, R.I., dated June 6, 1868.

21. Farquhar, 372.

22. Tabor Public Meetings, 76–77.

23. George Gaston Obituary in the *Lorain County News* (Ohio) dated June 12, 1873.

24. Farquhar, 374.

25. Two undated newspaper articles from the *Tabor Beacon* found in the Todd House Archives.

26. Todd genealogy, Oberlin College Alumni Files for James E. Todd, Oberlin College Archives.

27. Fremont, 711.

28. *Ibid.*

29. Oberlin College Alumni Files for James E. Todd, Oberlin College Archives.

30. Biographical Information of James E. Todd, Todd Collection, Kenneth Spencer Research Library, University of Kansas. Fremont, 711.

31. http://www.ukans.edu/~spencer/exhibits/darwin.html. Last visited 6/24/2001.

32. Tabor College Catalogue 1886–7.

33. Letter to Q.F. Atkins, Geneva, Ashtubula County, Ohio, from John Todd, Tabor, Iowa, dated June 18, 1857. A complete transcribed version of this letter is in the Appendix.

34. A Brief History of the Shenandoah Congregational Church by author. Also, notes of author on history of the Shenandoah Congregational Church. Brooks, 29.

35. Johnson, 272.

36. Letter to John and Martha Todd, Tabor, Iowa, from Mary Lynch, New Orleans, Louisiana, dated August 4, 1874.

37. Todd book, 21. Todd genealogy.

38. Article about Mrs. John Todd written by E.S. Hill in 1874, reprinted in the *Tabor Talisman* (Tabor College paper) in December of 1904.

39. Letter to John Todd, Tabor, Iowa, from G. G. Rice, Council Bluffs, Iowa, dated July 30, 1888.

40. Todd book, 21. Series of letters from Drakola, Kingsbury County, South Dakota, from John Todd to various people describing conditions in the area. These letters reside in the Todd House Archives.

41. Letter to John Todd, Tabor, Iowa, from Bertha Judson, Cleveland, Ohio, dated March 17, 1893.

42. *Tabor Beacon*, February 2, 1894. John Todd obituary.

43. *Ibid.*

44. Letters to William Brooks, Tabor, Iowa, from N.P. Dodge, Council Bluffs, Iowa, November 16, 1882, April 6, 1884. Brooks book, 32.

45. Johnson, 273.

46. *Tabor Beacon*, March 3, 1910.

47. *Council Bluffs Nonpareil*, February 2, 1929.

Bibliography

Books

Abels, Jules. *Man on Fire: John Brown and the Cause of Liberty.* New York: Macmillan Co., 1971.

Anderson, Galusha. *The Story of a Border City During the Civil War.* Boston: Little, Brown, and Company, 1908.

Ansley, Delight. *The Sword and the Spirit: A Life of John Brown.* New York: Thomas Y. Crowell Co., 1955.

Appanoose County History. Chicago: Western Historical Co., 1878.

Bigglestone, William E. *Oberlin from War to Jubilee: 1866–1883.* Oberlin, Ohio: Grady Publishing, 1883.

Blockson, Charles L. *Hippocrene Guide to the Underground Railroad.* New York, N.Y.: Hippocrene Books, 1994.

Blockson, Charles L. *The Underground Railroad: First-Person Narratives of Escapees to Freedom in the North.* New York, N.Y.: Prentice Hall Press, 1987.

Bordewich, Fergus. *Bound for Canaan: The Underground Railroad and the War for the Soul of America.* New York, N.Y.: Harper-Collins, 2005.

Boyer, Richard O. *The Legend of John Brown: A Biography and a History.* New York: Alfred A. Knopf, 1973.

Branch, E. Douglas, introduction by J. Frank Dobie. *The Hunting of the Buffalo.* Lincoln, Neb. and London: University of Nebraska Press, 1962.

Brandt, Nat. *The Town That Started the Civil War.* Syracuse, N.Y.: Syracuse University Press, 1990.

Brannan, John, ed. *Official Letters of the Military and Naval Officers of the United States During the War with Great Britain in the Years, 1812,13,14, and 15 With Some Additional Letters and Documents Elucidating the History of That Period.* Washington: 1823.

Britton, Wiley. *The Civil War on the Border.* New York and London: G.P. Putnam's Sons, 1891.

Brooks, William M. *The Story of Tabor College, Tabor, Fremont Co., Iowa.* Rochester, N.Y.: E.R. Andrews Printers, 1885.

Castel, Albert. *A Frontier State at War: Kansas, 1861–1865.* Ithaca, N.Y.: Cornell University Press, 1958.

Catton, Bruce. *The Civil War.* New York: Fairfax Press, 1980.

Cunningham, R.E., ed. *Southwest Iowa's Heritage: A History of Page and Fremont Counties.* World Publishing, 1973.

Dykstra, Robert. *Bright Radical Star: Black Freedom and White Supremacy of the Hawkeye Frontier.* Cambridge, Mass.: Harvard University Press, 1993.

Egle, William Henry. *Notes and Queries: Historical, Biographical, and Genealogical Relating Chiefly to Interior Pennsylvania.* Harrisburg, Pa.: 1896.

Fairchild, James H., *Oberlin Colony and the College, 1833–1883,* Oberlin: E.J. Goodrich, 1883.

Fairchild, James H. *Oberlin: Its Origin, Progress and Results.* Oberlin: Shankland and Harmon, 1860.

Fletcher, Robert Samuel. *A History of Oberlin College From its Foundation Through the Civil War, Vol. I and II.* Oberlin: Oberlin College, 1943.

Frazier, Harriet C. *Runaway and Freed Missouri Slaves and Those Who Helped Them.* Jefferson, N.C., and London: McFarland and Co., 2004.

Gara, Larry. *The Liberty Line: The Legend of the Underground Railroad.* Lexington: University of Kentucky Press, 1961.

Gara, Larry. *The Presidency of Franklin Pierce.* Lawrence, Kan.: University Press of Kansas, 1991.

Handy, Bob, and Gertrude Handy. *Someday: A Tale of Civil Bend by the River.* Interstate Publishers and Printers, 1973.

Hendrick, George, and Willene Hendrick. *Fleeing for Freedom: Stories of the Underground Railroad as Told by Levi Coffin and William Still.* Chicago, Ill.: Ivan R. Dee Publishers, 2004.

Hinton, Richard J. *John Brown and His Men.* Funk and Wagnalls, 1894.

History of Fremont County, Iowa. Des Moines: Iowa Historical Company, 1881.

Hutchinson, Stephen K. *Frontier Nebraska: Boone County Stories of Hardship and Triumph in the 1870s.* Lincoln, Neb.: Foundation Books, 1998.

Iowa: A Guide to the Hawkeye State. Compiled and written by the Federal Writers' Project of the Works Progress Administration for the State of Iowa. New York, N.Y.: Viking Press, 1936.

Jackson and Spence, ed. *The Expeditions of John Charles Frémont, Vol. I: Travels from 1838 to 1844.* Urbana, Chicago and London: University of Illinois Press, 1970.

Johnson, P. Adelstein. *The First Century of Congregationalism in Iowa, 1840–1940.* Cedar Rapids, Iowa: Torch Press, Congregational Christian Conference of Iowa, 1945.

Kennedy, John F. *Profiles in Courage.* New York: Harper and Brothers, 1956.

Larson, Kate Clifford. *Bound for the Promised Land: Harriet Tubman, Portrait of an American Hero.* New York: Ballantine Books, 2004.

Levine, Bruce. *Half Slave and Half Free: The Roots of Civil War.* New York: Hill and Wang, 1992.

Lord, Walter. *The Dawn's Early Light.* New York: W.W. Norton and Company, 1972.

Malin, James. *John Brown and the Legend of Fifty-Six.* American Philosophical Society, Independence Square, 1942.

McFeely, William S. *Frederick Douglass.* New York and London: W.W. Norton and Co., 1991.

Members of the Potomac Corral of the Westerners. *Great Western Indian Fights.* Lincoln, Neb.: Bison Books, 1960.

Merritt, W.W., Sr. *History of Montgomery County.* Red Oak, Iowa: Express Publishing, 1906.

Missouri: A Guide to the 'Show Me' State. Compiled by the Workers of the Writers' Program of the Work Projects Administration, New York: Duell, Sloan and Pearce, 1941.

Monaghan, Jay. *Civil War on the Western Border, 1854-1865.* New York, N.Y.: Bonanza Books, 1955.

Morton, Sterling J., and Albert Watkins. *History of Nebraska.* Lincoln, Neb.: Jacob North and Co., 1905.

Murphy, Dan, ed. *Old Courthouse.* St. Louis, Mo.: Jefferson National Expansion Historical Association, 1979.

Noble, Glenn. *John Brown and the Jim Lane Trail.* Broken Bow, Neb.: Purcells, 1977.

Oates, Stephen B. *To Purge This Land With Blood.* New York, Evanston and London: Harper and Row, 1970.

O'Flaherty, Daniel. *General Jo Shelby, Undefeated Rebel.* Chapel Hill, N.C.: University of North Carolina Press, 2000.

Parish, John C. *George Wallace Jones.* Iowa City: State Historical Society of Iowa, 1912.

Payne, Charles E. *Josiah Bushnell Grinnell.* Iowa City: State Historical Society of Iowa, 1938.

Pelzer, Louis. *Augustus Caesar Dodge.* Iowa City: State Historical Society of Iowa, 1908.

Peterson, Merrill D. *The Legend Revisited John Brown.* Charlottesville: University of Virginia Press, 2002.

Redpath, James. *The Public Life of Captain John Brown.* Boston: Thayer and Eldridge, 1860.

Richards, Laura, ed., notes by F.B. Sanborn. *The Letters and Journals of Samuel Gridley Howe.* Boston: Dana Estes and Co., 1909.

Rosa, Joseph G. *They Called Him Wild Bill: The Life and Adventures of James Butler Hickok.* Norman, Okla.: University of Oklahoma Press, 1964.

Roster and Records of Iowa Soldiers in the War of the Rebellion Together With Historical Sketches of Volunteer Organizations, 1861-1865, Vol. 5. Des Moines, Iowa: E.H. English, 1908.

Sage, Leland. *A History of Iowa.* Ames: Iowa State University Press, 1974.

Sanborn, F.B., ed. *The Life and Letters of John Brown, Liberator of Kansas and Martyr of Virginia.* Boston: Roberts Brothers, 1891.

Scott, John Anthony, and Robert Alan Scott. *John Brown of Harper's Ferry.* New York and Oxford: Facts on File Publishers, 1988.

Settle, William A. *Jesse James Was His Name, or Fact and Fiction Concerning the Careers of the Notorious James Brothers of Missouri.* Columbia: University of Missouri Press, 1966.

Sheridan, Richard B., ed. and comp. *The Underground Railroad in Lawrence and Douglas County, Kansas, 1854-1865: A Reader.* Lawrence: The University of Kansas, 1998.

Siebert, Wilbur H. *The Underground Railroad from Slavery to Freedom.* New York: Macmillan Company, 1898.

Silag, Bill, ed., Lord Richard Acton, Patricia Nassif Acton, and G. Galin Berrier. *Outside In: African-American History in Iowa, 1838-2000.* Des Moines: State Historical Society of Iowa, 2001.

Smith, Charles Edward. *The Underground Railroad in Iowa.* Unpublished manuscript for master's thesis from Northeast Missouri State College, 1971.

Speer, John. *Life of Gen. Jas. H. Lane, The Liberator of Kansas.* Garden City, Kan.: 1896.

Sprague, Stuart Seely, ed. *The Autobiography of John P. Parker, Former Slave and Conductor on the Underground Railroad.* New York and London: W.W. Norton and Co., 1996.

Swing, Albert Temple. *James Harris Fairchild or Sixty-Eight Years with a Christian College.* New York, Chicago, Toronto, London and Edinburgh: Fleming H. Revell, 1907.

Tibbles, Thomas Henry. *Buckskins and Blanket Days: Memoirs of a Friend of the Indian.* Chicago: Lakeside Press, reprint 1985.

Todd, John. *Early Settlement and Growth of Western Iowa or Reminiscences.* Des Moines: The Historical Department of Iowa, 1906.

Villand, Oswald Garrison. *John Brown: A Biography Fifty Years After.* Boston and New York: Houghton Mifflin; Cambridge: The Riverside Press, 1911.

Ward, Geoffrey C., Ric Burns, and Ken Burns. *The Civil War.* New York: Alfred A. Knopf, 1991.

Wedel, W., ed. *The Dunbar-Allis Letters on the Pawnee.* New York and London: Garland Publishing, Inc., 1985.

Periodicals

Abing, Kevin. "A Holy Battleground: Methodist, Baptist, and Quaker Missionaries Among Shawnee Indians, 1830–1844." *Kansas History.* Summer 1998.

Adams, Deacon (Samuel). "Tabor and Northern Excursion: Deacon Adams' Own Story." *The Annals of Iowa,* 3rd Series, No. 33, October 1955.

Author unknown, "A Pioneer Daughter." *The Oberlin Alumni Magazine,* Vol. 28, No. 3, December 1, 1931.

Connelley, William. "The Lane Trail." *Collections of the Kansas State Historical Society,* Vol. 13 (1913–1914).

Eldridge, Shaler, W. "Recollections of Early Days in Kansas." *Publications of the Kansas State Historical Society,* Vol. 2, 1920.

Farquhar, Catharine Grace Barbour. "Tabor and Tabor College." *The Iowa Journal of History and Politics,* October 1943.

Gara, Larry. "An Epic in United States History." *Underground Railroad.* Produced by the Division of Publication, National Park Service, Washington D.C., 1998.

Gaston, Robert. "Stoic Soldier, Precious Son." unpublished article.

Harnack, Curtis. "Underground Railroad." *The Iowan Magazine,* June-July 1956.

Lewis, Lloyd. "The Man Historians Forgot." *Kansas Historical Quarterly,* February 1939, Vol. 8, No. 1.

Minnick, A.A. "The Underground Railroad in Nebraska." *Nebraska State Historical Society Publication,* 2nd Series, Vol. 2, 73–74.

Morgans, James Patrick. "A Brief History of the Shenandoah Congregational Church."

Morrow, Robert. "Emigration to Kansas in 1856." *Transactions of the Kansas State Historical Society, Vol. 8, 1903–04.*

Platt, Elvira Gaston. "Reminiscences of a Teacher Among the Nebraska Indians, 1843–1885." *Transactions and Reports of the Nebraska Historical Society, Vol. 3.*

Platt, Elvira Gaston. "A Teacher Among the Pawnee." *Collections of the Kansas State Historical Society, 1915–1918, Vol. 14.*

Silbey, J.H. "Proslavery Sentiment in Iowa." *Iowa Journal of History,* Vol. 55, No. 4, October 1957.

Todd, J.E. "John Brown's Last Visit to Tabor," *Annals of Iowa,* April–July 1898.

Todd, John. "Christ's Last Passover," *Oberlin Review,* August 1846.

Van Ek, Jacob. "Underground Railroad in Iowa." *Palimpsest,* May 21, 1921.

Newspapers

Frank Leslie's Illustrated Newspaper, June 27, 1857.

Fremont Herald, December 4, 1858.

Nebraska City News, undated article.

Nebraska City News, August 13, 1859.

Liberator, October 21, 1859.

Taylor County Tribune, October 4, 1860.

St. Louis Democrat, undated article (reprinted in *Page County Herald,* November 9, 1860.)

Page County Herald, November 9, 1860.

Nebraska City News, November 24, 1860.
Lorain County News, Oberlin, Ohio, June 12, 1873.
Iowa State Register, February 16, 1887.
Iowa State Register, undated article, 1887.
Iowa State Register Morning Edition, ?, 6, 1887.
Tabor Beacon, February 2, 1894.
Tabor Beacon, June 26, 1903.
Tabor College Talisman, December, 1904.
Tabor Beacon, June 28, 1907.
Tabor Beacon, March 3, 1910.
Des Moines Capitol, May 7, 1924.
The Cardinal, Tabor College newspaper, December 8, 1925.
Council Bluffs Nonpareil, August 26, 1926.
Council Bluffs Nonpareil, February 2, 1929.
Tabor Beacon, Centennial Issue, July 23, 1952.
Milwaukee Journal Sentinel, January 31, 1999.

Letters

These letters and sermons all reside in Todd House Museum Archives unless otherwise noted. Many of the 2,000 letters, sermons and documents in the Todd House Museum Archives were consulted while doing this book. The items listed here were the letters, sermons and documents that were footnoted.

Letter to Pennsylvania Governor Snyder from Major General Nathan Watson of the Pennsylvania Militia from Baltimore, Md., September 20, 1814. Pennsylvania State Archives.
Letter to Mrs. Margaret Strohm, Dayton, Ohio, from John Todd, Oberlin, Ohio, February 21, 1842. Oberlin College Archives.
Letter to Q.F. Atkins, Cleveland, Ohio, from John Todd, Oberlin, Ohio, September 20, 1842.
Letter to Q.F. Atkins, address unknown, from "your fellow citizen," Detroit, Mich., September, 14, 1844.
Letter to Q.F. Atkins, Geneva, Ashtabula, Ohio, from A.R. Hanna, Mercer, Pa., March 19, 1846.
Letter to Mrs. Sally Atkins, Cleveland, Ohio, from her daughter, Martha Todd, Clarksfield, Ohio, December 29, 1846.
Letter to Q.F. Atkins, Geneva, Ashtabula, Ohio, from Martha and John Todd, Clarksfield, Ohio, June 15, 1847.
Letter to Q.F. Atkins, Cleveland, Ohio, from John and Martha Todd, Clarksfield, Ohio, January 29, 1849.
Letter to S. Atkins (Martha Todd's mother), Toledo, Ohio, from Q.F. Atkins, Cleveland, Ohio, May 4, 1849.
Letter to Q.F. Atkins, Cleveland, Ohio, from Martha and John Todd, Clarksfield, Ohio, May 11, 1849.
Letter Q.F. Atkins, Cleveland, Ohio, from John Todd, Granville, Illinois, June 10, 1850.
Letter to Sally Atkins (mother of Martha Todd) from Arthur Atkins, Chicago, Illinois, June 3, 1851.
Letter to John Todd, Gaston Fremont County, Iowa, from George Whipple, No. 48 Beckman St., New York, New York, September 9, 1851.

Letters to John Todd, Dawsonburg Post Office, Fremont County, Iowa, from David and James Todd, Granville, Ill., June 16 and June 21, 1852.

Letter to John Todd, Dawsonburg Post Office, Fremont County, Iowa, from David Todd, Granville, Ill., June 26, 1852.

Letter to John Todd, Dawsonburg Post Office, Fremont County, Iowa, from James Todd, Granville, Ill., July 8, 1852.

Letter to John Todd, Dawsonburg Post Office, Fremont County, Iowa, from George Whipple of the American Missionary Association, New York, New York, May 22, 1853.

Letter to John Todd, Dawsonburg Post Office, Fremont County, Iowa, from James Todd, Granville, Ill., July 13, 1853.

Letter to Q.F. Atkins, Wolcott, New Haven Co., Conn., from Martha Todd's sister, Bertha Judson, postmarked Cleveland, Ohio. However, Bertha indicates the letter was written from Brooklyn, no state given, July, 26, 1853.

Letter to Q.F. Atkins from John Todd, Dawsonburg Post Office, Fremont County, Iowa, January 3, 1854.

Letter to John Todd, Dawsonburg Post Office, Fremont County, Iowa, from S.L. Jocelyn and George Whipple of the American Missionary Association, New York, New York, March 9, 1854.

Letter to Cleveland Morning Leader newspaper from Q.F. Atkins, Tabor, Iowa, May 25, 1854.

Letter to Q.F. Atkins, address unknown, from Jonas Jones, Tabor, Iowa, September 5, 1854.

Letter to Q.F. Atkins, address unknown, from John Todd, Tabor, Iowa, March 26, 1856.

Letter to John Todd, Tabor, Iowa, from George Whipple of the American Missionary Association, New York, New York, June 3, 1856.

Letter to Thaddeus Hyatt, address unknown, from A.D. Searl, Tabor, Iowa, August 21, 1856. Kansas State Historical Society.

Letter to Sally Atkins, mother-in-law to John Todd, address unknown, from John Todd, Tabor, Iowa, September 12, 1856.

Letter to Q.F. Atkins, address unknown, from daughter Mary Atkins, Benicia, California, Sept. 28, 1856.

Letter to Q.F. Atkins, Racine, Wisconsin, from Mrs. John Todd and son James, Tabor, Iowa, December 25, 1856.

Letter to Q.F. Atkins, Racine, Wisconsin, from John Todd, Tabor, Iowa, January, 19, 1857.

Letter to Q.F. Atkins, address unknown, from John and Martha Todd, Tabor, Iowa, April 29, 1857.

Sermon by John Todd in Tabor, Iowa, titled "Oppression," May 10, 1857.

Letters to Q.F. Atkins, Geneva, Ohio, from John Todd, Tabor, Iowa, May 18 and June 18, 1857.

Letter of recommendation for William Brooks from Oberlin College Professor James Monroe, June 10, 1857.

Letter of recommendation for William Brooks from Oberlin College Professor John Morgan, June 11, 1857.

Letter of recommendation for William Brooks from Oberlin College Professor Charles Penfield, June 19, 1857.

Letter to John Brown, Tabor, Iowa, from William A. Phillips, Lawrence, Kansas Territory, June 24, 1857. Kansas State Historical Society.

Letter to Mary Brown (Mrs. John Brown), address unknown, from John Brown (Nelson Hawkins), Tabor, Iowa, August 17, 1857. Kansas State Historical Society.

Letter to Genl. John Brown, Tabor, Iowa, from James Lane, Falls City, Nebraska, September 29, 1857. Kansas State Historical Society.

Letter to Genl. Jas. H. Lane, Falls City, Nebraska, from John Brown, Tabor, Iowa, September 30, 1857. Kansas State Historical Society.

Letter to John Brown, Tabor, Iowa, from S.(Samuel) L. Adair, Osawatomie, Kansas Territory, October 2, 1857. Kansas State Historical Society.

Letter to John Brown, Tabor, Iowa, from Henry H. Williams, Osawatomie, K.T., October 12, 1857. Kansas State Historical Society.

Letter to Q.F. Atkins, Geneva, Ashtabula, Ohio, from John Todd, Tabor, Iowa May, 3, 1858.

Letter to William Brooks, Oberlin, Ohio, from Edwin Hill, Tabor, Iowa, November 28, 1858.

Letter to William Brooks, Oberlin, Ohio, from Edwin Hill, Tabor, Iowa, January 10, 1859.

Letter to William Brooks, Oberlin, Ohio, from John Todd, Tabor, Iowa, January 14, 1859.

Letter to William Brooks, Oberlin, Ohio, from George Gaston, Tabor, Iowa, January 27, 1859.

Letter to William Brooks, Oberlin, Ohio, from Jonas Jones, Tabor, Iowa, January 27, 1859.

Letter to John Todd, Tabor, Iowa, from E. Fraser, Kansas City, Missouri, November 15, 1860.

Sermon by John Todd in Tabor, Iowa, "Judgment for the Oppressed," April 28, 1861.

Funeral sermon for Jesse West given by the Reverend John Todd, November 3, 1861.

Letter to John Todd, Tabor, Iowa, from K. Day, Denmark, Iowa, February 6, 1862.

Letter to John Todd, Tabor, Iowa, from his brother, David Todd, Pine Bluff, Arkansas, June 6, 1864.

Letter to John Todd while chaplain of the 46th Iowa Infantry, Cairo, Ill., from Mrs. John Todd, Tabor, Iowa, June 30, 1864.

Letter to John Todd while chaplain of the 46th Iowa Infantry, Colliersville, Tennessee, from the Reverend Origen Cummings, Tabor, Iowa, July 7, 1864.

Letter to John Todd while chaplain of the 46th Iowa Infantry, Memphis, Tennessee, from James Pinnio, Tipton, Iowa, July 14, 1864.

Letter to John Todd while chaplain of the 46th Iowa Infantry, Memphis, Tennessee, from son James E. Todd, Ft. Stevens, Washington, D.C., July 19, 1864.

Letter to John Todd while chaplain of the 46th Iowa Infantry, Memphis, Tennessee, from Mrs. John Todd and daughters Maggie and Flora, Tabor, Iowa, July 27, 1864.

Letter to John Todd while chaplain of the 46th Iowa Infantry, Colliersville, Tennessee, from Lt. Alexander Rliedang, Memphis Officer Hospital, August 10, 1864.

Letter to John Todd while chaplain of the 46th Iowa Infantry, Colliersville, Tennessee, from his sister, Mary Sloan, Harrisburg, Pa., August 11, 1864.

Letter to John Todd while chaplain of the 46th Iowa Infantry, Colliersville, Tennessee, from L. Williams, Glenwood, Iowa, August 30, 1864.

Letter to John Todd, Glenwood, Iowa, from Dr. B. Henderson, Dubuque, Iowa, January 30, 1865.

Sermon by John Todd in Tabor, Iowa, "Western Book and Tract Society," June 23, 1867.

Letter to John Todd, Tabor, Iowa, from Jonathan Cable, Danville, Iowa, March 26, 1868.

Letter to John Todd, Tabor, Iowa, from Jonathan Cable, Philadelphia, Pa., April 13, 1868.

Letter to John Todd, Tabor, Iowa, from Jonathan Cable, Philadelphia, Pa., May 9, 1868.

Letter to John Todd, Tabor, Iowa, from Jonathan Cable, New York, New York, May 18, 1868.

Letter to John Todd, Tabor, Iowa, from Jonathan Cable, New York, New York, May 28, 1868.

Letter to John Todd, Tabor, Iowa, from Jonathan Cable, Providence, R.I., June 6, 1868.

Letter to the Reverend Theron Baldwin D.D., unknown address, from John Todd, Tabor, Iowa, July 11, 1868.

Letter to John and Martha Todd, Tabor, Iowa, from Mary Lynch, New Orleans, Louisiana, August 4, 1874.

Letters to Mrs. John Todd, Tabor, Iowa, from Wade Thomas, Tougaloo, Mississippi, January 26, 1880, March 23 and June 5, 1880.

Letter to Mrs. John Todd, Tabor, Iowa, from L.J. Hines, Tougaloo, Mississippi, February 16, 1880.

Letter to William Brooks, Tabor, Iowa, from N.P. Dodge, Council Bluffs, Iowa, November 16, 1882.

Letter to William Brooks, Tabor, Iowa, from N.P. Dodge, Council Bluffs, Iowa, April 6, 1884.

Letter to John Todd, Tabor, Iowa, from L.F. Parker, Iowa City, Iowa, February 19, 1887.

Letter to John Todd, Tabor, Iowa, from G.G. Rice, Council Bluffs, Iowa, July 30, 1888.

Letter to John Todd, Tabor, Iowa, from Bertha Judson, Cleveland, Ohio, March 17, 1893.

Miscellaneous Documents, Publications and Internet Sites

Unless otherwise noted these items reside in the Todd House Museum Archives. Items are listed in the order they appear in the book.

Gaston Manuscript. The material was gathered by W.E. Gaston, son of James Gaston, cousin to George Gaston. These were recollections of the Gaston, Cummings and Townsend family pioneers and their children on events in early Tabor history.

Robert Gaston Family Papers. These consist of various letters, reminiscences and newspaper articles concerning events in the Gaston family history and the history of Tabor.

Iowa Freedom Trail Program Proposal Publication, Department of Cultural Affairs, State Historical Society of Iowa, Community Programs Bureau, December 1999, Reference Chart in Fremont County showing percentage of inhabitants from slave states.

Records of Public Meetings in Tabor, Fremont County, Iowa.

John Todd's alumni file located in the Oberlin College Archives.

Martha Todd's alumni file located in the Oberlin College Archives.

David Todd's alumni file located in the Oberlin College Archives.

Muster roll of the 2nd Regiment, 1st Brigade, Pennsylvania Militia, September 14, 1814. Pennsylvania State Archives, Harrisburg, Pa.

Todds of Hanover Genealogy Chart.

Prosecuting attorney's summation from Harlan County, Kentucky, case involving David Todd, September 26, 1842.

"Political Economy of Slavery," handwritten copy of John Todd's commencement address at Oberlin College, 1841. University of Kansas, Kenneth Spencer Research Library.

Copies of John Todd's ordination papers, both handwritten and printed.

Maria Cummings Gaston alumni file located in the Oberlin College Archives.

Maria Gaston's handwritten autobiography.

Platt Family Papers, 1848–1960, Biographical Sketches, Oberlin College Archives.

Lowell Blikre, "Phase 1 Intensive Survey of Seven Potential Historical Archeological Properties in the Civil Bend Vicinity, Benton Township, Fremont County, Iowa. Prepared for State Historical Society of Iowa.

Historical reminiscences from the Dale Mathews family papers.

Articles of Incorporation for Tabor Literary Institute.

Fugitive Slave Act, 1850, Sections 5,6,7.

Tabor Congregational Church History 1852–2002, Compiled by Mrs. Leland Smith.

Anti-slavery journal of John Todd, newspaper and other articles that were pasted into a journal covering slavery and abolitionist topics.

"Sale of a Family of Slaves in Washington City, A Tract for Sabbath Schools." Pamphlet. Author unknown, published by American Reform Tract and Book Society.

"Is It Expedient to Introduce Slavery Into Kansas: A Tract for the Times, Respectfully Inscribed to the People of Kansas." Pamphlet. Author: Daniel B.Goodloe (Daniel Reaves) of North Carolina. Published by American Reform Tract and Book Society, Cincinnati, Ohio.

"Duty of Voting: For Righteous Men for Office." Pamphlet. Author unknown, published by American Reform Tract and Book Society.

Photocopy of a handwritten notice for an anti-slavery meeting in Sidney, Iowa. Original is in the Iowa State Historical Society.

Tabor Historical Pageant, Episode IV, June 9–12, 1917.

File on S.F. Nuckolls located at the Morton-James Library in Nebraska City, Nebraska.

Fremont County, Clerk's Office, Court Case No. 30 *Henry Garner vs. S.F. Nuchols* [sic], etc. March Term District Court, 1859. Transcribed court docket.

Federal Census, 1860.

File on Alexander Majors located at the Morton-James Library in Nebraska City, Nebraska.

Register of marriages performed by the Reverend John Todd located at the Tabor, Iowa Library.

Photocopies of military documents from the Headquarters Military District of Washington, January 8, 1863, giving John Todd a pass within the lines of the United States Forces. Another document from the Office of the Provost Marshal, Camp Hamilton, Va. notifying guards to pass the Reverend Todd. Tabor Public Library.

James E. Todd alumni file, Oberlin College Archives.

John Todd muster papers from the Union Army.

"History of Tabor College" presentation by William Brooks given at the Quarter Centennial Anniversary of the Tabor Congregational Church, October 11, 1877.

Biographical information of James E. Todd from the Kenneth Spencer Research Library, University of Kansas.

Tabor College Catalogue 1886–7.

Notes on the history of the Shenandoah Congregational Church by author.

WEB SITES

http://www.oberlin.edu/~archive/WWW?files/platt. Last Visited 1/19/01.

http://www.sos.mo.gov/archives/localrecs/conservation/dredscott/into.asp Last Visited 4/25/2004.

http://www.hitchcockhouse,org/conductor.htm. Last visited 1/17, 2004.

http://www.ukans.edu/~spencer/exhibits/darwin.html.Last visited 6/24/01.

Index